Word Order in Toposa
An Aspect of Multiple Feature-Checking

SIL International and
The University of Texas at Arlington
Publications in Linguistics 142

Publications in Linguistics are published jointly by SIL International and the University of Texas at Arlington. The series is a venue for works covering a broad range of topics in linguistics, especially the analytical treatment of minority languages from all parts of the world. While most volumes are authored by members of SIL, suitable works by others will also form part of the series.

Series Editors

Donald A. Burquest
University of Texas at Arlington

Mary Ruth Wise
SIL International

Volume Editors

Eugene E. Loos
Rhonda Hartell Jones

Production Staff

Margaret González, Compositor
Barbara Alber, Graphic Artist

Word Order in Toposa
An Aspect of Multiple Feature-Checking

Helga Schröder

SIL International
and
The University of Texas at Arlington

© 2008 SIL International
Library of Congress Catalog No: 2007-929937
ISBN: 978-1-55671-181-7
ISSN: 1040-0850

Printed in the United States of America

All rights reserved. No part of this publication may be reproduced, stored in a retrieval system, or transmitted in any form or by any means—electronic, mechanical, photocopy, record, or otherwise—without the express permission of SIL International. However, short passages, generally understood to be within the limits of fair use, may be quoted without written permission.

Copies of this and other publications of SIL International may be obtained from

International Academic Bookstore
SIL International
7500 W. Camp Wisdom Road
Dallas, TX 75236-5629
Voice: 972-708-7404
Fax: 972-708-7363
Email: academic_books@sil.org
Internet: http://www.ethnologue.com

I dedicate this work to my father
in gratitude for all that he has done for me.

Contents

Acknowledgements xi

Abbreviations. xiii

1 Introduction 1
   1.1 Background to the Study 2
   1.2 Basic Language Features 3
       1.2.1 Phonology 3
       1.2.2 Grammar 4
   1.3 Statement of the Problem 7
   1.4 Objectives 8
   1.5 Hypotheses 8
   1.6 Rationale 9
   1.7 Scope and Limitation 9
   1.8 Literature Review 10
   1.9 Research Methodology 16
   1.10 Significance of the Study 18

2 Theoretical Framework 21
   2.1 The Minimalist Program 21
       2.1.1 Philosophical background 22
       2.1.2 From lexicon to interface level 23
       2.1.3 The morphology drive 26
       2.1.4 The word-order parameter 34
       2.1.5 Topic and focus 36

2.2	The Nominative-Accusative and Ergative-Absolutive Parameter	36
2.3	The Pro-Drop Parameter	39
2.4	Discourse Configurationality: Topic and Focus	40
2.5	Basic Constituent Order	43
2.6	The Notion of Subject	44
2.7	Summary and Outlook	46

3 Morphosyntactic Representations 49

3.1	The Basic Sentence Structure	49
3.2	The Nominative-Accusative Case-Marking System	56
3.3	Morphological Ergativity	58
	3.3.1 Passive	58
	3.3.2 The split cross-reference pronominal system	59
3.4	Argument-Changing Processes	65
	3.4.1 Argument-increasing processes	65
	3.4.2 Argument-decreasing processes	73
3.5	Applied and Direct Object	78
3.6	Summary	82

4 Complex Verb Morphology and Word Order 85

4.1	Co-occurrence of Argument-Increasing Devices	85
4.2	Co-occurrence of Argument-Increasing and Argument-Decreasing Devices	97
	4.2.1 Combinations with passive	97
	4.2.2 Combinations with reflexive	101
4.3	Alternatives to the Double Object Construction	106
4.4	Summary	108

5 Complex Verb Morphology in Discourse 109

5.1	The Principle of Reference	110
	5.1.1 Subject and object pronouns in discourse	111
	5.1.2 Causative and applicative in discourse	116
5.2	The Principle of Focus	121
	5.2.1 Personal pronouns and focus	123
	5.2.2 Causative/applicative and focus	125
5.3	Contrastive Focus	130
5.4	Defocalised Information	138
5.5	Inherent Focus	140
5.6	Summary	142

6 The VS/VO Ergative Word Order. 145
6.1 The Principle of Reference in Complex Sentences 146
6.2 Ergative Tendencies in Complex Sentences. 148
6.3 Argument-Reducing Processes 153
6.4 Syntactic Ergatives 154
6.5 Summary. 160
6.6 Conclusion 161

Appendix A: From Lexicon to Interface 165

Appendix B: Nyepido 175

References 189

Acknowledgements

First of all, I would like to thank my lecturer Professor Irene Philippaki-Warburton of the University of Reading who introduced me to the concepts of Government and Binding during the years of 1993 and 1994 and alerted me to the complications of dealing with VSO languages in that framework. Her encouragement inspired me to apply these concepts to Toposa as a VSO language.

Next, I wish to thank the Summer Institute of Linguistics (now SIL International); it was under their auspices that my husband and I first entered Toposaland to do basic language research at the request of the Regional Ministry of Education in Juba which kindly granted us all the necessary permits.

Within SIL, special thanks go to the Department of Academic Affairs for their encouragement, including the financial support I received from them, which helped us to pay part of the cost for this whole enterprise.

During the years in Sudan, I elicited data with various language assistants, mainly Marko Lolimo and Chief Paulo Lopyem. After the spreading of hostilities between 1983–1985, the work continued in Juba with Chief Paulo, later supplemented by Lino Lokine and Peter Kagol, and, most recently, by Christine Ligie and her husband James Omo Nachek. I thank all of them for their patient work during the sometimes tedious language sessions, and for the many stories, procedural and hortatory texts they produced and edited for us, which served as a corpus of data after we had to leave the country in 1988 and moved to Nairobi. I also thank the Toposa Language Committee of those early years for their feedback on matters of orthography and voiceless vowels.

Among all the language assistants, my special thanks go to Pastor James Lokunda Kandaya who helped me throughout the research for this study (between 1995 and 2001) to recheck older data and to collect lots of new language material. He helped me very patiently, together with my husband, to elicit and recheck the complex tone class system that marks case on nouns and the tonal person-tense-aspect marking on verbs. I am also grateful for the practical suggestions made by Oliver Stegen, who showed us how to pinpoint tone more precisely and how to deal with register shifts.

I especially thank my husband Martin, who patiently took on the tedious task of editing all the complex language data and elaborate diagrams. He spent countless hours with me in front of my computer, helping me to get this work ready for submission.

Some very special thanks go to Professor Bureng Nyombe, Lecturer and Chairman of the Department of Linguistics and African Languages at the University of Nairobi, who supervised my research and writing from 1995 right to the end of my study program in 2001. He helped me through endless discussions to disentangle the complexities of the Toposa language, to put them into the Minimalist framework for descriptional adequacy, and he encouraged me to develop new ideas within these parameters. I also thank him for all his valuable comments on my early drafts.

In closing, I thank my three children, Daniel, Markus, and Sonja, for their patience in putting up with their very busy mother.

Abbreviations

Abbreviations used in text and tree diagrams:

AGR	agreement
AGRo (AGRoP, AGRo')	agreement object
AGRs (AGRsP, AGRs')	agreement subject
BEN (BENP, BEN')	benefactive
ben obj	benefactive object
C (CP, C')	complementiser
CAUS (CAUSP, CAUS')	causative
COMP	complement
dir obj	direct object
DP	determiner phrase
ERG (ERG')	ergative
FI	full interpretation
F (FP, F')	focus
FCM (FCMP, FCM')	focus-case-marking
GB	Government and Binding
INFL	inflection
INS (INSP, INS')	instrumental
INS/P (INS/PP, INS/P')	instrumental prepositional phrase
IP	inflectional phrase
LF	logical form
MUH	Morphological Uniformity Hypothesis
NEG (NEG')	negation
NP	noun phrase
NPb	noun phrase/benefactive
NPc	noun phrase/causative
NPo	noun phrase/object
P (PP, P')	preposition
PAS (PASP, PAS')	passive
PF	phonological form
QUE (QUE')	question

RES(NIC)	residue of the Nominative Island Conditions
RFL (RFLP, RFL')	reflexive
S1, S2, S3	sentence 1/2/3
SPEC	specifier
tb	trace/benefactive
tc	trace/causative
ti	trace/instrumental
TNS (TNS')	tense
to	trace/object
tpp	trace/prepositional phrase
ts	trace/subject
tv	trace/verb
UG	Universal Grammar
UTAH	Uniformity of θ-Assignment Hypothesis
VP (V', V)	verb phrase
XP (X', X)	"any phrase"

Abbreviations used in glosses:

1, 2, 3	1st/2nd/3rd person
ABL	ablative ("itive")
ACC	accusative
ALL	allative ("ventive")
BEN	benefactive
CAUS	causative
D	diminutive
DER	derivator
F	feminine
GER	gerund
HAB	habitual
IDEO	ideophone
IMP	imperfective
IV	imperative
INS	instrumental
INST	instrumentalizer
LOC	locative
M	masculine
NEG	negative
NOM	nominative
OBJ	object
PAS	passive
PER	perfective
PL	plural
RFL	reflexive
SEQ	(narrative-)sequential
SG	singular
SIM	simultative
STV	stative
SUB	subject
VOC	vocative
?	unidentified segment

1
Introduction

The purpose of this book is to provide a feature-checking approach to sentence structure and language typology within the generative framework, based on Toposa, a highly inflectional Eastern Nilotic language of Sudan.

It was a common belief among generativists that in Universal Grammar (UG) the sentence is derived through a grammatical subject and its position in the inflectional phrase (IP) and the verb phrase (VP) that has a c-commanded object. This book suggests that factors beyond sentence level play an important role in the conceptualisation of sentences. The book claims that sentence structure is determined by a multiple feature-checking process, and that the computational process is driven by the interaction between morphology, syntax, and discourse functions. Until recently it was not common to make discourse considerations part of the process for forming sentence structure. However the findings of Li and Thompson (1976) have demonstrated that there are languages where the formation of sentences is not only motivated by structural constituents of grammatical subject and object, but also by discourse functions such as topic. Kiss (1995) followed up the thinking of Li and Thompson and showed that there are indeed languages where the discourse functions of topic and focus determine the sentence structure. While Kiss still saw the discourse functions of topic and focus as isolated syntactic features, this work proposes to go a step further to view morphology, syntax, and discourse functions as merged in a multiple feature-checking process that is responsible for sentence structure and word order.

The feature-motivated interrelation of morphology, syntax, and discourse explain the occurrence and absence of the grammatical subject, the object and verbal constituents in discourse and leads to an ergative VS/VO word order in Toposa, where the preferred argument structure is to have only one argument after the verb. This contrasts with older analyses of a VSO word order for Toposa (Dimmendaal 1983b:130; Creider 1989:35; Givón 1976:73–74).

The complex relationship between morphology, syntax, and discourse is demonstrated through the morphology of the passive, the reflexive, the subject prefixes in the verb, the causative and the applicative—in isolation, in complex combinations, and in discourse.

Although this study presents data from Toposa, it contributes to aspects of general linguistic theory. For this purpose, the Minimalist Program (Chomsky 1993/1995) has been used as the framework.

1.1 Background to the Study

Toposa is classified as belonging to the Teso-Turkana subgroup of Eastern Nilotic (Vossen 1981, 1982, 1983).[1] It is spoken by an estimated 100,000–200,000 people in the southeastern corner of Southern Sudan. Other members of the Teso-Turkana dialect continuum are Jie in Sudan; Nyangatom in Ethiopia; Karimojong, Jiye, Dodos, and Teso in Uganda; and Turkana and Teso in Kenya. Karimojong, Nyangatom and Turkana are the most closely related dialects and are mutually intelligible with Toposa (Dimmendaal 1983a), although they are ethnically distinct. All members of Teso-Turkana are verb-initial languages.

This study concentrates on the western dialect of Toposa as it is spoken in the Riwoto section of Kapoeta District in what used to be Eastern Equatoria Province and relies on fieldwork and data elicitation which has been carried out between 1982 and 2001 (for the details see section 1.9).

There are few accounts of the language: a first attempt to describe the verb (Schröder and Schröder 1986), two articles on phonological aspects (Schröder and Schröder 1987a, Schröder and Schröder 1987b), a paper on narrative discourse (M. C. Schröder 1989), a collection of traditional texts (M. C. Schröder 1993a), a study of word order problems (H. Schröder 1994) and a dictionary with about 9000 entries (M. C. Schröder 2000). Apart from these, Toposa is usually mentioned merely in passing

---

[1]Vossen presents a detailed overview of the whole Nilotic language family, which consists of three branches, Western, Eastern, and Southern Nilotic (1982:273). Eastern Nilotic comprises about thirty related languages and dialects spoken by about two million people in six countries: Democratic Republic of the Congo, Congo, Ethiopia, Uganda, Kenya, and Tanzania.

by other authors in the context of comparative studies within the wider language family (mainly Dimmendaal, Creider, and Givón).

1.2 Basic Language Features

1.2.1 Phonology

Toposa has sixteen consonant phonemes: all consonants, except the glides /w/ and /y/, occur palatalised and labialised and are written in the data as *ty, cy, tw, cw,* etc.[2]

Toposa has nine vowels belonging to two different tongue root positions: advanced tongue root [+ATR], which is the marked position, and the normal (unmarked) position [−ATR]. The vowel /a/ is neutral with respect to vowel harmony because it occurs with [−ATR] and [+ATR] vowels in the same word, and when it does so, it is opaque and blocks vowel harmony processes from spreading through it. In terms of harmony sets, however, /a/ should be counted with the [−ATR] set because phonetically it becomes impossible to distinguish different tongue root positions in a maximally open vowel and because it is more logical for a neutral vowel to be counted under the unmarked set (for a description of Toposa vowel harmony and a more detailed discussion of the status of /a/ see Schröder and Schröder 1987a).

All vowels also occur as voiceless vowels word finally and are written as underlined, for example *i̠, u̠*. All vowels, except the voiceless ones, occur lengthened and are analysed and written as double vowels.

The palatal nasal /ɲ/ will be written as *ny* throughout this book as in Toposa orthography, a choice made by the Toposa Language Committee in 1986. The symbol *c* is used throughout for a voiceless postalveolar affricate, and *j* is used for a voiced postalveolar affricate.

Toposa has the following tones: high (H) and low (L), a fall (F) at the end of words, and a rise (R) which is rare and also occurs only at the end of words. These tones will be marked as *á à â ǎ,* respectively. There is a mid tone (M) which is restricted to sequences of HML and LMH or MH and is interpreted as a variant of H. Due to morphotonemics, raised highs and lowered lows also occur (marked by upward and downward arrows ↑ ↓, respectively).

Utterance-final voiceless vowels are not realized as voiced and therefore do not bear a detectable tone and have been left unmarked, as the

---

[2]The consonant phonemes are /p, t, k, b, d, g, s, c, j, l, r, m, n, ny, ŋ, w, y/.

determination of the underlying tonal height was not within the scope of this research.

1.2.2 Grammar

As this study concentrates on word order questions related to morphology, syntax, and discourse, it is not intended to present a comprehensive description of Toposa grammar. Nevertheless, it is appropriate to briefly consider some basic structural features of the language in order to provide some background information. More detailed features like the tense system and verbal morphology will be described later in those sections where they contribute to the progression of the argument.

Toposa, like other related Eastern Nilotic languages, is a consistent head-modifier or head-first language and typically is dependent-marking on phrase level (in the sense of Nichols 1986), but head-marking at sentence level.

Most nouns in Toposa follow a three-way gender distinction in the singular: masculine, feminine, and diminutive. In plural the contrast between masculine and diminutive is neutralized, as the following table of gender-number prefixes for class 1 nouns shows:

	singular	plural
masculine	nye-	ŋi-
diminutive	nyi-	ŋi-
feminine	nya	ŋa-

There is a second class of nouns which only distinguishes between masculine and feminine:

	singular	plural
masculine	lo-	ta-lo-
feminine	na-	ta-na-

A third very small and closed class of nouns (mostly kinship terms) exhibits no gender prefixes at all.

The noun phrase either has a noun or a pronoun as its nucleus. In the noun phrase (NP) all relative constructions, adjectives, demonstratives, and numerals follow the head noun in unmarked contexts and agree with it in number and gender.

1.2 Basic Language Features

Note the following NP paradigm, where adjectives, numerals, and the relative pronoun agree in gender and number with the head noun:

(1) a. nyá-bé⁺rú   nyà-pèì³
       F/SG-woman F/SG-one
       'one woman'

   b. nyá-bé⁺rú   nà-kà-pìpìl-àni⁴
       F/SG-woman F-DER-beautiful-SG
       'the beautiful woman'

   c. nyé-kìlé   ló-cyê
       M/SG-man M/SG-another
       'another man'

   d. ŋí-kí⁺lyók   lù-kà-àl-àk⁵
       M/PL-men   M/PL-DER-many-PL
       'many men'

   e. nyá-bé⁺rú   nà   é-lòs-í
       F/SG-woman who 3SG-go-IMP
       'the woman who went'

   f. nyá-bé⁺rú   ŋìnà
       F/SG-woman that
       'that woman'

Prepositions however, precede the noun:

(2)   tóòmá   lò-kále
       inside   M/LOC-home
       'inside the home'

Note how the language follows the general principle of right-branching on word order level (VSO) and on phrase level (nucleus-modifier). The

---

³The raised high tone in *nyábé⁺rú* 'woman' is caused by morphotonemics.

⁴A downward arrow marks extra low tone. In a limited sample of adjectives investigated so far, the last low tone in a series of low tones is either extra low or is realized as a rising tone as in (3) and (4).

⁵The singular of *ŋi-kily-ok* 'men' is *nye-kile*. In addition to their number-sensitive gender prefixes, many nouns have number suffixes which sometimes have become fused with the root. These number suffixes will not be segmented for the purpose of this study but the English gloss will reflect the number of each noun.

right-branching head-modifier relationship, as well as the dependent-marking strategy for phrases and head-dependent marking at sentence level has also been reported for Turkana (Dimmendaal 1983b, 1986, 1996) and for Eastern and Southern Nilotic (Creider 1989).

Toposa does not have any adjectival or adverbial phrases. All adjectives, except a closed class of colour terms, are derived from verbs, so that adjectives as a separate independent word category do not exist. Adjectives are modifiers of the noun and agree with it in gender and number.

The adjective gender prefixes are as follows:

	singular	plural
masculine	lo-	lu-
feminine	na-	nu-
diminutive	ni-	ni-

Normal adjectives have the following form: gender prefix, followed by a derivational prefix ka-, the root and a number-sensitive suffix: -ani̱/-oni̱ for singular and -ak/-ok in the plural. Compare (3) with (5).

(3) lò-kà-mòn-ǎni̱
     M/SG-DER-hot-SG
     'hot (adjective in M/SG)'

Note word order and agreement within the NP:

(4) nyé-ˈrót lò-kà-twòn-ǒni̱
     M/SG-road M/SG-DER-difficult-SG
     'the difficult road'

As adjectives occur only in derived forms, they cannot have any function as complements in verb phrases (VPs). Instead, the language expresses adjective phrase, adverb phrase or prepositional phrase (PP) functions not as complements of 'to be', but as stative verbs, as (5) illustrates.[6]

(5) è-món-à
     3SG-hot-IMP
     'it is hot'

---

[6]Dimmendaal (1983a:332) suggests for Turkana that the low occurrence of adjectives indicates a shift from adjectives to verbs, where adjectives are more and more used in a verbal sense.

Adverbs are very rare. The most frequent ones are temporal adverbs, followed by a number of locative adverbs. There are only two modal adverbs, *looi* 'very much', and *nabo* 'again'. The function of the modal and of temporal adverbs is to modify the verb. They either follow the verb (6a), or occur sentence finally (6b), if in unmarked constructions. Temporal adverbs also occur sentence initially, if they are marked (6c).

(6) a. Tém-a̱   nàbô   nyébù,...
       said-ABL again hyena
       'Again, Hyena said,...'

   b. Tó-sûk   nyébù   lóòwŏy.
      SEQ-run hyena   very
      'Hyena ran very hard.'

   c. Bèén   à-lòs-í   Lókáì lò-rê.
      yesterday 3SG-go-IMP   Lokai M/LOC-village
      'Lokai went to the village yesterday.'

The basic sentence structure will be dealt with later.

1.3 Statement of the Problem

The word order of VSO languages presents a problem to the concept of VP in Chomsky's Government and Binding (GB) theory (1981) as well as in his Minimalist Program (1993). The insertion of the NP subject between the verb—which functions as the head of the VP—and its complement, the NP object, violates the basic principle of government theory, namely the definitions of government and c-command. It also breaks the rule of case-assignment, which takes place under government in the VP. In the Minimalist Program the violation against the concept of government in the VP is no longer significant, as government theory is dismissed, but the questions of proper word order in VSO languages and case-assignment of the subject remain.

Resulting from these observations, the following research questions arise for Toposa (and for VSO languages in general):

1. What is the underlying sentence structure, VSO or SVO?

2. Where is the subject generated?

3. Where does the subject move in order to produce the VSO structure?

4. How does the case-checking of the subject take place?

1.4 Objectives

In pursuing these questions, the following objectives guided the research:

1. To study the Toposa verb morphology in order to determine its relationship to the argument structure of the verb.

2. To investigate the word order of finite and nonfinite sentences in order to establish the basic sentence structure of the language.

3. To examine the tonal case-assignment in order to find out whether it triggers verb movement with respect to feature-checking as proposed by the Minimalist Program.

4. To investigate the pro-drop parameter in subject and object position in order to see whether a relation exists between morphology and VSO word order.

5. To find out whether any relationship exists between discourse-related concepts like topic and focus and how these influence word order.

1.5 Hypotheses

In the process, the following hypotheses are tested:

1. Toposa does not have an underlying SVO but a VSO word order structure.

2. The subject is base-generated in the specifier of the VP as an argument of the verb.

3. Argument-related affixes of the Toposa verb morphology determine the argument structure of the VP (in terms of the occurrence and non-occurrence of arguments).

4. For Toposa the checking theory of the Minimalist Program is adequate to describe verb movement and the case-assignment of the subject, object, and incorporated objects.

5. The subject moves to the specifier of the subject agreement phrase (AGRsP) for case assignment.

6. The order of the projections of tense and agreement has to be changed to reach the VSO word order structure.

1.6 Rationale

The word order question is central to syntactic theories, because word order parameters are used as criteria for creating a typology of the world's languages. As VSO languages only represent one third of the world's languages, the parameters and concepts determining these languages have not yet been studied very widely. Also, in Generative Grammar, the word order question raised by verb-initial languages has not been solved very satisfyingly.

1.7 Scope and Limitation

This study concentrates on the following areas in order to answer the research questions (cf. 1.3):

- the word order parameter of finite and nonfinite sentences, to establish the basic sentence structure,

- the verb morphology and the argument structure of the verb, in order to understand the verb-subject-object relationship,

- the tonal case assignment, to find out whether it triggers verb movement with respect to feature-checking as suggested by the Minimalist Program,

- the pro-drop parameter, to establish whether a relationship exists between morphology and word order.

The verb morphology is to be examined closely because it also determines the absence and presence of various constituents, particularly subject, object, and applied objects, and thus directly affects the VP and word order questions. Discourse considerations are taken into account where they affect the sentence structure. This seems to happen in regard to the presence and absence of the subject, the object and the applied object because all of them can have their antecedents (referents) beyond the basic sentence.

The focus system of the language is also taken into consideration as it affects the position of the subject in the VP, and because it influences the presence or absence of the subject and of the direct and applied object.

1.8 Literature Review

Since its inception in 1957, the theory of Generative Grammar has undergone a series of fundamental changes, culminating in the Minimalist Program of 1993 and 1995. The different stages of development were all triggered by deepening insight and, above all, new data.

In his first book *Syntactic Structures* (1957) Chomsky introduced the notions of Generative Grammar and rewriting rules, arguing for a separation between phrase structures and transformations which alter them.

Based on this model, in his *Aspects of the Theory of Syntax* (1965), he developed the notion of deep structure and surface structure, the latter being derived from the former by transformations. At the same time, he introduced the distinction between competence and performance. This model is also known as "Standard Theory."

In the eighties, this theory underwent significant changes, which were conceptualized in GB theory, described in Chomsky's *Lectures on Government and Binding* (1981). This new approach, also known as "Principles and Parameters," became necessary as more language data were brought into the research program and forced the theory into parametrisation. This model is still phrase-structure based and retains the concept of deep structure and surface structure, but additionally it develops autonomous and interrelating modules such as X-bar theory, θ-theory, case theory, binding theory, bounding theory, control theory, and government theory.

X-bar theory projects the phrase structure from the lexicon onto the deep-structure level. θ-theory and case theory explain how the semantic roles or case markings are assigned to core constituents on the sentence level. Binding theory describes the relations of anaphors, pronouns, names, and variables to possible antecedents. Bounding theory is

1.8 Literature Review

concerned with the local restrictions on grammatical processes. Control theory deals with the referential dependency between an unexpressed subject PRO and an argument, and government theory describes the head-complement relationship of a phrase. The interaction of these subtheories provides the basis for the frameworks of "Filters and Control" and "On Binding." GB theory also incorporates analyses of other languages, particularly Romance languages, using the pro-drop parameter. Further, GB touches upon some resulting issues like the residue of the Nominative Island Conditions [RES(NIC)] problem and the theory of indexing. All these conceptual and empirical discussions of Generative Grammar take place in the philosophical context of the origin and nature of language and language acquisition.

Chomsky's book *Knowledge of Language* (1986a) resumes the discussion of the philosophical framework of UG and language acquisition. The book tries to answer intricate issues such as what is the origin and nature of language. Language is understood as an innate property of the brain, also called "knowledge of language." This internal language underlies and determines the use and understanding of language. The book also examines the different stages of language learning, showing that the Principles and Parameters approach of UG offers an adequate model for language acquisition at its different stages.

Chomsky's monograph *Barriers* (1986b) presents a further development of GB theory, discussing possible barriers to government and movement in the subtheoretical framework of X-bar theory, theory of movement, and government. It also explores two concepts of barriers, namely maximal projection and minimality conditions, and their manifestations and implications for proper government, subjacency, island violations, vacuous movement, parasite gaps, and α-chains.[7]

Up to this point, the theory has never addressed the morphology of a language adequately. The fundamental intention of Generative Grammar was to explain the syntactic relationships between the constituents of the sentence. So it is foreign to the theory to explain morphology and its bearing on syntactic relations. In fact, the relationship between morphology and syntax was not seriously dealt with in the generative framework until Marantz' monograph *On the Nature of Grammatical Relations* published in 1984. Marantz claims that morphology has to be considered as a

---

[7]Liliane Haegeman's *Introduction to Government and Binding Theory* (1994) presents one of the most extensive introductory works to the Principles and Parameters approach of syntactic theory. The second edition has been updated throughout, paying attention to issues like Functional Heads, Head Movement, Relativised Minimality, Chain Formation, and the new Minimalist Program. Another textbook is *Chomsky's Universal Grammar* (1996) by Cook and Newson; it covers the basic principles of Government and Binding and the Minimalist Program, but is not as exhaustive as Haegeman.

subtheory of the GB system, and that morphemes can directly influence the logico-semantic structure of a sentence. Marantz' model has three main levels of syntactic representation: the logico-semantic structure, the syntactic structure, and the surface structure. This model is no longer committed to derivation in that it does not rely on a deep-structure-to-surface-structure model; rather, a Mapping Principle preserves the grammatically important relations from one level to the next. The lexicon contains roots and affixes and information about argument structure, transitivity, and semantic roles. The level of logico-semantic structure corresponds more or less to GB's level of θ-structure, and the surface structure is GB's phonological form. The Mapping Principle is an important cornerstone of Marantz' theory. It guarantees that the logico-semantic relations have a syntactic counterpart. A further important principle is the Merger Principle which takes care of the morpho-syntactic processes. Affixes like causative or applicative merge with the root of the main verb and build a new verbal stem that creates logico-semantic and syntactic relationships.

Another attempt to relate morphology to syntax is Baker's work *Incorporation* (1988) in which, building on Chomsky's Barrier model (1986a), morphological processes are viewed in terms of syntactic functions. Baker's starting point is the analysis of noun incorporation in terms of syntactic movement into the verb. He continues with the incorporation of verbs and prepositions. All these incorporation processes are function-changing processes which are dealt with as movement of lexical heads, mostly into the verb (Baker 1988:19). Thus, the fundamental idea of incorporation theory is that one semantically independent word is incorporated inside another. A side effect of this word movement is grammatical function-changing. One of the main concepts of incorporation theory deals with the movement of words (X_0) rather than with the movement of phrases (XP). The theory relies on concepts like Move-α of X_0, the Empty Category Principle, and the Uniformity of θ-Assignment Hypothesis (UTAH). The Empty Category Principle guarantees that the traces left behind by the word movement are properly governed. The UTAH ensures that the thematic relationships between words and morphemes are guaranteed, and that there is a direct link between morphology and syntax, in that UTAH explains the change in grammatical functions as caused by morphology. In all cases the incorporated element is in itself the head of a phrase. Baker arrives at his conclusions by considering passives, antipassives, causatives, applied verb constructions, and possessor raising in terms of word movement. Additionally, he also advances the Mirror Principle (1988:13) which says:

1.8 Literature Review

(7) Morphological derivations must directly reflect syntactic derivations (and vice versa).

A big step forward towards an integration of morphology into UG was Pollock's article *Verb Movement, Universal Grammar, and the Structure of IP* (1989) in which he demonstrates that differences in the sentence structure between languages are conditioned by presence and absence of morphology. Coming from French, he shows that its verb morphology requires a split IP and forces verb movement (unlike English where verb movement is not triggered). Subsequently, he separates the IP into an agreement phrase (AGRP) and a tense phrase (TNSP), where the AGRP is a complement of tense (TNS) or negation (NEG), which also occurs as negation phrase (NEGP). To prove his claim of a split IP, he considers sentence negation, questions, adverbs, floating quantifiers, and "quantifications at a distance." The discoveries of the article had, as rightly predicted by himself, theoretical consequences for the analysis of case-assignment and proper government. Consequently, Pollock's concepts have now been incorporated into the Minimalist Program.

The latest Chomskyan model, the Minimalist Program (Chomsky 1993, 1995) retains the overall goal to make statements about languages as simple and as general as possible. What is radically new, however, is the integration of morphology into syntax. The Minimalist Program addresses problems of inflectional morphology and integrates the Split Hypothesis of Inflection (INFL), which leads to new projections of AGR and TNS. The Minimalist Program thus manifests that all the information of the sentence is contained in the VP. It also explores the Principles of Economy and Derivation, first mentioned in Chomsky 1991, and the Principle of Full Interpretation (FI), first mentioned in Chomsky 1986a, and their determination for movement. The Minimalist Program further shows that the specifier-head relationship is central for case-assignment and that the concept of 'chain' explains the structure of intricate phrases more adequately than previous models. It finally presents a simple explanation of focus as it has now been integrated into the feature-checking process.

Another weakness of Generative Grammar (apart from not addressing issues of morphology before the Minimalist Program) was that it never dealt specifically with word order problems, except a few works like those of Emonds (1980, 1985), Koopman (1984), Jones and Thomas (1977), Harlow (1981), and Sproat (1983). Emonds tries to solve the VSO word order problem as Move-α between deep structure and surface structure, where VSO languages have an underlying SVO structure. He also suggests to divide languages into two parameters, the N-parameter and the non-N parameter. The N-parameter basically consists of SVO/SOV languages, i.e., the unmarked order, and the non-N parameter of VSO languages, which has marked status (1980:35). According to this parameter, SOV languages do not derive their structure (see also den Besten 1983 for German and Dutch) but fit into the N- framework with a modified rule for VP. In addition to the word order parameter, Emonds introduces the Structure Preserving Constraint and the General Head Restriction (Emonds 1980, 1985), both of which perpetuate and manifest the idea that VSO languages have an underlying SVO word order. Koopman (1984), Jones and Thomas (1977), Harlow (1981), and Sproat (1983) arrive at the same conclusion with respect to underlying SVO. All these authors appear to have a European bias by making VSO a modification of SVO languages, instead of granting them an independent status with independent properties.

With respect to VSO languages, Chomsky in his early work (1965) does not even mention any of the theoretical problems that VSO languages impose on the basic generative principle of head and complement relationship. In his Principles and Parameters model (1981), he takes a very broad approach to language typology by dividing the spectrum into head-first and head-last languages (Radford 1992:273–278, commenting on Chomsky 1981). In regard to VSO, Chomsky refers to the work of Aoun (1979, 1994) who tries to tackle the VSO word order of Classical and Lebanese Arabic in terms of underlying SVO and verb movement. He conceptualises the VP as discontinuous, which has marked status against the VP in the SVO order (Chomsky 1981:145, 151). In his latest model, the Minimalist Program, Chomsky again pays more attention to SVO languages than VSO ones, concentrating mainly on a variety of Indo-European languages.

However, there have been other attempts to conceptualise VSO languages other than as a derived word order from an underlying SVO order. For example, Modern Greek has been analysed in the framework of GB as having a nonderived VSO order (Philippaki-Warburton 1985, Catsimali 1990, and Tsimpli 1995).

Philippaki-Warburton argues that Greek has an independent VSO order, and that SVO is derived from it due to subject thematisation. She is thus one of the first authors to question the traditional view of Modern Greek as SVO and to challenge the basic assumptions of GB concerning VSO languages.

Alternatively, Catsimali (1990) analyses the Greek VP as a flat structure. As yet another approach, Tsimpli analyses the VSO structure on the basis that TNS is dominating AGR, thus the verb always precedes the

1.8 Literature Review

subject situated in [S/AGRP] (1995:177). This is the solution that has also been suggested by Ouhalla (1991) for Arabic.

The first to apply GB theory to a Nilotic language was Nyombe (1987), who applied Baker's Incorporation Theory to the argument-bearing affixes of Bari. Later on, Creider (1989) examined some Nilotic languages in the GB framework, focusing on the problem of verb movement and word order. He relates the difference between VSO and SVO structures in Nilotic to finite (VSO) and infinitival (SVO) sentences. Assuming that verb movement is triggered by nominative case-assignment, he expects no movement for infinitival sentences and claims that they represent the basic SVO structure of the language. He then suggests that the verb moves into the complementiser phrase (CP) in order to create the typical VSO word order, as also suggested by Borer and Tuller (1985) for German and Dutch.[8]

Another author to reject SVO as underlying sentence structure is McCloskey (1983:12), who examines Irish, a typical VSO language. According to him, INFL is spread over more than one syntactic category, e.g., INFL also contains the progressive particle. McCloskey separates the progressive particle as a distant constituent with maximal projection. As the progressive particle always occurs first, if used together with the main verb, the typical VSO structure is preserved, as the verb has to move into the progressive phrase.

The first author who devises a radically different approach to VSO languages is Ouhalla (1991) who presents data from Arabic and a wide selection of VSO languages across the world. He demonstrates that one of the properties of VSO languages is that AGR resides inside TNS (p. 110). This assumption changes the order of projections. Thus, the TNSP selects and c-commands the AGRP. Therefore, the TNS projection heads the sentence, and the VSO order is preserved, as the verb moves into AGR and TNS to pick up its inflectional features.[9]

Black (2000) adopts the Verb Movement proposal for obtaining VSO order in Quiegolani Zapotec. Her work, which utilizes a Principles and Parameters approach, cites negation constructions as evidence in support of this choice.

Among the non-generativist approaches to word order, Greenberg, known for his work on language typology and universals, predicts for

---

[8]In response to Creider's approach, I (H. Schröder 1994) refute the thesis that there are infinitive sentences in Teso-Turkana; I try to solve the question of VSO word order by making the subject an adjunct to V. That analysis, however, is superseded by this study.

[9]In recent years more and more scholars have come to recognise that verb-initial languages are not an off-shoot of SVO languages, but have to be analysed with their own verb-initial properties, where language-specific categories determine the VSO sentence structure. See the collection of articles in Carnie and Guilfoyle (2000).

VSO languages that they have SVO as an alternative (1963: universal #6). He also relates word order of sentences to the word order of NPs and predicts that in VSO languages nouns precede the modifier in normal and genitive constructions, and that VSO languages tend to have prepositions instead of postpositions. Although most of Greenberg's predictions have proven valid, Keenan (1978) observed postpositions in some South American VSO languages.

A data-oriented non-generativist approach to the typology of verb-initial languages is that of D. Payne (1990). Working on Yagua, a language of northeastern Peru, she works out a typology of verb-initial languages. She partly bases her observations on Hawkins (1983) and specifically on Keenan's word order typologies of verb-initial languages (1978) and discusses an extensive list of observations typical for verb-initial languages in the area of morphology, basic word order, sentence-level syntax, the NP, and the VP.

1.9 Research Methodology

This study is both data-oriented and theoretical. The first time I gathered Toposa data was during two extended periods of field work carried out together with my husband between January 1982 and October 1984 at Riwoto (in Kapoeta District in Eastern Equatoria Province) in the western section of Toposaland, and again between March 1986 and May 1988 among Toposa refugees in Juba (the provincial capital). This fieldwork was carried out as part of a literacy project under the joint auspices of SIL International and the Institute of Regional Languages, both under what was then the Regional Ministry of Education of the semiautonomous Southern Sudan. The bulk of research for the purposes of this study was done between 1995 and 2001, mostly with displaced Toposa speakers in various locations in Kenya.

During the earlier periods I elicited data with various language assistants, mainly Marko Lolimo, Chief Paulo Lopyem, and Lino Lokinei.

Towards the end of that time, in 1986, a Toposa Language Committee was formed among the refugees in Juba which consisted of a group of dedicated teachers and educated Toposa. With the help of this committee an alphabet based on our analysis was established for use in primary education, and teachers were trained in the use of the following materials: an ABC book (H. Schröder 1988a), a primer (H. Schröder 1988b), two readers (H. Schröder 1988c, M. C. Schröder 1993b), a spelling guide (M. C. Schröder 1988), and a handbook for teachers (H. Schröder 1988d).

1.9 Research Methodology

On the linguistic side, our efforts resulted in a first attempt to describe the verb (Schröder and Schröder 1986), an article on vowel harmony (Schröder and Schröder 1987a), one on voiceless vowels (Schröder and Schröder 1987b), and a paper on narrative discourse (M. C. Schröder 1989). This joint research formed the basis of my knowledge of Toposa and led to my M.A. thesis on word order problems (H. Schröder 1994).

Furthermore, all words and phrases we encountered during our years of fieldwork were collected in a database. The resulting Toposa-English dictionary of about 9,000 entries (together with a computer-generated reversed index) was put in the public domain as a photocopied trial edition (M. C. Schröder 2000). This dictionary database served as an additional source of language material for this book.

Over the entire period, we elicited a collection of traditional texts of various genres such as narrative, hortatory, procedural, expository, and prophetic. The texts were mostly recorded on tape and then transcribed and cleaned up[10] with the help of native speakers. A much smaller number of texts were written down by Toposa on paper, and later, on computer. These were usually edited by the authors themselves. These texts were later compiled and published by my husband (M. C. Schröder 1993a) and served as the basis for my investigation of sentence constructions in the contexts of higher levels of discourse.

All my work between 1994 and 2001, i.e. the research conducted for this study, was carried out based in Nairobi, but also involved a number of visits to the "liberated Toposa areas" around Narus, to Kakuma in northern Kenya, where many Toposa refugees lived in an UNHCR (United Nations High Commissioner for Refugees) camp, and to Kitale, where there is a small team of Toposa working in a Bible translation and literacy project.

During the research for this study, I mainly worked with Peter Kagol, Christine Ligie, and her husband James Omo Nachek, but above all with James Lokuuda Kadanya, who also helped to verify all the other data used in this book.

For the purposes of this study, a number of methodological considerations were important. First back in 1982, Toposa was not yet a written language with a standardized orthography, so we employed Pike's method of listening and writing down utterances in phonetic script and analysed the data according to the procedures of phonemics (Pike 1975). Our approach to syntax at that time was merely descriptive, and it was

---

[10]Editing from the oral stage to the written style usually involved taking out repetitions and other redundancies, as well as choosing from alternatives in instances where the narrator corrected himself/herself. Apart from this "streamlining," the written texts do not deviate from the oral version in any significant way.

not until 1994 that I began to investigate the word order problem in Toposa in the framework of generative models of grammar.

Second since all languages undergo change, the data collected twelve years earlier had to be verified. While it was not to be expected that the syntactic structure had changed within this period, it was necessary to recheck all the earlier data, and to augment the corpus as the direction of the research demanded. At the same time it was necessary to analyse tone, especially with respect to the marking of case on nouns.

Third the data represent a fair cross-section of the speakers of the language. Although the main language assistants were from the younger generation, my data were also checked with middle-aged speakers and older people, both men and women, wherever this was feasible.[11]

Fourth this study concentrates on the western dialect of Toposa as it is spoken in the Riwoto section where we first lived. As far as I could establish, Western and Eastern Toposa are so similar that dialect differences do not affect the conclusions of this research in any way.[12]

1.10 Significance of the Study

This study is significant in a number of ways. Primarily, it seeks to contribute to the development of generative theory as it deals with unresolved questions of the VP in verb-initial languages, such as what the underlying structure is for VSO languages, where to base-generate the subject, what the case-assigner of the subject is, whether a VP exists in verb-initial languages, and how morphology interrelates with the discourse principles of Reference and Focus for word order questions.

It supports the hypothesis of the Minimalist Program that word order is determined by morphosyntactic features rather than by syntactic constituents alone. At the same time it shows that in languages with complex morphophonological processes the Minimalist Program presents an adequate explanatory model.

---

[11]It appears that the main differences are a change in the awareness of the quality of underlying voiceless vowels, a tendency among the younger speakers to use contractions without knowing the older fuller forms, and the extended use of the verb 'he came' to mark narrative progression. None of these differences have any relevance to this study.

[12]Eastern Toposa differs from Western Toposa mainly in that it has less of a tendency to contract in fast speech but retains the fuller forms, especially reduplications, and the lexical inventory of Eastern Toposa is a little closer to Turkana, no doubt due to its closer geographical proximity.

1.10 Significance of the Study

Finally, the research also contributes towards Nilotic language studies in that it makes data from Toposa, a language on which very little has previously been published, available to a wider audience.

These data also provide proof that Toposa has a number of ergative features, which is a novum among Eastern Nilotic languages. This is significant in the light of the fact that until recently a number of authors have claimed that there are no ergative characteristics found in African languages (for instance Plank 1979 and 1985, Dixon 1979, Mallinson and Blake 1981). Since the late eighties, more and more evidence has surfaced to show that ergativity is not absent from the African continent,[13] and this study will provide further evidence to support this claim.

---

[13] Anderson (1988) reports that Päri has a fairly consistent marking of morphological ergativity, but also some features of syntactic ergativity. Some marginal features of syntactic ergativity are found in Luwo (Buth 1981) and in Anywa/Anuak (Reh 1996). Miller and Gillley (2001) report morphological ergativity for Shilluk. Tennet, a member of the Surmic language family, shows traces of ergativity on the morphological level (Randal 2000).

Päri, Luwo, Anywa, and Shilluk all belong to the North-Western branch of Nilotic and are found mainly in Southern Sudan. Tennet is spoken in Eastern Equatoria, Southern Sudan, where it is surrounded by various members of North-Western and Eastern Nilotic.

Apart from this concentration of ergative features in the Nilotic phylum of languages, there are reports of marginal features of erativity in Loma, a Mande language (Rude 1983) and in Mandara, a Chadic language (Frajzyngler 1984)—both cited in Anderson 1988:footnote 1.

2
Theoretical Framework

In order to describe and explain Toposa word order, the following fundamental and interrelating concepts will be used: selected ideas of the Minimalist Program, the ergativity parameter, the pro-drop parameter, and topic and focus as two relevant concepts of discourse configurationality. Beginning with the fundamental ideas of the Minimalist Program, this chapter will introduce all these concepts as the theoretical framework for this study.

2.1 The Minimalist Program

The Minimalist Program is no longer driven by the interaction of rules and modular principles as was common in GB, but is reduced to general principles which guarantee that a linguistic expression is well represented at interface level only (Chomsky 1993:5). The interface level contains the phonological form (PF) and the logical form (LF). Several processes and guiding principles are involved in transporting lexical or morphological information from lexicon to interface. Before looking at these basic concepts, however, it will be good to briefly outline the philosophical background of generativist theory.

2.1.1 Philosophical background

Language and language use have been studied from various points of view. Generative Grammar, for example, treats language as part of the natural world. Man is equipped with a language faculty which is an innate property of the human mind. This language faculty comprises a general component called grammatical competence, also known as I-language, and performance, also known as E-language. Grammatical competence is the speaker's actual knowledge of the language. It provides him with the ability to perceive relationships of linguistic elements and to analyse, generate, and describe the structure of his language in a grammar. He can then produce an infinite number of sentences using only a finite number of rules. Competence also allows the native speaker to make assessments about the grammaticality of expressions, whereby his intuition helps him to judge the well or ill-formedness of grammatical sentences.

Performance is the actual use of the language in concrete situations (Chomsky 1965:4). It builds upon the structure of the language for proper language usage and focuses more on cultural and conventional normative concepts than on the grammaticality of sentences. Performance as language behaviour is the subject of psychology and other interlinguistic disciplines such as ethnography, sociolinguistics, pragmatics, and conversational analysis, to mention only a few (cf. Schiffrin 1994).

In reality, the boundaries between grammatical and pragmatic competence are not clearly marked. Such a sharp distinction only exists under ideal speaker-listener conditions in a completely homogeneous speech community (Chomsky 1965:3). Chomsky himself does not see a strict distinction between competence and performance. For him, both concepts are interrelated and contribute to investigating universal grammar (UG) and the human mind (Chomsky 1982:201–202).

Based on these premises and presuppositions, generative grammar meets the conditions for an adequate grammatical model. First of all, it achieves observational adequacy in specifying the difference between grammatical and ungrammatical sentences on phonological, morphological, syntactic, and semantic grounds. Second, it strives for descriptive adequacy by formulating the rules and regulations of the language structure which are based on the native speaker's intuition about well-formedness properties. Thirdly, explanatory adequacy is achieved by providing good reasons for the rules of the grammar. According to Chomsky (1986a:53), every grammar of a specific language has to meet these conditions. Additionally, Chomsky is searching for a universal theory of language where

2.1.2 From lexicon to interface level

After these more philosophical considerations, the model itself will be described, i.e., the "computational process" from the lexicon to the syntactic representation.

The lexicon contains all the lexical and morphosyntactic information about nouns and verbs. A set of morphosyntactic and lexical items is taken from the lexicon in a process called numeration. A computational process, the merge, takes place to combine the elements into projections and partial trees. Merge is part of the structure-building process that takes place to transport the information from the lexicon to the interface level (what used to be the surface level in GB). Note that the structure-building process in the Minimalist Program pursues a different concept from that of the Projection Principle in GB. There the level of deep structure was postulated as functioning as an internal interface between the lexicon and the syntactic representation. The information of the lexicon was then projected onto the deep-structure level. Under the Minimalist Program, however, the structure-building process eliminates the Projection Principle and the deep structure level of GB's T-model (Chomsky 1981:5; 1993:3) which represented the generated information from the lexicon.

The Minimalist Program keeps the specifier-head and head-head relationships of X-bar theory (Chomsky 1993:6). The lexical items from the lexicon are typically transformed into a specifier-head or head-complement relationship:

(8)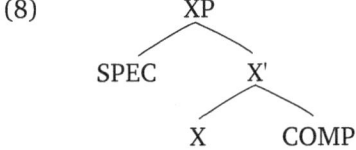

This typical structure, formerly known as maximal projection (Chomsky 1981:29), preserves the idea that representations are projected from the lexicon into a master plan for all phrases and presupposes a cross-categorial symmetry for all of them. The structure-building process is different from the Projection Principle: it is driven by necessity. Structures are only built if they are licensed by the morphosyntactic or lexical information of the lexicon, i.e., by morphological or lexical evidence of the language. Thus language can produce partial trees with a head and no complement if there is no need for case-assignment under the specifier-head relationship. Consequently, the new model does not allow any vacuous positions.

In GB the concept of movement, also known as Move-α, mediated between the deep structure and surface structure levels.[1] This movement was triggered by different syntactic phenomena. Wh-movement was caused by word-order change, V-movement by AGR, and TNS features and constituent movement by case-assignment and word order changes, particularly in passive constructions. In the Minimalist Program, by contrast, words are moved around for checking purposes. The necessity for checking creates the positions in the structure-building process; for example, the specifier (SPEC) position is only relevant as constituents exist that require case-checking. The movement of the checking process is no longer determined by the nature of INFL (Haegeman 1994:591), since it is now a checking process where the abstract inflectional features of the verb are checked for their correctness against the syntactic positions in the sentence structure. The same holds for the nouns and their morphology: the case features of the nouns are checked in the appropriate specifier position. Consequently, the new theory develops a different understanding of AGR and TNS. Now TNS and AGR have two functions. According to the Split-INFL-Hypothesis, INFL no longer exists (Pollock 1989), but is separated into TNS, subject agreement (AGRs) and object agreement (AGRo) projections. The functional heads AGR and TNS do not dominate inflectional morphology any longer but are bundles of abstract features. Movements to AGRs, TNS, and AGRo are feature-checking processes that eliminate the abstract features so that they are not visible at PF. The TNS and AGR projections ensure that the properties of the verb are checked by raising them, and the case features also check the properties of the NP, now also referred to as determiner phrase (DP), by raising them to the specifier positions of AGRs and AGRo. Thus the checking process ensures that NP and VP are properly paired. The checking can take place at any stage of derivation to PF and LF.

Movement is directed by the interacting Principle of Economy, the Minimal Link Conditions, and the Principles of Procrastinate and Greed. Reformulating the Principle of Relativised Minimality, the Minimal Link Conditions state that movement is only possible into the nearest relevant position (Rizzi 1990, Chomsky 1993, 1995). Procrastinate makes sure that movement only takes place if there is need for it and if it is licensed

---

[1] Lasnik and Saito in their 1992 book deal with all aspects of Move-α, describing in detail the subjacency conditions on movement and requirements on traces (The Empty Category Principle).

2.1 The Minimalist Program

by any morphosyntactic or lexical evidence from the language. Additionally, the Last Resort Principle guarantees that a short movement is preferred over a longer one. Related to the Last Resort Principle is the Greed Principle, which is some sort of a self-serving Last Resort. It ensures that movement is only possible if the requirements for movement of the element are satisfied in terms of spell-out and convergence (Chomsky 1995:200).

After tree-structure building, the computational process spells out the information of the lexicon onto PF and LF. The process of spell-out becomes most relevant as it sorts out the phonological and semantic information for the structural descriptions. No kind of phonological information is allowed to appear at LF; neither can logical information appear at PF. Thus a derivation crashes if the phonological or semantic information is mixed on the respective levels and the final structure turns out to be ungrammatical. However, if the conditions of PF and LF are met, the derivation converges.

The two independent representations of the interface are no longer represented by GB's traditional T-model, but by the following diagram:

(9)

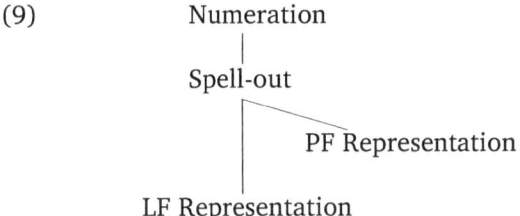

Within this new interface representation, the Principle of FI has been integrated into the process of spell-out and is now also linked to the Principle of Economy. This principle constrains the structure-building process, so that no superfluous element appears, i.e., any element that is not licensed, either lexically or morphologically, is filtered out. It is obvious how this principle goes hand in hand with the idea of spell-out. As the spell-out process sorts out the semantic from the phonological information, spell-out is likewise guided by the Principle of FI, so that no unlicensed element appears on interface level. The Principle of FI replaced the earlier Principle of θ-criterion (Cook and Newson 1988:327), because the θ-criterion turned out to be insufficient and arbitrary (Chomsky 1993:21).

Languages also work on the Principle of Economy (Chomsky 1993:44; 1995:150) which interacts with the other principles in the computational process before spell-out into PF and LF. The economy concept is also channelled by Procrastinate and the Least Effort Condition which further constrains the representational and derivational process. Procrastinate is economical in terms of X_0 movement. It makes sure that movement only takes place if there is need for it and if it is licensed by any morphosyntactic or lexical evidence from the language. The Least Effort Condition ensures that the derivations are as economic as possible: no superfluous step in the derivation is allowed, so that no superfluous symbol appears in the representation. In simple words, languages are lazy, and if one element does the job in representing the interface level, any other element expressing the same meaning is redundant.

Within the derivational process, one question arises: when exactly should spell-out take place? Spell-out can only take place after numeration and after the structure-building process, so that spell-out can do its sorting job according to the Principle of FI for semantic and phonological information. If spell-out takes place too late, for example after PF and LF, the representations on both levels are mixed up. Or, if lexical items are inserted after spell-out, spell-out cannot split the relevant information into the correct levels of interpretation.

2.1.3 The morphology drive

Morphology plays an important role in the new theory. Chomsky states that operations in the computational system are driven by morphological necessity (Chomsky 1993:32). In other words, the amount of movement that takes place in the structure-building process depends on how rich or weak the morphology of a language is (Chomsky 1993:8).

There is a significant difference between the role which morphology plays in GB and in the Minimalist Program. Under GB, the morphosyntactic features were not placed onto the deep structure level. A verb, for example, was selected in its root form from the lexicon and generated in the VP under its lexical head. The inflectional morphemes (person, number, and tense) were then generated under their respective inflectional heads. The reason for verb movement was to pick up these morphological features, so that on surface structure level the verb appeared grammatically correct. In this way morphology and syntax were split in GB. The Minimalist Program, however, in its morphosyntactic nature assumes that the inflectional properties are given to the verbs and nouns in the lexicon, and the already inflected verbs and nouns with their case morphology are generated in the VP under their respective heads. There is no longer any need for verbs and nouns to be projected at deep structure level in order to pick up their features and to appear grammatically correct on surface structure level. Thus, the division between deep structure and surface structure is eliminated.

In other words, the lexicon is no longer a collection of roots and stems for verbs and nouns but it also contains all the relevant inflectional morphology of these categories. Therefore, the process of verb movement is not determined by the nature of INFL (Haegeman 1994:591) but is now a checking process in which the abstract inflectional features are checked for their correctness against the syntactic positions in the sentence structure. The same holds for nouns and their morphology: the case features of nouns are checked under their appropriate positions.

Under the Minimalist Program the elements TNS and AGR are incorporated into the verb in the lexicon; they are called V-features. The function of these V-features is to check the properties of the verb, after it is selected from the lexicon, and before it appears at PF and LF.

With respect to AGR, the Minimalist Program sees languages as having either strong or weak AGR. Strong AGR becomes visible at PF, whereas weak AGR does not. In other words, languages with strong AGR force verb movement to eliminate the abstract feature bundles before spell-out into PF and LF, while languages with weak AGR do not force verb movement, since no features have to be checked. Thus, the verb appears right away at PF and LF.

This way of handling morphology with its direct bearing on verbal inflection and case-marking is reflected in the new basic sentence structure (Chomsky 1993:7), as seen in (10).

In example (10) AGRs and AGRo are bundles containing features (gender, number, person), which distinguish the agreement-marking of the two functional roles of AGR, subject and object. Thus, the new program also takes languages into consideration which have morphological object case-marking. (Extensive work on case-marking and case-assigning was done by Blake 1994.)

(10)
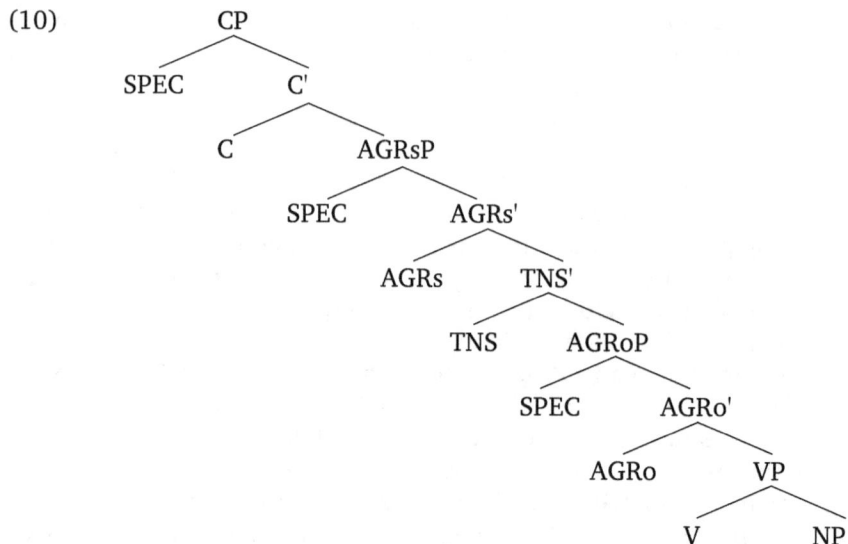

In many languages, the morphology of verbs extends beyond AGR and TNS and has to deal with phenomena like benefactive and instrumental (commonly subsumed under the term 'applicative') and causative constructions. These were dealt with under 'exceptional case-marking' (Baker 1988), but continued to pose a problem to the common generative analysis. One of the central questions that concerned GB analysts was the conflict of how to assign case in double object constructions which typically occur with applicative and causative. The common assumption was that, according to the case filter, one case-assigner is responsible for the case-assigning of one element. The case-assigning of a double accusative object, therefore, posed a problem. Under the Minimalist Program this is taken care of by the checking theory which determines that every affix has its own head, so that double accusative case-assigning is no longer a problem, because the specifiers of the respective heads take care of case-marking.

In the past, applicatives have been handled mainly in two different ways.[2] Marantz (1984) approaches applicatives in terms of merger. According to him, the transitive verb merges with the benefactive suffix into

---

[2]Outside of GB, Cole and Saddock have handled the problem in their Relational Grammar under the terms 3-to-2 Advancement or Oblique-to-2 Advancement (1977). Grammatical function rules derive (or sanction) the applicative constructions by taking an oblique PP and changing it into the direct object of the clause. As by-products of this rule, the basic object automatically ceases to be a direct object, and the verb is marked with the applied affix.

2.1 The Minimalist Program

a ditransitive verb root and heads the benefactive NP and the direct object NP:

(11)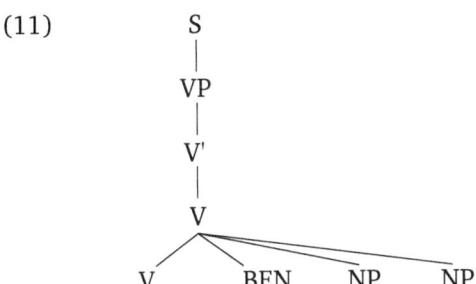

It is part of his merger theory that the merged verb already occurs in the lexicon with the applicative construction.

Baker deals with applicatives in the following way: the benefactive suffix functions as the preposition of the NP, and it is this preposition which case-assigns the accusative case to the NP and θ-assigns the role of recipient to it (1988:230–268). Thus, the prepositional relationship and the thematic relationship can be diagrammed as follows:

(12)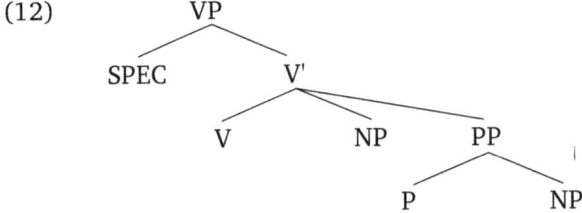

In order to ensure that the preposition governs the NP and remains case-assigner at surface structure level, Baker adduces the UTAH which moves the preposition into the verb and leaves a trace of P behind:

(13)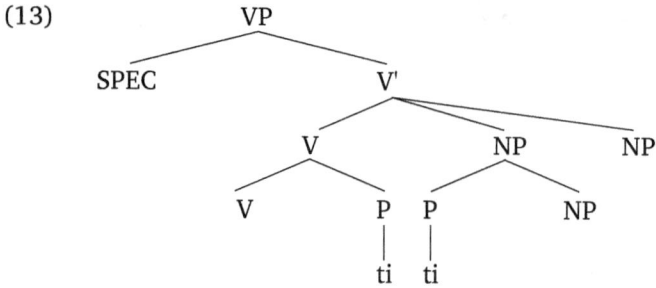

At this stage the Empty Category Principle plays an important role in Baker's theory. It demands that traces are properly governed, and the only proper governor is an argument in θ-position. Barriers to government are full projections. The proper governor of the trace P is V, and there is no full projection blocking the government, because PP does not enter the complex construction as a PP but as a NP.

Note that the Minimalist Program has several advantages over the merger theory of Marantz and the incorporation theory of Baker. Because the Minimalist Program suggests to split the IP into morphological projections, which require feature-checking, the merger and the complicated mapping onto three levels is no longer necessary. The structure-building process also supersedes the complex incorporation processes of Baker, for example the transfer from deep structure to surface structure and the rules guarding this process, i.e., the various principles like the UTAH, the Empty Category Principle, and the complications with proper government are all eliminated, as all these complex principles are replaced by the much simpler checking theory.

Another question with double object constructions is the following: Which one is the direct and which one is the applied object? Again, Marantz (1984) solves the problem in terms of merger. The applicative affix merges into a new applicative stem which heads both the applied object and the basic object. The result of this merger is a derived predicate structure with a derived semantic logical structure where the applied object becomes the goal object, and the basic object retreats to the position of indirect object (Marantz 1984:235). The applied affix remains the head in this lexical structure and assigns the semantic benefactive role to the direct object. Thus the benefactive advances to the derived direct object, while the patient object shifts to the function of an indirect object. Baker refers to this phenomenon as Marantz's generalisation (Baker 1988:249).

Baker's incorporation theory poses questions whether the verb can assign case to two objects. The original case filter says that one argument can assign only one case. Therefore, Baker (1988:246–264) asks what is the case-assigner of the second object. He adduces the Case Frame Preservation Principle, which says that a lexical category, whether derived or underived, can assign only one case. In the light of this constraint, the theory faces a serious problem in that two conditions have to be met: a second type of case-assigning has to be activated that will satisfy the visibility needs for the basic object, and it must become clear that this second type of indexing cannot refer to the applied object. Baker argues that every language handles the problem differently, but basically languages have two options: either the object is incorporated into the verb, which means that no case-assignment is needed, or the verb assigns two cases. He also points out that applicative constructions have always raised problems for the second object in terms of case filter (cf. Hornstein and Weinberg 1981, Kayne 1983, and Oerhle 1975 as cited by Baker 1988:280). It seems that there has never been an elegant and easy solution to this problem. Incorporation theory cannot separate the applicative affix as a case-bearing unit, because it merges with the verb and the verb becomes the case-assigner; and Marantz's theory faces the same theoretical problem, because after the merger of the main verb and its benefactive affix the verb becomes the case-assigner, but cannot properly assign two cases to the double objects.

The Minimalist Program resolves these difficulties by separating the applicative affix as a case-bearing unit. In this way, the basic object receives its case features through the specifier of AGRo and the applicative gets its features through the specifier of the applicative phrase. Thus there is no longer any question about multiple case-assignment. Furthermore, no question is raised about the proper government of the traces, because government theory has been eliminated under the Minimalist Program. Note also how Baker was forced to discuss the Empty Category Principle in detail after the P had moved into the verb and left a trace behind (1988:51–63), because the trace has to obey the Empty Category Principle, a fact which complicates the matter.

Another advantage of the Minimalist approach is that it also cancels the UTAH because it is not concerned with θ-assignment. It replaces the θ-theory by introducing the Principle of FI, which guarantees that the morphological elements of the verb and its syntactic relations appear at PF and LF after they have been properly case-assigned. Proper case-assignment takes place through the specifier-head relationship of the respective heads.

The Minimalist Program comprises a number of other developments. The subject is no longer base-generated in the [SPEC/INFL] because the subject no longer relies on any independent deep-structure level criterion such as θ-marking (Chomsky 1981:47). From now on the subject is placed in the [SPEC/VP] following the Subject-Internal-Hypothesis (Larson 1988) which departs from the concept that a verb has an internal and an external argument (Chomsky 1981:101–103).[3] Under the new scenario it is the VP which contains all the information of the sentence, and the verb has two internal arguments. From now on sentences are the extended projection of VP and not of INFL (Chomsky 1981:52).

To summarise the new approach, the transfer of information from lexicon to interface to PF and LF deletes the deep structure level, the surface structure level, and the concept of government (a fundamental concept held onto since 1965). Consequently, all other principles that applied at deep structure level and surface structure level, such as the θ-criterion and the Projection Principle (deep structure phenomena), case theory and binding theory (surface structure phenomena) have been disposed of.[4] Case theory is reformulated to become a checking process[5] and the

---

[3]For an extensive discussion of argument structure from a logical point of view, see Allwood et al. (1977) and McCauley (1970). For a discussion of the classification of verbs in traditional literature, see Burton-Roberts (1986), Huddleston (1976), and Quirk et al. (1985).

[4]The original thought of creating a deep structure level was that the operation called Satisfy selected an array of items from the lexicon and mapped them onto deep structure level to satisfy the conditions of X-bar. Chomsky thus postulated an additional level beyond the two external levels PF and LF. Deep structure functioned as an internal interface between the lexicon and the computational system. Certain principles of UG apply then to deep structure, expecially the Projection Principle and the θ-criterion. The computational system maps the information of deep structure onto surface structure through Move-α, and then branches off into PF and LF, thus producing the typical T-model of UG. Binding theory, case theory, and the pro-module apply at surface structure.

[5]Case theory was supposed to apply at surface structure, for morphological case-marking of an NP was mapped onto deep structure and through movement an NP received its structural case-marking. Under the Minimalist Program an NP receives its case-marking from the lexicon, depending on the choice of the verb, and is put into the VP of a sentence. The morphological case-marking of the subject and the object are checked against the various positions, as the NPs move to the specifier positions of AGRsP and/or AGRoP. This movement can happen overtly, before spell-out, or covertly, after spell-out.

2.1 The Minimalist Program

θ-criterion[6] is taken over by the Principle of FI.[7] The binding conditions[8] are left to apply at LF without any structural principle.

The elimination of government solved a long-standing problem. The concept of government had always remained arbitrary because the relationship of the governor to its governee could often not be identified precisely. The concept was either fixed too narrowly, as was the case in its

---

[6]In early versions of the Principles and Parameters framework, the concepts of θ-theory turned out to be difficult. There are particularly two areas where the θ-criterion does not cover the data of English, for example. One area is adjectival constructions as "John is easy to please" where John is occupying a non-θ-position and hence cannot appear at deep structure level, but only at PF level, and thus the θ-filter is violated (Chomsky 1993:21). Secondly, NPs with multiple semantic roles violate the θ-criterion which states that one argument can only bear one θ-role. A typical example for one argument bearing more than one θ-role is "John left the room angry", where John is not only the one who left the room, but he is also angry. Chomsky himself realised that linguistic expressions which have no place at deep structure level but are interpreted only at LF (also Reinhardt 1991) led to the disposal of deep structure, as it loses its "credibility" (Chomsky 1993:21). Also Jackendoff (1990:59–61), working on a theory of meaning, tries to tackle the insufficiency of the roles and θ-criterion for NPs that have more than one θ-role or multiple NPs that hold a single θ-role. He points out that the richness of semantic roles cannot be squeezed into such a rigid parameter as one θ-role. The θ-theory and its principles turned out to be very weak, so Chomsky replaced its concepts. He retained the idea that semantic information has to be integrated into the syntactic framework, but the θ-theory is no longer the mediator; rather, the Principle of Full Interpretation (1986a:98) is: "Every element of PF and LF, taken to be the interface of syntax with systems of language use, must receive an appropriate interpretation—must be licensed in the sense indicated."

[7]The Principle of FI shifts the concepts of θ-theory, like θ-roles, into the area of the lexicon. As stated before, it is in numeration that the elements are selected from the lexicon and get ready for structure-building. The semantic information previously conceptualised in the θ-theory is now part of the lexicon. Thus, transitive verbs determine the semantic role of an agent and a patient and are selected from the lexicon with their semantic characteristics, for example take the verb 'drink'. It has the following structure: agent–drink–patient. When 'drink' is selected from the lexicon, it determines that the subject of the sentence can only have the semantic role of an agent and the object the role of a patient.

[8]The disposal of surface structure eliminates a lot of unsolved problems in binding theory. At LF the wh-material is in its proper wh-position. As a consequence, non-wh-material which is overtly moved along with a wh-element is reconstructed into its original position, and only wh-elements undergo covert movement to wh-positions at LF.

original GB version (Chomsky 1981),[9] or it was fixed too widely, as in Chomsky's barrier model (1986b).[10] In either version it allowed a wide range of relationships and raised obvious empirical problems.[11] Consequently, the concept of government has now been replaced by the specifier-head relationship and by checking theory. The case theory of GB had already partly conceptualised the specifier-head relationship. For example, the specifier-head of INFL assigned nominative case to the subject, and the head-complement relationship of the verb assigned accusative case to the object. In the new program case-assignment has been completely unified through the specifier-head relationships of AGRs and AGRo.

2.1.4 The word-order parameter

The notion of feature-checking results in a simple cross-linguistic parameter of word order, in that feature-checking requires all languages to have verb movement, i.e., all languages move their verbs to the inflectional nodes, and NPs are moved to the specifier of AGRsP and AGRoP for feature-checking. Languages differ as to when these movements take place: before or after spell-out. If a language has morphological features in the verb, movement takes place before spell-out, because the features have to be checked before they result in the PF. Here is where the Principle of Procrastinate comes in. It makes sure that verb movement only takes place if forced to do so by evidence from the language. Languages that have no morphological features in the verb delay movement until after spell-out, just before LF. If movement takes place before spell-out the language is said to have "overt movement;" if it takes place after spell-out the language is said to have "covert movement." In earlier versions of

---

[9]The minimal c-command conditions (Chomsky 1981:163) were:
α governs ß and if and only if
(a) $\alpha = X_0$
(b) α c-commands ß and if γ c-commands ß then γ c-commands α or is c-commanded by ß.

[10]The maximal c-commands conditions (Chomsky 1986b:8) were
α governs ß if and only if
(a) α m-commands ß and
(b) every barrier for ß dominates α.

[11]For example, it allowed a verb to govern the specifier of its complement and therefore to assign case to a wh-element in this position, which also resulted in a chain formed by the moved wh-element. The wh-word received at least two cases, because the original trace of the wh-element sat in a case-marked position, but the moved element received case, too. Further, it did not make sense that AGR governs the specifier of TNSP, and therefore can assign case to this specifier. It remains unclear why the subject should move into the specifier of AGRP to receive nominative case, as it is already in a case-marked position in the TNSP.

2.1 The Minimalist Program

Generative Grammar, verb movement was only triggered by the absence or presence of INFL (especially Pollock 1989). This concept led to a division between French-type and English-type languages. In French-type languages, the verb has to move to INFL in order to pick up its inflectional features, whereas English-type languages do not have to raise the verb due to their weak AGR system. The French-type languages have a so-called strong AGR versus the English-type languages which have a weak AGR. This division based on verb movement versus no verb movement has been modified; under the Minimalist Program all languages have to move the verb for feature-checking, but there is now a new distinction between overt and covert verb movement.

As already pointed out in section 1.8, word order differences, such as SVO/VSO versus SVO/SOV, were formerly solved through the theory of deep structure and verb movement. The Minimalist Program, however, has created a somewhat simplified version of word order, because it leaves the determination of word order to morphology (Chomsky 1993:31). The dichotomy created through the criteria of weak and strong AGR for word order differences remains unsatisfactory because there are SVO as well as VSO languages with rich verb agreement. For example, Kiswahili is SVO but has a strong verb agreement system (Bearth 1995) both in terms of subject and object agreement, and Toposa is a VSO language with a strong subject-verb agreement. Therefore, the concept of overt and covert verb movement does not resolve the fundamental differences between VSO and SVO languages.

Another area where the approach of the Minimalist Program leaves open important questions is ergativity. Chomsky tries to capture the difference between nominative-accusative and ergative-absolutive languages through feature-checking and verb movement. Thus, the distinction between ergative and non-ergative now depends on which of the agreement systems is active and which one is inert only. In ergative-absolutive systems, for example, the specifier of AGRoP is more active than the specifier of AGRsP, since it is visited for the absolutive case-marking; in nominative-accusative systems it is the other way round. Again, Chomsky leaves the difference to what he terms "a trivial question of morphology" (Chomsky 1993:9).

Although Chomsky has sought to take care of ergativity in clearer terms than in previous models of grammar where ergativity was captured in terms of deep structure and NP movement, the new approach is still not complex enough because it does not specifically deal with split systems and syntactically ergative languages.

2.1.5 Topic and focus

The last area of word order phenomena that needs to be dealt with is that of topic and focus.

Again, the Minimalist Program merely touches on this issue and does not even make a distinction between topic and focus. Under GB, topicalisation and focus were treated as left-dislocated constituent movement to the specifier of CP, similar to the wh-movement (Chomsky 1981:158ff., Rizzi 1982, particularly Lasnik and Saito 1992:1ff. and 75ff.)[12] Note that because the new approach is driven by morphological necessity, it assumes that the operator feature of CP is morphologically strong so that it attracts movement. Topicalisation and focus are also left to morphologically strong CP features (Chomsky 1993:32). A strength of the new approach is that it simplifies the complex wh-movement theory; it bypasses all the complicated syntactic constraints on movements for syntactic barriers (Lasnik and Saito 1992:1ff.) and the wh-island constraint (Chomsky 1981, 1986b, Rizzi 1982, Lasnik and Saito 1992) and it also simplifies the left-dislocation complications associated with focus and topic.

2.2 The Nominative-Accusative and Ergative-Absolutive Parameter

We have examined the theoretical framework of the Minimalist Program, particularly those aspects that deal with word order. The next sections (2.2–2.6) will look at a number of independent frameworks that are relevant to this study. The first one to be dealt with is the nominative-accusative and ergative-absolutive parameter.

All languages distinguish between transitive and intransitive sentences in terms of the number of their constituents and their case-marking. Case-marking is accomplished either in terms of word order (which is also referred to as syntactical case-marking), or with morphological case-marking, or both. If it is done in terms of word order, usually the verb identifies both constituents so that there is no doubt which constituent is the subject and which one is the object. English is such a language where the SVO word order nicely separates the subject from the object through the intervening verb. Those languages which have both subject and object on the same side of the verb, e.g., VSO and SOV languages,

---

[12]Lasnik and Saito (1992:75ff.) discuss topicalisation and left dislocation, claiming that topicalisation is not always left dislocated, particularly as topic can be an adjunction to IP.

2.2 The Nominative-Accusative and Ergative-Absolutive Parameter

tend to employ morphological case-marking. Whatever the marking strategy is, it is either pursued within a nominative-accusative or an ergative-absolutive system. The term "ergative-absolutive" is used to describe a grammatical pattern in which the subject of an intransitive sentence is marked in the same way as the object of a transitive sentence, while the subject of the transitive sentence is marked differently. Under this scenario, the term "ergative" refers to the subject of the transitive sentence, over against the term "absolutive" which denotes the subject of the intransitive sentence and the object of the transitive sentence. An estimated twenty-five percent of the world's languages use this strategy (Dixon 1994:2).[13]

As ergativity is not found in Europe, except in Basque (Dixon 1994:2) which is not Indo-European, traditional European grammars (e.g., Quirk et al. 1985) generally do not talk about ergative, but characterise grammatical core relations in terms of "nominative" and "accusative," where the term nominative specifies the subject of both transitive and intransitive sentences, and accusative indicates the object of a transitive sentence. As an increasing amount of work in non-Indo-European languages was carried out at the beginning of the seventies and more ergative-absolutive systems were discovered, the basic concepts of subject and object relating to nominative and accusative were not enough to cover the grammatical relations. Hence, linguists began to use the three primitives S, A, and O to capture grammatical relations in transitive and intransitive sentences, where A refers to the agent/subject of the transitive sentence, O to the patient/object of the transitive sentence, and S describes the single core relation of the intransitive sentence (Dixon 1994:9, Comrie 1989:110ff). Based on this three-way distinction, the difference between nominative-accusative and ergative-absolutive systems is best defined in terms of the constituents that are marked in the same way, and are thus grouped together, as shown in (14).

(14)

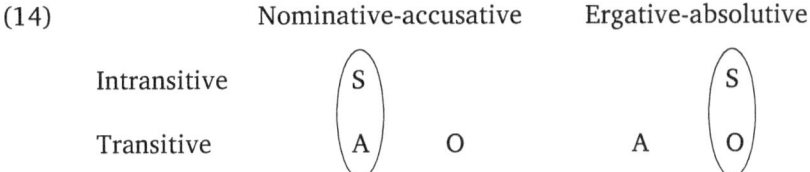

	Nominative-accusative	Ergative-absolutive
Intransitive	S	S
Transitive	A O	A O

In other words, in nominative-accusative systems, S and A are marked identically, but O is treated differently, whereas in ergative-absolutive

---

[13] A very small number of languages have both nominative-accusative as well as ergative-absolutive features. These are also referred to as languages with a split system (see next footnote and section 3.3).

systems S and O are marked in the same way, while the A of the transitive sentence is marked separately (Dixon 1994:9, T. Payne 1982:78).

Ergative languages which employ case-marking to signal the core syntactic relations are generally referred to as languages with "morphological ergativity" (Dixon 1994:39), whereas those that mark the ergative-absolutive relationship in terms of word order are defined as having "syntactic ergativity."

Many languages exhibit either morphological ergativity or syntactic ergativity; very few show signs of both (like Toposa). If a language morphologically case-marks its NPs, it is likely also to have a cross-reference system which is based either on an accusative-nominative or an ergative-absolutive system.[14] Any language that shows signs of syntactic ergativity is likely to have ergative characteristics at the morphological level as well (Dixon 1994:177), whereas not all languages that have morphological ergativity also show syntactically ergative features.[15]

Generative grammarians have written very little about ergative case-marking, but the term "ergative verbs" does occur in the literature. For example, Burzio (1981) refers to ergative verbs as forming a subset of intransitive verbs in Italian. These verbs have only one internal argument and behave like passives.[16] They are also classified as "unaccusative verbs" or "ergative causative verbs."

On a more theoretical level, Marantz (1984:196) attempts to handle ergativity in the following way: the deep structure subject in ergative languages is S and O, while the deep structure object O is the A of the transitive sentence, as shown in (15).

---

[14]See Dixon 1994:42–45 for a detailed discussion of how languages cross-reference their basic constituents either on an ergative-absolutive or nominative-accusative or on a split cross-reference basis, where both accusative-nominative and ergative-absolutive features occur together. Dixon also shows that there are languages where no congruence exists between the cross-reference and the case-marking system: such languages have a split system in which the cross-reference system works on a nominative-accusative basis, whereas the case-marking system is ergative-absolutive, or vice versa.

[15]According to Dixon, there is no language that works on syntactic ergativity alone (1994:52, 177). However, it is possible that languages have only morphologically ergative case-marking without any feature of syntactic ergativity.

[16]Some linguists depart from Burzio's analysis and do not put the ergative verbs in the same group as passives (Haegeman 1994 following a suggestion of Belletti 1988, also Hale and Keyser 1986, and den Besten 1985, who works on Dutch and German).

(15)

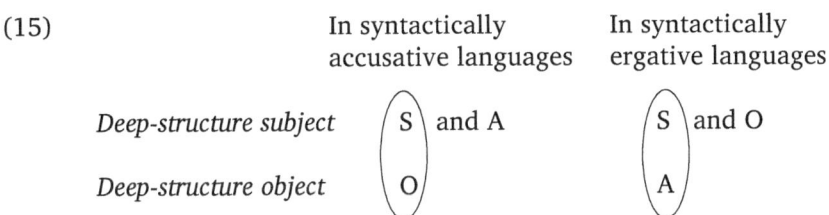

	In syntactically accusative languages	In syntactically ergative languages
Deep-structure subject	S and A	S and O
Deep-structure object	O	A

It seems awkward, however, to link O with subject properties and A with object properties, even at deep-structure level. Marantz also regards the ergative-absolutive system as an off-shoot of the nominative-accusative system. Furthermore, his approach is unable to take care of split systems.

2.3 The Pro-Drop Parameter

The next framework relevant to word order is the pro-drop parameter which describes the property of natural languages to omit the pronominal subject on sentence level. This parameter is based on the idea that if the pronoun is dropped, its content must be recovered or identified by other means. It has been shown that the nominal features of person, gender, and number attached to the verb (also called the ph-nominal features) are rich enough to recover the content of the missing subject. This idea was formulated in the Standard Theory (Jaeggli 1982, Rizzi 1982, and Chomsky 1982) and was later modified by the Morphological Uniformity Hypothesis (MUH) that related a morphologically uniform inflectional paradigm to pro-drop languages (Jaeggli and Safir 1989).

Huang (1984) also dealt with pro-drop from a Chinese perspective and gives an account of the problem of zero subjects and objects. He claims that the pro-drop in object position is an empty topic which forces the theoretical framework of generative grammar to set up a maximal projection for topics. His analysis leads him to postulate a new language typology which distinguishes between discourse-oriented languages (i.e., languages with an empty topic) and sentence-oriented languages (i.e., languages without an empty topic).

Neither of these theories covers all instances of pro-drop languages, for example, the MUH is questioned by English which is not a pro-drop language and has an inflectional paradigm. Consider also languages like Danish, Norwegian, and Swedish which are morphologically uniform and yet do not allow pro-drop at all (Y. Huang 1994).

2.4 Discourse Configurationality: Topic and Focus

There are various approaches to discourse and the discourse function of topic and focus which are relevant for this study. These will be considered in this section.

Discourse has been viewed from many different perspectives (cf. Schiffrin 1994). A perspective which is of particular interest for the discussion in this book is the difference between the formalist and the functional approaches to discourse. The formalist camp (represented by Hymes 1974, Grimes 1975, Chafe 1976, Chomsky 1981, Givón 1984, Harris 1988) concentrates on the structure of discourse, how the units that make up the structure of discourse relate to each other, and how these relationships are formally marked. The formalist approach regards discourse as a unit above the sentence, views language as a syntactically hierarchical order, and is interested in how the different levels of morphology, sentence, complex sentence structure, and discourse relate to each other. The functionalists are more interested in language use (especially Labov 1972, Fairclough 1989, and Fasold 1990)[17] and how the different discourse features are best interpreted from a sociolinguistic point of view.

In this study, discourse is viewed from a formalist vantage point, but it should be noted that even in the formalist camp there are different ways of noting how syntactic phenomena are related to discourse. Two discourse features which always receive special attention are focus and topic.

Topic and focus are not easy to define and are sometimes hard to detect. Often only tendencies can be observed because as soon as one leaves the syntactic realm of the sentence, the concepts tend to get more fuzzy.

In the following, the different approaches to these two concepts will be surveyed. There are a number of different schools of thought with regard to the phenomena of topic and focus (see Vallduví 1992:28–52 for a good presentation of the different views). They all have in common that they recognise that there is a mechanism in the sentence to highlight information and that some pieces of information are more important than others. The more informative parts of the sentence are marked either structurally or morphologically, or both.

The theme-rheme school—mainly represented today by Halliday (1967)—originated with the Prague school. (See Firbas (1960). He and others credit Mathesius (1915) as the originator of the notion of theme-rheme.) Theme is "what is being talked about...the point of

---

[17]A characteristic functional statement of discourse is the following (Fasold 1990:65): "The language issues treated within discourse analysis are myriad: in a sense the study of discourse is the study of any aspect of language use."

2.4 Discourse Configurationality: Topic and Focus

departure" (Halliday 1967:212–213). Rheme is the informative part of the sentence.

A similar idea is the division of the sentence into "topic" and "comment" (especially Li and Thompson 1976, but also Kuno 1980 and Reinhart 1982). This approach divides the sentence into what the speaker wants to talk about, the topic, and what is said about it, which is the comment. Li and Thompson (1976) developed these basic ideas further into a language typology of subject and topic-oriented languages, adducing languages in Indonesia which are predominantly topic-comment oriented rather than subject-oriented.

A more open school of thought is best subsumed under the term "focus-propositional" (especially Chafe, Prince, and Grosz and Sidner cited in Vallduví 1992:36–42). The focus-propositional approach sets the highlighting of the information structure into the focus framework, where focus represents the informative part of the sentence, and the open-proposition is the anchoring part. Topic plays only a subsidiary role in the system as topicalisation is achieved by fronting the focused constituent. Within this framework, different types of focus are admitted.[18] The focus-propositional approach also made its way into generative grammar; the focus could be anchored into the concept of transformation (Chomsky 1971, Jackendoff 1972). In this GB approach, the focused constituent is moved to its structural position at the front of the sentence.

Although focus had its place in Generative Grammar in relation to wh-movement, topic orientation had been neglected for a long time. Since its inception, Generative Grammar has mainly dealt with syntactic relations at the sentence level. Apart from the definition of the sentence (through its phrase structure, the grammatical subject, VP dichotomy, and the c-command by a single operator position that also functions as the landing site for wh-movements), little attention has been paid to the pragmatic factors determining sentence structure and language typology. Kiss (1995) is one of those who depart from this tradition when she suggests that focus and topic be considered for determining word order and language typology. She proposes the following properties for discourse-configurational languages (p. 6):

A. The (discourse-) semantic function "topic," serving to foreground a specific individual that something will be predicated about (not

---

[18]Watters found that focus in Aghem is marked in four different ways: by word order, by verbal morphology, by the particle *nò,* and by cleft sentences. When applied alone or in combination these means produce the following types of focus: unmarked focus, assertive focus, counter-assertive focus, exhaustive listing focus, polar focus, and counter-assertive polar focus.

necessarily identical with the grammatical subject), is expressed through a particular structural relation (in other words, it is associated with a particular structural position).

B. The (discourse-) semantic function "focus," expressing identification, is realised through a particular structural relation (that is, by movement into a particular structural position).

In other words, discourse-configurational languages are either topic-oriented or focus-oriented. Most languages clearly fall into one of these two categories, but in some languages topic and focus interrelate.

Among non-generativists, topic is often defined in the following way: "topic...denotes the function of the constituent that the sentence is about" (Kiss 1995:7, T. Payne 1997:270, Comrie 1989:69, Dixon 1994:41). Often the topic is identical with the subject of predication, because it denotes what the sentence wants to talk about (Rothstein 1983, Wiesemann 1996:121, and Dik 1978:19). However, other authors like T. Payne (1997:150) extend the concept of topic and do not only identify the subject with topic, but talk about a "topic-worthiness"[19] that ranges between subjects and objects, agreement-marking, personal pronouns, and human, animate, and inanimate NPs. These different categories are arranged on a scale, where the constituents listed on the left show more topic-worthiness than the inanimate NPs placed on the right. This hierarchy is also known as "agentivity hierarchy" or "animacy hierarchy."[20]

A very practical approach to topic and focus is found in Wiesemann (1996, based on Watters 1976). She approaches the somewhat confusing terminology of topic and focus from a practical point of view. Supported by language data, she differentiates between "topic" and "marked topic," where the marked topic is left dislocated and/or marked by a topic marker. She also develops a differentiated view of focus, dividing it first of all into "inherent focus" and "marked focus." Marked focus has an assertive element which answers an explicit or presupposed information question. Another type of marked focus is "selective focus." It presupposes a choice of requested information and signals which information has been selected. Wiesemann also introduces the notion of "tail information" that works antifocally. She further demonstrates that focus comes in

---

[19]Comrie (1989:198) suggests that distinctions often explained in terms of an animacy hierarchy (such as pronoun, non-pronoun, proper name and common noun) do not directly reflect animacy, but might be better explained in terms of topic-worthiness.

[20]T. Payne (1997:150) observes that "agentivity hierarchy" and "animacy hierarchy" are not really accurate terms, as they have nothing to do with animacy or agentivity. Verb agreement, pronouns, and proper names for example can refer to biologically animate or inanimate, agentive or non-agentive entities.

degrees: marked focus, inherent focus, and defocalised elements. The inherent focus is less marked than the marked focus, and the least degree of focus is manifested by defocalised elements.

In Generative Grammar, markedly different from the practical approach of Wiesemann, the discussion on focus concentrated on the issue of an operator expressing identification. Several theories have been developed about how the focus operator fits into the sentence structure, and what the focus-assigner is (Horvath 1981, 1995; Brody 1990). Further issues (discussed in Horvath 1995) are whether focus can be assigned by a functional head, INFL or C, according to cross-linguistic features, or whether the feature [+ FOC] can be transmitted by INFL or C into a position governed by one of these two. Another option might be that focus is assigned by INFL or C under specifier-head agreement (see Kiss 1995:21, 23, 24).

Chomsky himself does not speak explicitly about focus or topic, but assumes that C has an operator feature and that this feature has morphological properties which require checking in its checking domain (1995:32).

2.5 Basic Constituent Order

Several attempts have been made to classify the world's languages according to word order. Word order deals with the order of constituents in the sentence, namely, how subject, verb, and object are grouped together.

Greenberg (1963) studied 30 different languages and produced a survey of correlations between word order, order of constituents, and adpositions which has remained relevant until now and is often cited for word order typology. He suggests six language types based on word order: SVO, SOV, VSO, VOS, OVS, and OSV, with a heavy concentration on the first three, among whom the first two are much more widespread than the third.

The discussion of word order is divided into two opposing camps (cf. Dixon 1994:49). On the one hand, there are those who regard the main active declarative sentence with subject and object as a clear reflection of the dominant word order (Greenberg 1963, Hawkins 1983, Mallison and Blake 1981). On the other hand, there are those who look for other factors outside the matrix clause that could influence word order, as they argue that restricting the search to the main declarative sentence has several weaknesses. First of all, it is no longer considered proven that the basic word order of a language is laid down in main clauses. Emonds (1976), Hopper and Thompson (1973), and Green (1975) have demonstrated that subordinate clauses also play an important role in determining the sentence structure of a language. Secondly, main clauses are likely to have more root transformations and changes, thus the basic word order is often best preserved in subordinate clauses. The latter camp further rejects the assumption that the basic word order has two overt NPs. This approach taken in Generative Grammar and other syntactic models (Dik 1978) has been contradicted by much recent work which shows that the co-occurrence of subject and object is not always the normal case in natural discourse (Derbyshire 1986, Du Bois 1985, Lambrecht 1987, T. Payne 1997). This means that two overt NPs is the marked status of a sentence; the normal case is that a sentence has one constituent. This suggests that this whole area of research calls for a sensitivity towards discourse pragmatic criteria, i.e., clausal-independent criteria like topic, focus, and "given" and "new" information, as well as the relation between subject and object in coordinated and subordinated sentences[21] that determine the basic word order. So far, only Kiss (1995), C.-T. J. Huang (1984),[22] and Philippaki-Warburton (1985)[23] have considered word order within the framework of GB from a more pragmatic angle.

2.6 The Notion of Subject

Not only is basic word order hard to pinpoint, it is even far from easy to define one of the basic constituents, the subject, because there is no general agreement on what exactly constitutes a subject (Comrie 1989).

The most common notion of subject is to define it in terms of topic and agent (Comrie 1989, T. Payne 1997). The reason why topic and agent are subsumed into the notion of subject is that humans have a strong tendency to select more agentive entities (rather than inanimate ones) as

---

[21]D. Payne (1990:25) opts to depart from the common conservative approach and to consider basic word order in the light of language typology that considers syntactic and pragmatic factors. She distinguishes between (a) languages in which order is primarily used to establish syntactic relations, (b) languages in which order is primarily used to signal discourse-pragmatic functions (e.g., identifiability, focus, and contrast), and (c) languages in which order displays a good mixture of both syntactic and discourse-pragmatic functions. Many African languages probably are found in the second or third category, while most Indo-European languages are members of the first group. Payne considers these distinctions as a continuum between languages with almost fully syntactic order on the one end and almost fully pragmatic factors at the other end.

[22]C.-T. J. Huang develops a more pragmatic approach to clauses for Chinese regarding the zero-topics in object positions. Languages that allow zero-topics bound to a variable are "discourse-oriented," over against "sentence-oriented" languages, which do not permit empty topics in object positions.

[23]Philippaki-Warburton (1985:115–117) suggests for Modern Greek that one should consider pragmatically affected and non-pragmatically affected clauses in order to find out the "neutral," i.e., most basic discourse order.

2.6 The Notion of Subject

topics of discussion. This leads to a natural correlation between agent and topic. Hence, the notion of subject simply reflects the grammaticalisation of this expected coincidence. This also explains why so many languages have a grammatical relation definable in its core as the intersection of agent and topic (Comrie 1989:120).

T. Payne warns about subsuming topic and agent under subject by pointing out that the subject can have more than one role. Besides agent, it can occupy the semantic roles of instrument, force, and patient (1997:49). He also tries to reconcile the grammatical, the semantic, and the pragmatic roles of the subject. He argues that it is difficult to find a one-to-one mapping of these three levels. If it comes to discourse, the subject is often found in the role of topic, and on that level the concept of agent and topic needs to be combined.

Dixon attempts his own universal definition of subject based on the idea of agency and control (1994:115). For most multi-participant events, there is just one participant who potentially initiates or controls the activities. So in a transitive sentence the subject would be the most likely candidate to exercise control of the situation. This participant is identified as being in the A function if we consider the three primitives S, A, and O as basic building blocks for grammatical relations (cf. section 2.2). If the A from the tripartite system fulfils the role of agent, the question arises about the roles that S and O perform. And if the A is identified as subject, another question arises as to what grammatical functions should be attributed to S and O? Dixon shows that in most languages the S of the intransitive sentence also fulfils the role of agent, as it exercises control over the events (consider motion verbs like 'go', 'walk', 'jump', 'run', etc.); other verbs like 'yawn', 'die', etc. however do not have an S in controlling function. (See Keenan (1978) for a statistical approach to defining and conceptualising the notion of subject.)

In Generative Grammar the subject was first defined simply through its structural position and in correspondence to case-marking and θ-marking. Quite differently from GB, the subject under the Minimalist Program is now placed in the [SPEC/VP] following the Subject-Internal-Hypothesis (Larson 1988) from where it then moves to its specifier of AGRs to receive its case-marking. This new development is a departure from the concept that a verb has an internal and external argument (Chomsky 1981:101–103). (For an extensive discussion of argument structure from a logical point of view, see Allwood et al. (1977) and McCawley (1970). For a discussion of classification of verbs in traditional literature, see Burton-Roberts (1986), Huddleston (1984), and Quirk et al. (1985).)

2.7 Summary and Outlook

This chapter discussed the theoretical frameworks that will be employed in this book. It described the morphosyntactic Minimalist Program (making reference to the older GB model where appropriate), Marantz's theory of grammatical relations, and Baker's incorporation theory. It examined the word order parameter from several theoretical viewpoints, evaluated theories about topic and focus, explained the nominative-accusative versus the ergative-absolutive parameter and the pro-drop parameter, and concluded with a discussion of basic constituent order and the notion of subject.

After having considered these different frameworks, this study suggests a multiple feature-checking approach to Toposa sentence structure. It does not regard the formation of sentence structure and the word order question as a single simple syntactic decision, as suggested by Greenberg (1963), Dik (1978), Chomsky (1981), and others. Neither does it go along with the merely structural approach of Baker's *Incorporation* (1988), Marantz's *Grammatical Relations* (1984), Chomsky's *Government and Binding* (1981), or other generative proposals which did not address the relationships between morphology, syntax and discourse as interrelated feature-checking processes. Although Kiss considered topic and focus in her *Discourse Configurational Languages* (1995), neither of the theories discussed there fit Toposa, as it has an elaborate focus system that is also best interpreted as a feature-checking process[24] because it is related to the complex verb morphology. (This will be elaborated in chapter five).

This study also supports the claim that some African languages have ergative features, and it will show that Toposa employs a morphological nominative-accusative case-marking system with traces of ergative-absolutive case-marking in the passive, as well as ergative features in the split cross-reference system (see section 3.3). It will also demonstrate that Toposa has syntactic ergative features (chapter 6).

For the examination of multiple feature-checking processes in Toposa, the Minimalist Program has been selected, as it is the only theory that is able to explain the relationship between morphology, syntactic categories, and discourse functions adequately, i.e., these relationships are seen as feature-motivated rather than structurally motivated.

As the Minimalist Program however is unable to explain how to derive the proper order of constituents in a VSO language, it will be supplemented by the VSO theory of Ouhalla (1991) (see section 3.1). The

---

[24]Note that Horvath (1995) also regards focus as a grammatical feature and not only as a structural position. He points out that [+FOC] represents a syntactic feature that is cross-linguistically not bound to any category but requires a special category that is determined by the specific language (1995:47).

2.7 Summary and Outlook

Minimalist Program also does not elaborate on discourse concepts. Therefore a Principle of Reference and a Principle of Focus will be set up for the discourse domain to explain the morphosyntactic processes more adequately within the context of discourse.

In the following, the multiple feature-checking processes in Toposa will be displayed step by step, showing the complexity of the morphological system (chapter three) and displaying the structure-building process for the sentence (throughout chapters three to six). The next chapter begins with the basic morphosyntactic features of the language.

3

Morphosyntactic Representations

This chapter discusses the basic sentence structure in Toposa and how it is influenced by a number of argument-increasing and decreasing devices. Before these can be examined, however, it will be necessary to first demonstrate the nominative-accusative case-marking system and to analyse some traces of morphological ergativity in the passive and the cross-reference system.

3.1 The Basic Sentence Structure

The basic sentence structure under the Minimalist Program is (Chomsky 1993: 7), shown in (16).[1]

This sentence structure works well for all SVO languages, because the subject moves out of the VP to have its nominative case features checked under the specifier of AGRs. The verb moves to [TNS/TNS'] and to [AGRs/AGRs'] for tense and agreement checking.

Toposa, however, is a verb-initial language in which the verb heads the sentence in all intransitive and transitive sentences and all complex sentence structures; see the example of an intransitive sentence in (17a) and a transitive sentence in (17b).

---

[1]Building on Pollock's theory of verbal inflection (1989).

(16)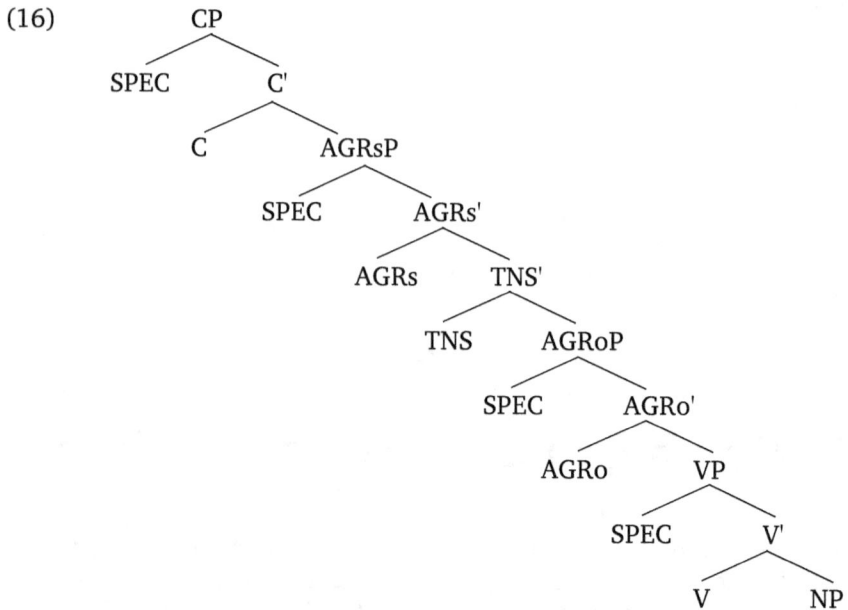

(17) a. È-kèr-í   nyí-kókû.[2]
     3SG-run-IMP D/SG-child/NOM
     'The child is running.'

   b. È-mín-á   nyá-bérù   nyí-kòkù.[3]
     3SG-love-RFL F/SG-woman/NOM D/SG-child/ACC
     'The woman loves the child.'

In complex sentence structures, the verb heads all sentences, as in (18).

(18)   Tó-tûk nyé-bù   ŋá-kílê,   kí-ŋìt nàbó
       SEQ-take M/SG-hyena/NOM F/PL-milk/ACC SEQ-ask again

       kwèě,...
       jackal/ACC
       'Hyena took a mouthful of milk, [and] he asked Jackal again...'

---

[2]Phonetically, the tones on *nyikoku* 'child' in the nominative case are high-mid-fall (HMF) before pause and high-mid-low (HML) elsewhere (see example (21b)), which are best interpreted as underlying HHF and HHL respectively. (Note though that not all underlying HHL patterns on nouns with CVCV nouns are realized as HML.)

[3]The tones on *nyaberu* 'woman' in nominative case are *nyábérû* (HMF) before pause, and *nyábérù* (HML) elsewhere—except for situations where the following context raises the final tone to extra high (*nyábé⸢rú,* cf. examples (1a and b) in chapter one, footnote 3 there).

3.1 The Basic Sentence Structure

The intransitive sentence (17a), the transitive sentence (17b), and the coordinate sentence construction (18) do not fit into the basic sentence structure of (16), because the subject has to move into the specifier of AGRs and thus the subject heads the sentence and does not result in the required verb-initial word order. To produce the desired VSO structure, a change in the order of projections has to take place, so that the verb has to move into TNS of TNSP.

The normal Toposa verb is marked for tense and aspect. The tense system is the typical past and non-past type found in many African languages. Tense is marked by the tone pattern that extends over the entire verb and varies according to verb class, person, number, and tense.[4] In addition to the tone pattern, the tense prefix a-[5] occurs in the third-person singular and plural.

(19) a. É-múj-ì   áyòŋ   nyá-kírîŋ.
       1SG-eat-IMP I/NOM   F/SG-meat/ACC
       'I am eating meat.'

   b. Ì- múj-ì   íŋèsi̱   nyá-kírîŋ.
       3SG-eat-IMP he/NOM   F/SG-meat/ACC
       'He is eating meat.'

   c. È- múj-î   áyòŋ   nyá- kírîŋ.
       1SG-eat-IMP I/NOM   F/SG-meat/ACC
       'I was eating meat.'

   d. È-mùj-í   íŋèsi̱   nyá-kírîŋ.
       3SG-eat-IMP he/NOM   F/SG-meat/ACC
       'He was eating meat.'

Note how the tone pattern changes between first-person singular non-past (19a) which has the tone pattern HHL, and the first-person singular past with the tone pattern LHF (19c), indicating the change from non-past to past. In a similar way, the third-person singular has LHL in non-past (19b), and LLH in past (19d).[6]

Additionally, Toposa has two aspects: imperfective and perfective. Imperfective aspect is indicated by the suffix -i, as shown in the above

---

[4]Non-past is the unmarked tense and past is marked.
[5]Note how the person agreement prefix i- in (19b) changes to e- in (19d), indicating that i- 'third person' and a- 'past tense' have become fused together, resulting in e-.
[6]Dimmendaal (1995) claims that the tonal difference in the above paradigm—here referred to as past and non-past—is related to an imperfective/perfective tonal contrast in Eastern Nilotic.

data. It has an allomorph -e before the plural suffix -te, used in second- and third-person plural. First-person plural uses the suffix -i with the plural suffix -o. The perfective aspect is indicated by the suffix -iti:[7]

(20) É-múj-îti̱   áyòŋ   nyá-kírîŋ.
      1SG-eat-PER I/NOM   F/SG-meat/ACC
      'I have eaten meat.'

Tense and aspect usually occur combined together. Past tense always marks events that are past and have ended. Non-past is normally used for events that are present or present continuous, and sometimes future (although future can also be marked more distinctly by the auxiliary edikino).

However, there is a group of verbs that require a perfective aspect suffix but have continuous meaning when combined with a non-past tone pattern, for example *ecamit* 'he wants', *etwarit* 'he is herding'. These verbs never occur with the imperfective suffix. With the past tone pattern, the meaning of *acamit* is 'he wanted' i.e., the same as the combination past/imperfective on regular verbs. In some rare cases the perfective aspect suffix (together with non-past tone-pattern) signals inchoative meaning, for example *ecumit* 'I am going to spear', or *alosit* 'I am going to leave' (versus *ecumi* 'I spear/am spearing' and *alosi* 'I leave/am leaving').

In other words, the lexical combinations of these verbs in the framework of tense and aspect signal different time structures, but shall not be described in more detail here, because they are not relevant for the overall discussion of this study.

Both the tonal tense features and the morphological aspect features are checked under TNSP.

In the person agreement system usually the verb agrees with the subject of the sentence:

(21) a. È-pèr-í   nyí-kókû.
        3SG/SUB-sleep-IMP   D/SG-child/NOM
        'The child is sleeping.'

   b. È-màs-í   nyí-kókù   ŋá-kîlê.
        3SG/SUB-drink-IMP   D/SG-child/NOM   F/PL-milk/ACC
        'The child is drinking milk.'

---

[7] In the first-person plural the suffix -iti̱ ~ -it is followed by the first-person plural suffix -ae; in second and third person it is followed by the plural suffix -o. The voiceless vowel is elided in both plural forms (and other suffix combinations).

3.1 The Basic Sentence Structure

The agreement prefix *e-* 'he/she/it' refers to the subject of the intransitive sentence (21a) and the subject of the transitive sentence (21b).[8]

Both inflectional features, tense/aspect and agreement, are normally checked under their respective inflectional heads, which results in the typical SVO sentence structure laid down in (16), which however does not reflect the actual VSO word order of examples in (21). An easy solution would be to go back to an earlier concept (Koopman 1984, den Besten 1985 and many others) and claim that all VSO languages have an underlying SVO structure. However, further insight like the Mirror Principle (Baker 1988:13) might help to find a more elegant solution. The Mirror Principle states that the succession of the verbal affixes determines the order of the arguments (cf. section 1.8). This leads to the question at which point tense needs to be checked, because it is a suprafix. As the tonal pattern extends over the entire verb, logically it should supersede the affixation and therefore it can be checked last. Consequently, one can conclude that Toposa has agreement inside TNS, which forces TNS to c-command AGRs, because the tone on the verb is checked last. Thus, TNSP precedes the AGRsP, and the checking process results in the desired VSO order.

This solution is supported by Ouhalla (1991:105–110), who suggests that one of the properties of VSO languages is that AGRs resides inside TNS, i.e., TNS heads AGRs. This typical VSO property is also found in the Toposa tense and agreement system. (See also Tsimpli (1995) for Modern Greek, where the tense affix precedes the agreement suffix.) In other words, examples (17) to (21b) cannot be generated using the basic sentence structure of the tree in (16). Since in Toposa TNS heads the AGRsP, the diagram has to be revised in such a way that the TNSP heads the AGRsP. The tree in (22) shows how this is done for (21b).[9]

---

[8]The basic person agreement prefixes appear in TO-class verbs in non-past tense (all in the order of 1st/2nd/3rd person SG and 1st/2nd/3rd person PL): *a-, i-, e-, i-, e-*. In KI-class verbs, these prefixes are fused with a petrified root-initial *i*, resulting in *e-, i-, i-, i-, i-*. In past tense, a tense prefix *a-* (which exists only for 3rd person SG and PL) is additionally fused into the person agreement prefix, resulting in *a-, i-, a-, e-, i-, a-* for TO-class verbs and *e-, i-, e-, i-, i-, e-* for KI-class verbs. For the purposes of this study only the resulting surface forms are shown and segmented.

[9]For a more detailed description of the computational processes between lexicon and interface, see appendix A, together with the explanations provided in section 2.1.2.

(22)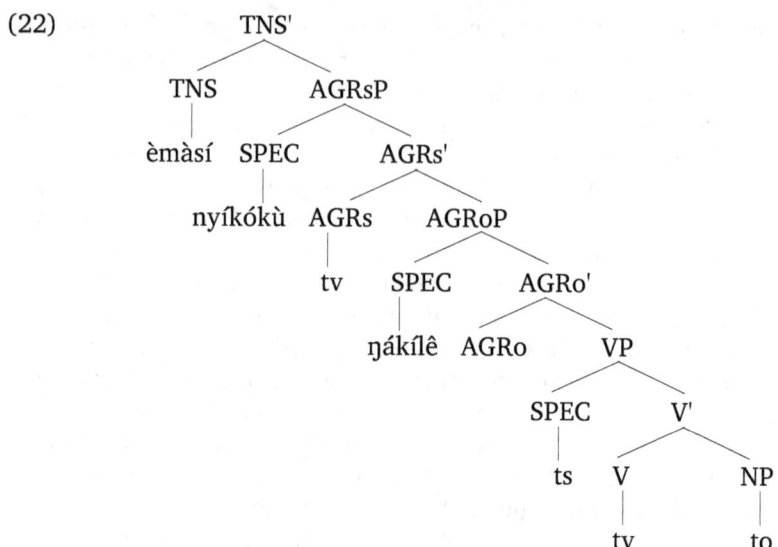

Now the verb moves from its position in the sentence first to [AGRs/AGRs'] to check its AGR features, and then to [TNS/TNS'] to check its TNS features.

The movement of the NP is determined through nominative case-checking to the specifier of AGRsP, and through accusative checking to the specifier of AGRoP. After the verb and NP movements are completed, the word order results in VSO. (Nominative case-checking will be demonstrated in the next section.)

To complete the sentence structure for Toposa, it is necessary to consider the placement of CP. As in most other languages, the CP in Toposa heads the sentence. For example, in the case of wh-questions, the question words *nyô* 'what?' and *ŋáĕ* 'who?' head the sentence, as in the examples in (23).

(23) a. Ŋáĕ   è-lós-ì   lò-ká<u>l</u>e?[10]
    who/NOM 3SG-go-IMP M/LOC-home
    'Who is going home?'

  b. Nyô   ì-múj-ì   nyá-bérù?
    what/ACC 3SG-eat-IMP F/SG-woman/NOM
    'What is the woman eating?'

---

[10]The rising tone ˇ (R) in the word *ŋáĕ* is very rare in Toposa and has not been fully analysed yet.

3.1 The Basic Sentence Structure

However, the CP features of Toposa are not very strong because the language has very few sentence connectives, for example *tarai* 'but', *kotere* 'because', *na* 'when', and *ani* 'if/when'. Consider (24) with *tarai* and *kotere*:

(24) Kí-ír-à-sí   nàì   ŋí-ᵗtyáŋ   dáànḭ
     SEQ-hear-RFL-PL then   M/PL-animals/NOM all

nyé-rúy-é   kéŋḛ,
M/SG-roar-GER/ACC   his

tàràì ny-ì-ŋár-âkìn-à   ìŋésḭ,   kòtèré
but   NEG-3PL-help-BEN -PL   him/ACC because

è-kùryán-ìt-ò   íkèsḭ   ìŋésḭ.
3PL-afraid-IMP-PL   they/NOM   him/ACC

'All the animals heard his roaring, but they did not help him, because they were afraid of him.'

The tree diagram of (23b) completes the basic sentence structure of Toposa by adding CP as seen in (25).

(25)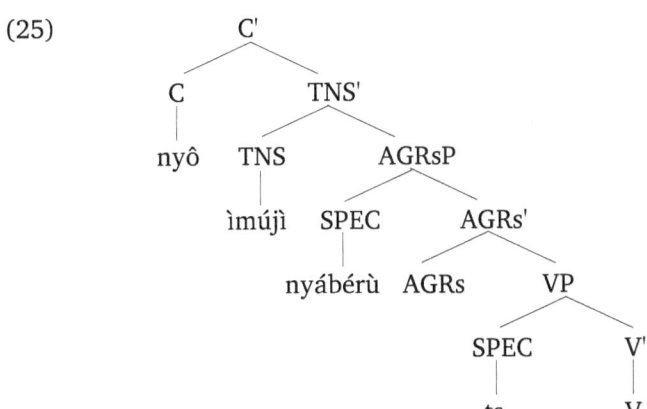

Note that the CP is also relevant as contrastive focus position, which will be described later in section 5.3.

3.2 The Nominative-Accusative Case-Marking System

Toposa has a nominative-accusative system and marks case by different tonal patterns on the noun. Consider the tone patterns in the following VS and VSO constructions:

(26) a. È-kèr-í   nyí-kókû.
     3SG-run-IMP D/SG-child/NOM
     'The child is running.'

   b. È-mín-á   nyá-bérù   nyí-kòkù.
     3SG-love-RFL F/SG-woman/NOM D/SG-child/ACC
     'The woman loves the child.'

   c. È-màs-í   nyí-kókù   ŋá-kîlê.
     3SG/SUB-drink-IMP D/SG-child/NOM F/PL-milk/ACC
     'The child is drinking milk.'

The word *nyikoku* 'child' shows in the subject position of the intransitive sentence (26a) the tone pattern HHF which marks the nominative, and in the subject position of the transitive sentence (26c) the pattern HHL, also marking nominative case.[11] In the object position of the transitive sentence (26b), *nyíkòkù* shows a different tone pattern: HLL for accusative case.[12] In this way the subjects of the intransitive sentence (26a) and of the transitive sentence (26c) are grouped together as nominatives and the object of the transitive sentence (26b) is marked as accusative. This marking strategy constitutes a typical nominative-accusative system (cf. (14) in section 2.2).

In Toposa the accusative case represents the unmarked form, while the nominative case is the marked form. The accusative case is also used when either of the constituents S or O is fronted for focus, and it is the form used when nouns are cited in isolation.

Turkana and several other Nilotic languages are reported to have such a marked nominative/unmarked accusative system (Tucker and Bryan

---

[11]Toposa also marks locative and genitive case, which do not need to be considered here. The tone change from F to L is morphotonemically conditioned: *nyíkókû* is found before pause and *nyíkókù* occurs in other contexts. Other nouns ending in F follow the same pattern.

[12]Not all nouns have the same tone patterns for nominative and accusative, as Toposa nouns fall into many different tone classes.

3.2 The Nominative-Accusative Case-Marking System

1966, Dimmendaal 1986:130, Anderson 1988:131, Dixon 1994:65).[13] Dimmendaal interprets the tonal case inflection as an areal feature which probably goes back to an early tone-bearing morpheme (ibid.).

The nominative case-checking takes place under the specifier of the AGRs head, and the accusative case-checking under the specifier of the AGRo head. Thus the subject moves from the specifier VP position to [SPEC/AGRs] to check its nominative case features, and the object moves from the NP position in the verb to [SPEC/AGRo].

This leads to the diagram in (27), using (26c) as an example (after the verb and the NPs have gone through their case-checking processes):

(27)

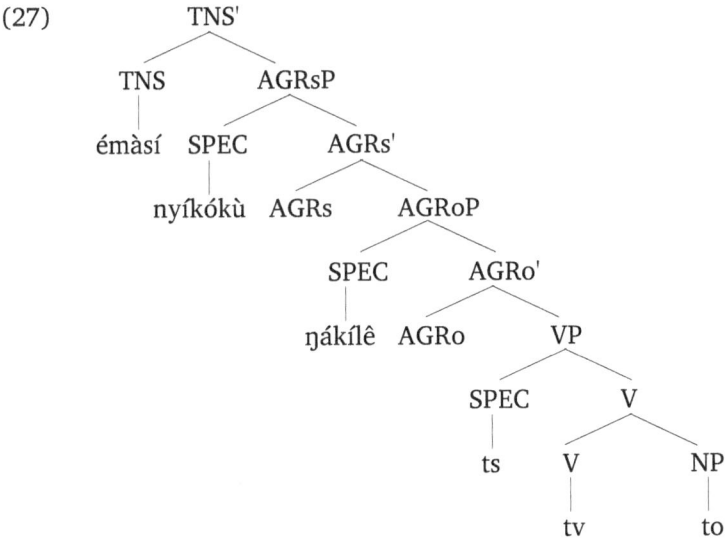

The verb moves from inside the VP to [AGRs/AGRs'] to check its AGR features and then to [TNS/TNS'] to check its TNS features. The subject moves from the [SPEC/VP] to [SPEC/AGRsP] to check its nominative features, and the object moves from the verb to [SPEC/AGRo] to check its accusative features. In this way, the VSO word order is preserved, because TNS c-commands AGRs, and the verb finally moves to [TNS/TNS'], where it heads the whole sentence.

Note how the basic SVO sentence structure of (16) has been altered to a basic VSO sentence structure. From now on, (27) will be considered as the basic sentence structure for Toposa.

---

[13]Randal (2000) reports marked nominatives also for Tennet (Surmic) which is geographically close to several Western Nilotic and Eastern Nilotic languages.

3.3 Morphological Ergativity

Although Toposa has a nominative-accusative morphological case-marking system, there are traces of morphological ergativity in the passive and in the cross-reference system, which will be considered next.

The term "passive" in this study is used under the following conditions (Dixon 1994:146):

1. Passive applies to an underlyingly transitive clause and forms a derived intransitive clause.

2. The underlying O becomes S of the passive sentence.

3. The underlying S is omitted, although there is always the option of including it.

4. The passive is formally marked, generally by a verbal affix.

This study does not corroborate the second part of point 3, however, because in many languages, Toposa included, the S can never be stated.

3.3.1 Passive

Toposa has a morphological passive,[14] whereby the underlying transitive sentence is demoted to an intransitive one through the passive suffixes {-o ~ -ae ~ -oe},[15] a typical argument-reducing process (T. Payne 1997:196), for example:

(28) a. Ì-dés-ì   nyé-kílè   ŋá-átûk.
     3SG-beat-IMP M/SG-man/NOM   F/PL-cows/ACC
     'The man is beating the cows.'

---

[14] Recall the traditional passive concept in which the object of the underlying sentence is transferred to the subject of the passive sentence by movement (Chomsky 1981), a notion that has been dismissed in the Minimalist Program when the concepts of deep and surface structure were abandoned.

Under Minimalist theory, the sentence is generally regarded as a normal intransitive sentence, where the subject of the sentence is checked under the specifier of AGRs. Although Chomsky (1993) talks about passive as a 'nemoncritic', i.e., it is merely a formal phenomenon, the term passive is kept in this study, because in Toposa the passive shows exceptional case-marking.

[15] The suffix -o occurs after the imperfective suffix -i, whereas the alternating suffix allomorphs -ae ~ -oe are found after the perfective suffix -itį and in narrative-sequential verbs. The latter alternation is conditioned by vowel harmony.

b. Ì-dés-ít-àè   ŋá-átûk.
3PL-beat-PER-PAS F/PL-cows/ACC
'The cows are being beaten.'

As in most other languages with a morphological passive, the passive sentence (28b) is structurally an intransitive sentence, where the accusative object of (28a) turns into the subject of sentence (28b) through the passive morpheme.

In Toposa however, a change from the normal nominative-accusative case-marking system to ergative-absolutive case-marking takes place: the subject of the intransitive sentence does not show the expected nominative case-marking, but has accusative case-marking. This can easily be supported with example (29).

(29) È-màs-é-tè   ŋá-àtùk   ŋá-kìpì.
      3PL-drink-IMP-PL F/PL-cows/NOM   F/SG-water/ACC
      'The cows are drinking water.'

If one compares sentence (28a) and (28b), it is apparent that the object ŋáátûk 'cows' of the transitive sentence (28a) displays the same accusative tone pattern HHF as the subject of the passive construction (28b), rather than the expected nominative marking HLL of the subject ŋáàtùk in the transitive sentence (29). This marking strategy indicates a typically ergative case-marking system (cf. (14) in section 2.2 above).

3.3.2 The split cross-reference pronominal system

Other morphologically ergative traces in Toposa are found in the cross-reference system. Usually the verb agrees with the subject of the intransitive and transitive sentence, which is typical for nominative-accusative systems.

(30) a. È-pèr-í   nyí-kókû.
        3SG/SUB-sleep-IMP D/SG-child/NOM
        'The child is sleeping.'

   b. È-màs-í   nyí-kókù   ŋá-kílê.
      3SG/SUB-drink-IMP D/SG-child/NOM   F/PL-milk/ACC
      'The child is drinking milk.'

c. È-màs-é-tè   ŋí-dè   ŋá-kílê.
   3PL/SUB-drink-IMP-PL   D/PL-children/NOM   F/PL-milk/ACC
   'The children are drinking milk.'

The agreement prefix *e-* 'he/she/it' refers to the subject in the intransitive sentence (30a) and the transitive sentence (30b), and the agreement prefix *e-* 'they' refers to the subject in the transitive sentence (30c). However, agreement is not consistently nominative-accusative in the pronominal system. Normally, in a nominative-accusative agreement system one can expect that the person agreement prefix always agrees with the subject, which would result in the paradigm in (31):

(31) a. À-lìm-ókín-î   áyòŋ   ìŋési.
       1SG/SUB-tell-BEN-IMP   I/NOM   him/ACC
       'I will tell him.'

   b. *E-lim-okin-i   íŋèsi   íyôŋ.
       3SG/SUB-tell-BEN-IMP   he/NOM   you/ACC
       'He will tell you.'

   c. *E-lim-okin-i   íŋèsi   áyôŋ.
       3SG/SUB-tell-BEN-IMP   he/NOM   me/ACC
       'He will tell me.'

   d. *I-lim okin-i   íyòŋ   áyôŋ.
       2SG/SUB-tell-BEN-IMP   you/NOM   me/ACC
       'You will tell me.'

However, examples (31b–d) are ungrammatical. The grammatically correct forms for these sentences are as follows:

(32) a. K-ì-lìm-ókín-î   íŋèsi   íyôŋ.
       OBJ-2SG/OBJ-tell-BEN-IMP   he/NOM   you/ACC
       'He will tell you.'

   b. K-à-lìm-ókín-î   íŋèsi   áyôŋ.
       OBJ-1SG/OBJ-tell-BEN-IMP   he/NOM   me/ACC
       'He will tell me.'

3.3 Morphological Ergativity

c. K-ì-lìm-ókín-î   íyòŋ   áyôŋ.[16]
   OBJ-2SG/SUB-tell-BEN-IMP   you/NOM   me/ACC
   'You will tell me.'

Note how in (32a–c) the prefix *k*- marks the object on the verb. Also note how, if the object of the transitive sentence is in first or second person, as in (32a) and (32b), the person prefix in the verb agrees with the object rather than with the subject, as in (30a–c) and (31a). This agreement with the object rather than the subject is typical of ergative-absolutive cross-reference systems (Dixon 1994:42–49).

Further note that example (32c) is an exception in the system. If subject and object occur in first and second person *together* (it does not matter whether the object is in first person and the subject is in second person or vice versa), the person agreement prefix on the verb reverts to subject referencing. The object-marking prefix *k*-, however, remains.

The same anomalies occur if the accusative pronouns are in the plural, for example:

(33)   K-ì-lìm-ókín-'é-tê   íkèsi   ìŋwóni
        OBJ-1PL/OBJ-tell-BEN-IMP-PL   they/NOM   us/ACC
        'They will tell us.'

In other words, Toposa displays a split cross-reference system that can be summarized as follows: if the object is a pronoun in third person, the person prefix on the verb agrees with the subject; if however the object is in first or second person, an object prefix *k*- indicates the shift to ergative-absolutive marking, and the person prefix agrees with the object. Thus, the *k*- can also be analysed as an ergative marker and will be glossed as such from here on. If both subject and object are pronouns in first and second person, the marking strategy becomes mixed in that subject agreement prevails, but the object marking *k*- remains.

These overlapping marking strategies seem to point to different stages in the evolution of the language from an ergative-absolutive to a nominative-accusative system.

These pronominal ergative-absolutive irregularities in an otherwise nominative-accusative case-marking system are further underscored by a change in word order: If the subject slot of the transitive sentence is occupied by a noun and the object slot by a pronoun in first or second person, the word

---

[16] Some speakers in careful speech add a copy-vowel, resulting in *aka-, iki-,* and *eke-* constructions. As the language seems to be in transition at this point, all data will be considered without the copy vowels, because this appears to be the more common pronunciation.

order changes from VSO to VOS. Also reported for Turkana (Dimmendaal 1986:131–132), note also the presence of the ergative-absolutive marker *k-*:

(34) K-à-lìm-ókín-î áyôŋ ló-káàtó káŋ.
 OBJ-1SG/OBJ-tell-BEN-IMP me/ACC M/SG-brother/NOM my
 'My brother will tell me.'

The same object-agreement-marking on the verb occurs in the following idiomatic expressions:

(35) a. K-à-nyám-íti áyôŋ nyá-kórò.
  OBJ-1SG/OBJ-eat-PER me/ACC F/SG-hunger/NOM
  'I am hungry.' Lit., 'Hunger is eating me.'

 b. K-é-rúm-ìt-ò áyôŋ ŋí-léèci.
  OBJ-1SG/OBJ-hold-PER-PL me/ACC M/PL-shame/NOM
  'I feel ashamed.' Lit., 'Shame is holding me.'

 c. K-è-mùrí-ákín-ìti áyôŋ nyé-kírò kèŋe.[17]
  OBJ-1SG/OBJ-escape-BEN-PER me/ACC M/SG-name/NOM his
  'I forgot his name.' Lit., 'His name is escaping me.'

In neighbouring Turkana, where no ergative-absolutive features have been reported, the change to ergative agreement-marking in these idioms and elsewhere is interpreted in terms of animacy and definiteness (Dimmendaal 1986:135, 143).

Finally, in passive constructions, the verb agrees with the object if it is a first- or second-person pronoun in a double-accusative construction.

(36) K-ì-ín-ít-àè ìsùá ŋá-kílê.
 OBJ-1PL/OBJ-give-PER-PAS we/ACC F/PL-milk/ACC
 'We were given milk.'

These ergative elements in the agreement system lead to a further change in the basic sentence structure, as it was presented in (27), due to the following considerations: The AGRo has strong morphological features, while the AGRs has no phonological features and therefore is weak and not occupied. Furthermore, the verb-initial *k-* is interpreted as an

---

[17]The *e-* is first-person SG/OBJ, but Toposa has two different sets of agreement markers, which we refer to as TO class and KI class, based on the class prefix of the verb in the imperative and narrative sequential forms. The KI class set has *e-* for first person and the TO class has *a-* for first person.

3.3 Morphological Ergativity

ergative marker whose features have to be checked under a head, in this case the ERG head, which also heads the sentence, because the verb moves into ERG projection, after it has checked the TNS features. The tree in (37) (from 32a) illustrates these changes; the ordering of the affixes follows the Mirror Principle of Baker (1988:13).

(37)
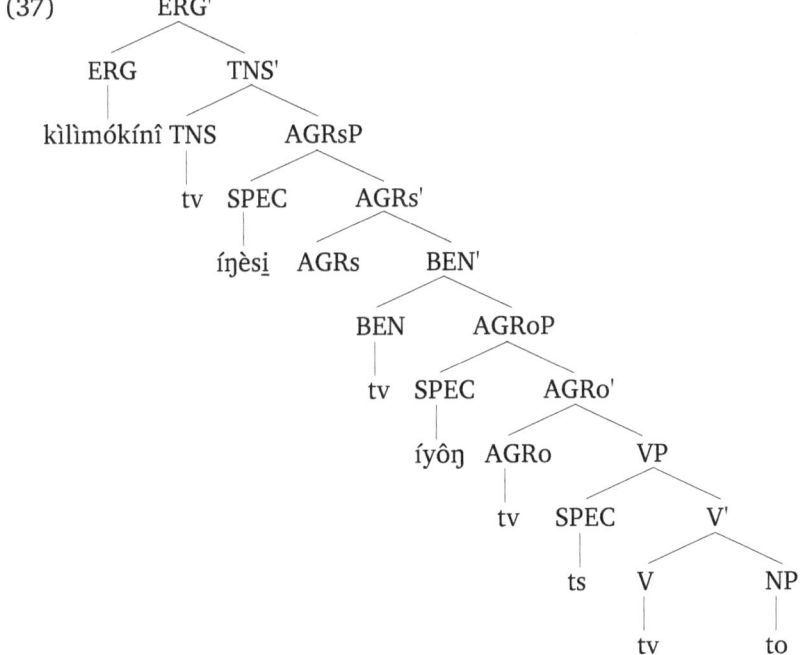

In other words, the verb moves from its place in the VP to [AGRo/AGRo'] to pick up the accusative agreement-marking, then to [BEN/BEN'] for benefactive checking (see next section), then to [TNS/TNS'] to check its TNS features, and then to [ERG/ERG'] to check the ergative marking feature. The tree accounts for the ergative system because the [AGRo/AGRo'] place was visited by the verb, when the accusative cross-reference features were checked under [AGRo/AGRo']. Note that the verb did not move to [AGRs/AGRs'] because the sentence has no subject agreement.

Building on the sentence structure (37) for (32a), the change in word order that occurs in (34), where the structure-building process changes the order of projections in the sentence, can now be discussed. In this case the AGRs and the AGRo projections trade so that AGRo heads AGRs, because the accusative object follows the verb and the sentence has a VOS order. The order of projection is supported by the Mirror Principle (Baker 1988:13) which states that the order of affixes determines the word order (cf. section 1.8).

According to this principle, the affixes on the verb must reflect the VOS structure of (34) and (35a–c), and justify that the AGRo and AGRs projections trade places, so that the object prefix, rather than the subject prefix, follows TNS, and the AGRo projection heads the BEN and AGRs projections. In this way, as the verb and the nouns move, the VOS sentence structure is preserved because the order of projections has changed as follows:

(38)

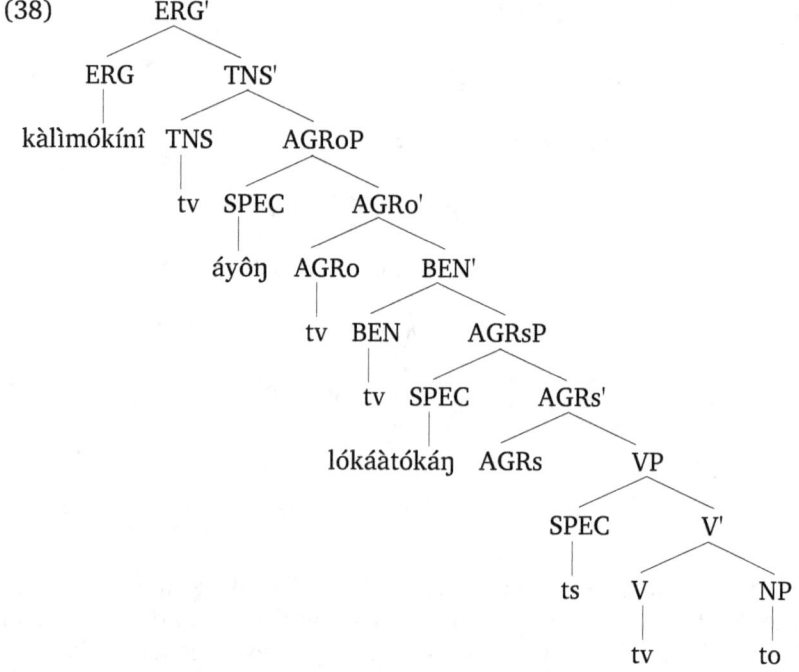

The verb moves from its place in the VP to [BEN/BEN'] for benefactive feature-checking, then to [AGRo/AGRo'] to pick up the accusative agreement-marking, then to [TNS/TNS'] to check its TNS features, and then to [ERG/ERG'] to check the ergative marking feature. Again, the tree displays an ergative system because the [AGRo/AGRo'] place was visited by the verb, when the accusative cross-reference features were checked under [AGRo/AGRo']. Note that the verb did not move to [AGRs/AGRs'] because the sentence has no subject agreement. The nouns move to their respective specifier of AGRo and AGRs.

3.4 Argument-Changing Processes

Toposa sentence structure is also influenced by a number of argument-changing devices which need to be considered next.

Normal verb roots in Toposa are either intransitive or transitive. Thus, a monovalent verbal root requires one argument, the subject, while a bivalent root requires two arguments, the subject and the object. However, argument-increasing and decreasing devices can change the valence of the root and require a new argument structure of the sentence.[18] Toposa has two such argument-increasing processes, applicative and causative, and two argument-decreasing processes, passive and reflexive.

The argument-increasing and decreasing devices are functional terms that are interpreted in the Minimalist Program[19] as case-bearing affixes which receive a head for feature-checking, because they are licensed morphologically and consequently build a specifier-head relationship for case-checking of the newly created argument.

3.4.1 Argument-increasing processes

3.4.1.1 The applicative

The morphological applicative in Toposa comprises the benefactive suffix {-akin ~ -okin ~ -ikin ~ -kin}[20] and the instrumental suffix {-a ~ -o ~ -re̯ ~ -re̯}.[21] Both suffixes restructure the verbal root and license an additional object for the sentence. The additional object carries accusative

---

[18]T. Payne (1997:172) reports that a survey done by Bybee (1985) showed that out of all the languages investigated, 90 percent had the valence marked on the verb.

[19]Chomsky specifically states that the difference between languages lies in their verb morphology and case morphology (1993:24).

[20]The variants of the benefactive and the instrumental suffixes are phonologically conditioned and depend on the harmony class of the verb root and its CV pattern. The a-containing variants harmonise with –ATR roots, while the o-variants assimilate to the +ATR root (see Schröder and Schröder (1987a) for a detailed description).

[21]The instrumental has several allomorphs, depending on aspect and voice. These (with their aspect-number combinations) are -a ~ -o when preceded by the imperfective aspect suffixes -i ~ -e, resulting in -io and -ea, respectively. These take the plural suffix -to ~ -ta, yielding -ioto and -eata in plural forms.

With perfect aspect, the instrumental suffix changes to -re̯. The preceding perfective variants are -ito, if the verb has no extensions, -oto if benefactive, ablative, or allative precede the aspect suffix, resulting in the sequences -itore̯ and -otore̯ in singular and itototore̯/-ototore̯ in the plural.

In passive constructions the instrumental suffix is -ere ~ -re.

This instrumental marker has also been reported for Turkana (Dimmendaal 1983a:189–192, 1986:137) under the heading 'subjunctive mood'.

case-marking. The case-bearing suffix receives its own feature-bearing head and heads the AGRoP in transitive sentences, because all applied objects directly follow the verb and precede the direct object in ditransitive sentences.[22] In intransitive sentences, the applied suffix head c-commands the VP and changes the sentence to transitive:[23]

(39) a. À-lím-ókín-î   lò-káàtó   káŋ
       1SG-tell-BEN-IMP M/SG-brother/ACC my

   ŋá-kíꜜró   ŋùnà.
   F/PL-matters/ACC these/ACC
   'I shall tell my brother about these matters.'

b. È-dès-é-á   nyá-tèlé   nyá-àtê.
   3SG-beat-IMP-INS F/SG-stick/ACC F/SG-cow/ACC
   'He is beating the cow with a stick.'

Constructions like (39a) are accounted for by the sentence structure in (40) which is representative of all transitive sentences with one case-bearing suffix (only the projection after the AGRs needs to be adapted according to the type of suffix):

Note that the instrumental suffix refers not only to instruments, but also to locatives and temporals. See (41b) for a locative example.

[22]The succession of the affixes determines the succession of the arguments in the sentence, in accordance with Baker's Mirror Principle (1988:13).

[23]Baker (1988:227) treats the applicative as PP incorporation (cf. section 1.8).

3.4 Argument-Changing Processes

(40)

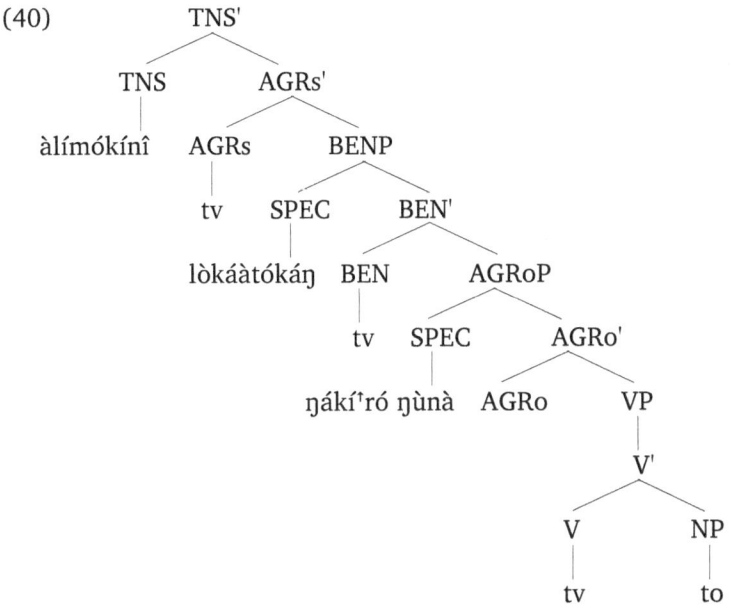

The verb takes two NPs as complements. The basic object NP ŋákìró ŋùnà moves to [SPEC/AGRoP] to check its accusative case features. The benefactive object receives its accusative case-marking in the specifier of BEN. The verb moves to [BEN/BEN'] to have its benefactive suffix checked, it passes through the [AGRs/AGRs'] for agreement-checking, and moves to [TNS/TNS'] to check its tone and aspect-marking.

Note that through the structure-building process which creates heads and specifiers that are licensed through the Principle of FI, the benefactive receives a feature head and a specifier for case-checking of the additional argument. In the representation of the structure-building process, the benefactive object is kept in the specifier of the benefactive for case-checking to avoid a double accusative construction in the VP. If the licensing of the specifier as case-checker and the case-checking are regarded as one computational process, it is justified to keep the applied object in the specifier of BEN. Since there is no overt subject, the specifier of the VP for the subject is not licensed and the specifier of the AGRsP is not built, because no case-checking takes place there.

In the case of intransitive verb roots, the applicative creates a normal transitive sentence pattern. The newly created object is the applied object that acts as the direct object and also appears as complement of the verb (see also the discussion on the applied object in section 3.5 below):

(41) a. À-pèr-í   nyá-bérù.
       3SG-sleep-IMP F/SG-woman/NOM
       'The woman was sleeping.'

   b. À-pèr-í-ó   nyá-bérù   nyé-pyêm<u>u</u>.
      3SG-sleep-IMP-INS F/SG-woman/NOM M/SG-bed/ACC
      'The woman was sleeping on the bed.'

The sentence structure of (41b) is the following:

(42)

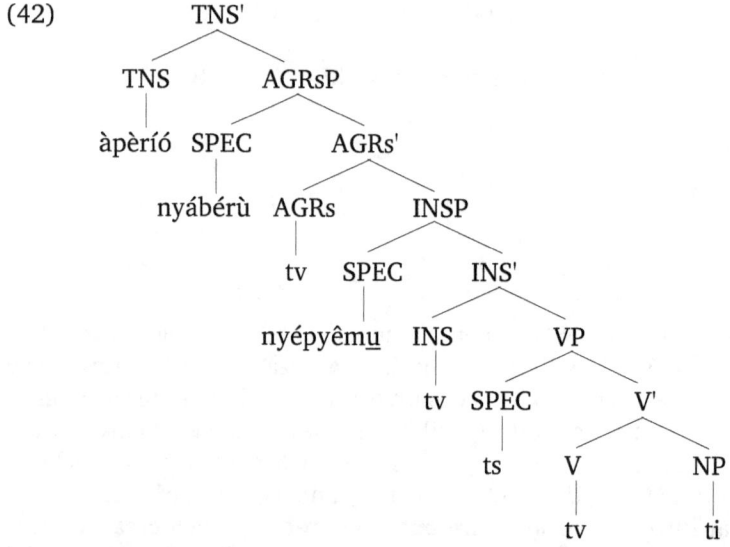

Note how the verb moves to [INS/INS'] to check its instrumental suffix, to [AGRs/AGRs'] for agreement-checking, and to [TNS/TNS'] for TNS and aspect-checking. The nominative subject is placed under [SPEC/VP] and moves to [SPEC/AGRsP] for nominative case-checking. The applied object raises to [SPEC/INSP] for accusative case-checking.

The structure-building process and the Principle of FI build an INS head and a specifier for the INS head, where the accusative case-checking takes place. No AGRo is built, because no direct object is overt. The sentence structure is grammatically transitive, however, since the incorporated object becomes the direct object.

The intransitive verb root also occurs with benefactive constructions, but the incorporated argument remains implied. Because the benefactive

3.4 Argument-Changing Processes

morpheme, however, licenses an extra object,[24] the inherent valency of the verb is changed from intransitive to transitive. Since in most cases intransitive verbs with a benefactive suffix have no overt object, the transitivity is only evident through the existence of the BEN head. The specifier of the BENP is not licensed, because no case-assigning takes place.[25] According to the structure-building and licensing of the FI, a specifier neither occurs in the BEN' nor in the AGRo head, because no overt incorporated or direct object exists and no case-assigning takes place under the specifier of BEN:

(43) a. È-pòr-í   nyá-pèsê.
     3SG-jump-IMP F/SG-girl/NOM
     'The girl is jumping.'

   b. É-pòr-ókín-ì   nyá-pèsé   kà ló-kóròt.[26]
      3SG-jump-BEN-IMP F/SG-girl/NOM at M/LOC-dance
      'The girl will dance at the dance.'

The structure of a sentence like (43b) is the following:

(44)
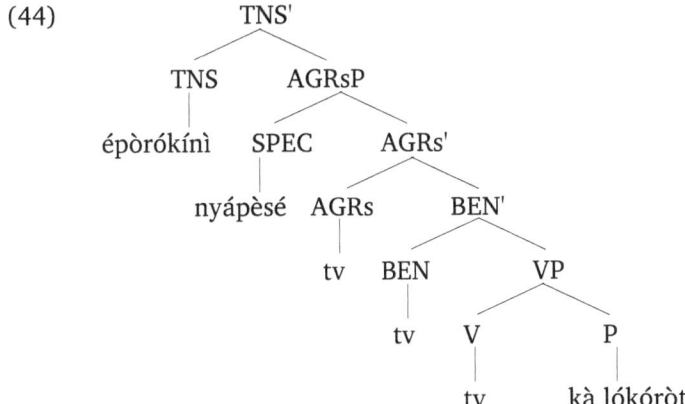

Note that the presence of the BENP points to a transitive verb root and a transitive sentence. The verb moves to BEN of [BEN/BEN'], to AGRs of

---
[24]The applicative process also has implications for the focus system, explained in chapter six (see 5.2–5.5).
[25]The theory no longer conceptualises empty categories because there is no deep structure versus surface structure. The extra object is not realised through the structure-building process.
[26]The tone pattern *nyápèsê* before pause changes to *nyápèsé* if followed by another noun phrase.

[AGRs/AGRs'], and to TNS of [TNS/TNS'] in order to have its benefactive, subject and tense and aspect features checked. The nominative *nyápèsé* moves to the specifier of AGRsP to have its nominative case-marking confirmed. An explanation of why benefactive extensions also occur without overt argument will be given in sections 4.1 and 5.1.2.

3.4.1.2 The causative

The other argument-increasing process in Toposa is the causative. The causative prefix is {*itV-*}.[27] Like the applicative, the causative occurs with both transitive and intransitive verb roots.

The causative prefix is represented as a full projection. It licenses an extra object, which changes the sentence structure in the following way: if the underlying sentence is intransitive, the subject becomes the object, and a new subject is introduced:

(45) a. È-pèr-í   nyí-kókû.
       3SG/SUB-sleep-IMP D/SG-child/NOM
       'The child is sleeping.'

    b. È-té-pér-ì   áyòŋ   nyí- kòkù.
       1SG-CAUS-sleep-IMP   I/NOM   M/SG-child/ACC
       'I put the child to sleep.'

The subject of sentence (45a) *nyíkókû* 'child' becomes the object *nyíkòkù* of (45b), and *áyòŋ* 'I' is introduced as a new subject.

If the underlying sentence is transitive, the reconstruction is as follows:

(46) a. È-màs-í   nyí-kókù   ŋá-kílê.
       3SG/SUB-drink-IMP D/SG-child/NOM   F/PL-milk/ACC
       'The child is drinking milk.'

---

[27]In the causative prefix *itV-*, the vowel V copies the vowel quality of the following root, e.g., *nyakiteper* 'cause to sleep' (root *per*), *nyakitamat* 'cause to drink' (root *mat*). The initial vowel *i* of the causative prefix is always fused into the preceding person agreement prefix.

Additionally, in KI-class verbs, which all have roots that begin with a petrified class prefix *i* that has become fused into the root, the causative prefix undergoes a number of ordered phonological rules such as vowel copy, vowel deletion, spirantisation and harmonisation. In this study only the fused and shortened surface forms of the causative will be segmented and glossed.

3.4 Argument-Changing Processes

b. È-tá-más-ì   (áyòŋ)   nyí-kòkú   ŋá-kílê.[28]
   1SG-CAUS-drink-IMP I/NOM   D/SG-child/ACC   F/PL-milk/ACC
   'I give the child milk to drink.'

The underlying subject *nyíkókù* of (46a) is demoted to incorporated object, and the causer *áyòŋ* 'I' enters as the new subject. Underlying subjects usually are demoted to the nearest empty syntactic slot (see Comrie 1989:165–184), which in Toposa is always the first accusative argument, directly following the verb. This slot is used for all argument-increasing applied constituents (see also section 3.4.1 on the benefactive and on the instrumental). The direct object remains *in situ*.

The following tree captures the causative construction of sentence (45b) with an intransitive verb root that was changed into a transitive one through the causative suffix:

(47)

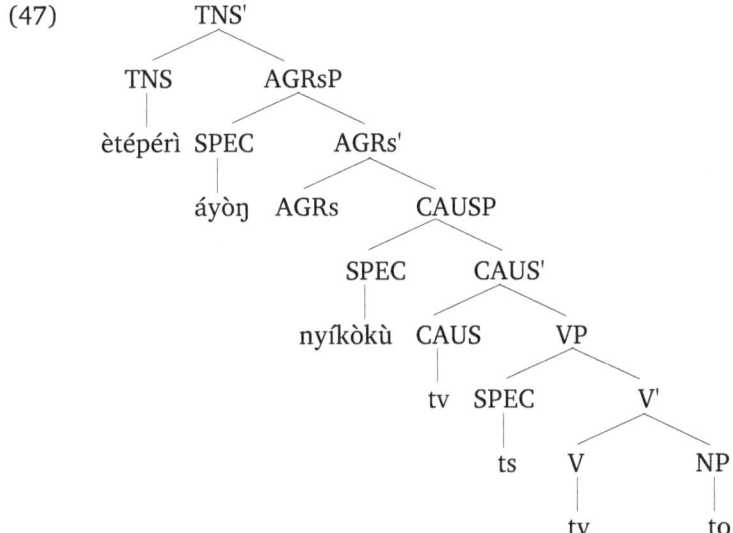

The above construction shows the causative sentence after the verb has moved from its V place in the VP, in order to have its causative features checked under [CAUS'/CAUS], then to [AGRs/AGRs'] to check its agreement features, and then to [TNS/TNS'] to have its tense and aspect

---

[28]Perturbations occur whenever two ACC objects are joined together. Note how the pattern HHL (HML) on *nyikoku* changes to HLH before another object. The nominative *áyòŋ* 'I' is in parentheses because it is very unnatural in the language to mention three constituents after the verb.

features checked. The causative object moves from its place in the VP into the specifier of CAUSP for case-checking.

The causative construction of (46b) with a transitive root is as follows:

(48)

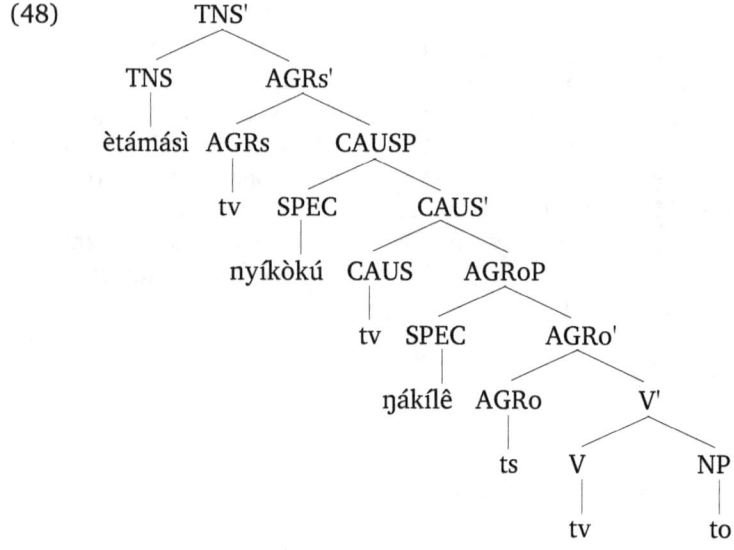

This construction shows the following verb movements for feature-checking: First, a move from V in VP to [CAUS/CAUS'] for causative checking, secondly to [AGRs/AGRs'] for agreement-checking, and finally to TNS of [TNS/TNS'] for tense and aspect feature-checking. The basic object ŋákílê moves to the specifier of AGRo to have its accusative case features checked, and the causative object receives its accusative features when it visits the specifier node of CAUSP. Note that there is no conflict in case-assigning for the double object, because the AGRo head is responsible for the accusative case-assignment to the basic object, and the causative prefix for the accusative case-assignment to the applied causative object.[29]

---

[29]Another approach to morphological causative is that of Marantz (1984) who explains it in terms of merger. In the merger process the verb root and the affix merge into one causative stem. The causative stem then heads the NP (the causer) and the NP (the causee) in transitive sentences. In intransitive sentences the causative stem heads the NP which is the causee.

Yet another approach is Baker's incorporation theory. He regards morphological causatives as incorporation of a verb that heads a complement. The causative construction is then created through verb movement to the main verb, where the causative affix attaches to the root and leaves a trace behind.

3.4 Argument-Changing Processes

Note the difference between the intransitive sentence (47) and the transitive sentence (48). In both cases the representation of the sentence appears with one complement of the verb. In tree (47) the intransitive verb adopts the applied object as the direct object and complement of the verb. In the transitive sentence the applied object stays in the specifier of the causative to avoid a double complement construction in the VP. Note that there is no specifier in the VP in (48) for the sentence has no overt subject.

The argument-increasing processes shown in this section turned out to be case-bearing affixes, which have their own projection in the sentence structure of the Minimalist theory.

3.4.2 Argument-decreasing processes

The next section will show that the argument-decreasing devices of Toposa are also marked on the verb. These are passive and reflexive.

The typical feature of argument-decreasing devices is that an argument is demoted to an oblique case, or it is dropped entirely. The functional argument-decreasing devices are captured as morphosyntactic case-bearing projections.

3.4.2.1 The passive

As already described in section 3.3.1, Toposa has a morphological passive which is marked through the allomorphs {-o ~ -ae ~ -oe} of the passive suffix on the verb. Passive in Toposa always produces a sentence that has one argument; the subject is never mentioned as in (49). This type of passive is also called 'agentless passive' (Dixon 1994:147, Anderson 1988:299):

(49) a. À-lèm-ùn-î nyá-bérù ŋí-jàmu̱.
   3SG-take-ALL-PAS F/SG-woman/NOM D/PL-skins/ACC[30]
   'The woman brought cowskins.'

  b. Tò-lém-ún-àè ŋí-jàmu̱.
   SEQ-bring-ALL-PAS D/PL-skins/ACC
   'Cowskins were brought.'

---

[30]Toposa has two directionals, which have been labelled ABL for ablative and ALL for allative in this study. These correspond to what Dimmendaal (1983a:109–112) refers to as 'itive' and 'ventive' and Heine (1981:76) as 'venitive' and 'andative' in their descriptions of Turkana.

The passive in Toposa employs ergative case-marking (as was already pointed out in section 3.3.1), i.e., the subject of the sentence (49b) is marked as accusative.

For the description of the passive sentence the basic tree structure of (27) has to be revised. First of all, the passive subject agrees with the accusative of the sentence, so the agreement features are checked under [AGRo/AGRo'], not under the [AGRs/AGRs']. The change of the agreement-checking from subject to object agreement is induced by the passive morpheme. As the suffix licenses the case-marking, the structure-building process creates a passive head that induces a specifier for accusative case-marking. The order of the projections is again determined by the Mirror Principle (Baker 1988:13), where the AGRo features take the place of the AGRs feature, following the tense features and heading the PASP. Thus, the tree is:

(50)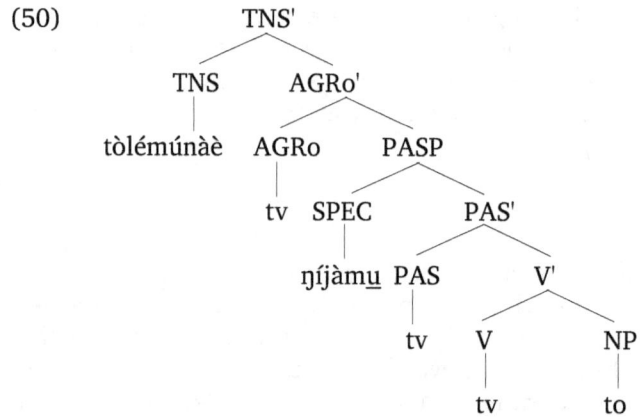

Because of passive feature-checking of AGRo, PAS, and TNS, the verb moves three times from its original place under V to PAS' to have the passive features checked, and then to AGRo' to pick up the object agreement features, and finally to TNS' for tense and aspect feature-checking. The accusative feature of the subject is checked under the specifier of PASP, to which the accusative subject moves from its complement position of the VP. Note that the structure-building process has created two novelties in the tree: first of all, the AGRoP has no specifier, since no overt object exists, and secondly, the specifier of VP is not built, for the sentence has no nominative subject.

Again, the Minimalist approach offers a better explanation for the syntactic change between active and passive than was the case under GB in that it no longer utilizes transformational rules, but the change of NP

3.4.2.2 The reflexive

The prototypical syntactic reflexive construction reduces the valence of the sentence by specifying that there are not two separate NP roles like subject and object involved. Rather, these two syntactic constituents collapse into one because there is an identity of reference between the antecedent subject and the reflexive object. Toposa has a morphological reflexive, whereby the suffix takes on the role of the object and is incorporated into the verb. A transitive sentence is changed into an intransitive one with only the NP subject role. In Toposa the reflexive is marked with the suffix {-a ~ -o ~ -i̱}.[31] Compare the following:

(51) a. Ì-dés-ì   nyá-bérù   nyí-kòkù.
       3SG-beat-IMP   F/SG-woman/NOM   D/SG-child/ACC
       'The woman is beating the child.'

    b. Ì-dét-à   nyá-bérù.
       3SG-beat-RFL   F/SG-woman/NOM
       'The woman is beating herself.'

Examples (51a) and (51b) show that compared to transitive sentences reflexive sentences have no overt object, because the reflexive object morpheme is incorporated into the verb.

Since the structure-building process and the FI force the morphological features to be checked under a head, the morphological reflexive requires a head for feature-checking. I here suggest that the reflexive features be checked under the AGRo head, because the reflexive suffix represents the object of the sentence. Thus, the following tree structure in (52) is established for (51):

---

[31] The -a ~ -o variants occur in finite verbs without extensions, the variant -i̱ is found in finite verbs with extensions (directionals and benefactive) and in imperatives and narrative-sequential verbs.

(52)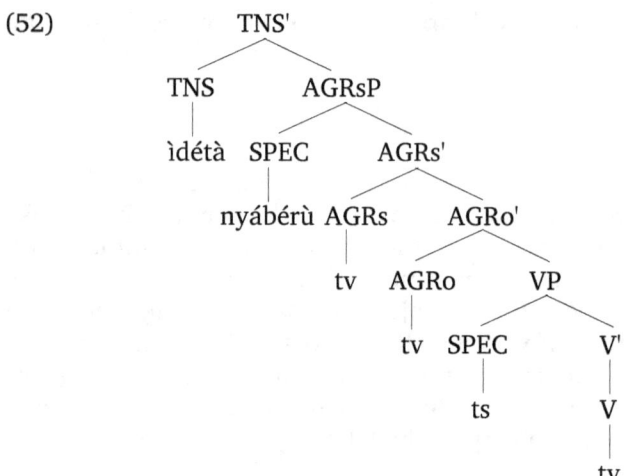

The verb has moved for checking purposes from its place under V to [AGRo/AGRo'] for the reflexive features, to [AGRs/AGRs'] for the subject prefix, and to [TNS/TNS'] for the TNS features. Note that reflexive verbs are only inflected for tense and not for aspect. No binding conditions apply in the case of morphological reflexives, since there is no overt referent for the antecedent. However, the relationship between the subject of the intransitive sentence and the reflexive suffix is expressed through the fact that the feature-checking takes place under [AGRo/AGRo'], because [AGRo/AGRo'] represents the object agreement-marking.

Toposa uses the reflexive also with transitive verbs that keep an overt NP object. For example, the verb *kyan* 'laugh' is transitive (corresponding to English 'laugh about'). When the reflexive is used with such transitive verbs the antecedent of the incorporative pronominal is the subject, as is the case in (51b), where the reflexive verb has no overt object.

(53) Tó-kyán-âr-i̱   nyé-kílè   nyí-kàlé.
     SEQ-laugh-ABL-RFL M/SG-man/NOM D/SG-goat/ACC
     'The man laughed at/about the kid goat.'

Since the anaphoric pronominal represents the object, and a direct object is overt in a transitive sentence, the object pronominal cannot be checked under the AGRo head, because this head is reserved for the case-checking of the object under the specifier-AGRo-head relationship. The FI licenses and the structure-building process creates a head for the

3.4 Argument-Changing Processes

reflexive feature. Consequently, the reflexive features are checked under the [RFL/RFL'].

The syntactic representation of (53) is the following:

(54)

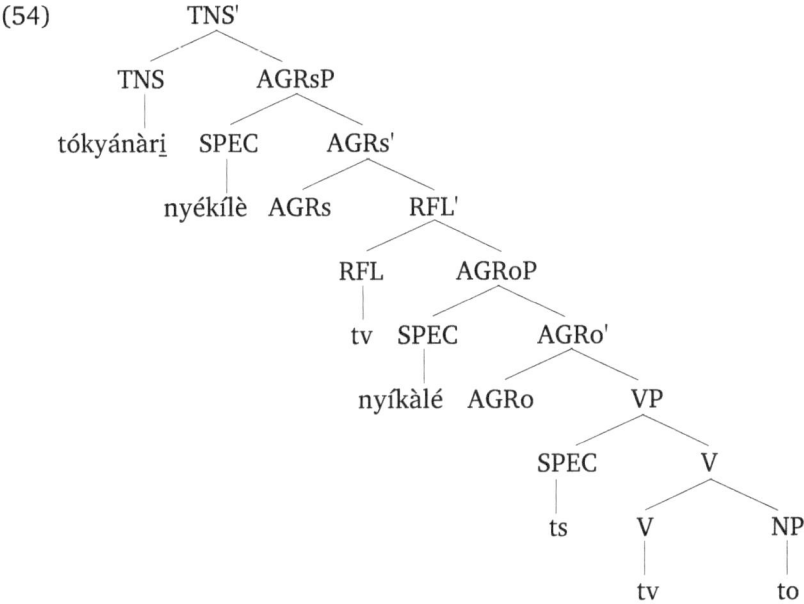

The movement of the verb is as follows: it moves from the V in the VP to [RFL/RFL'] to check the reflexive features, to [AGRs/AGRs'] to have its agreement features checked, and to [TNS/TNS'] for TNS feature-checking. The accusative object moves from the NP in the verb phrase to [SPEC/AGRoP] to have its accusative case-marking checked, and the nominative subject moves from the [SPEC/VP] position to [SPEC/AGRsP] to have its nominative case features checked.

The difference between (52) and (54) is the creation of the reflexive head in (54), where the AGRo is occupied by the object *nyíkàlé*. Consequently, the reflexive has to be checked under an extra head.

In some instances, Toposa uses the reflexive in a passive sense. This is not uncommon for languages; Spencer describes the same phenomenon for French, German, and Slavic (1995:241).

(55) Kù-gòr-ó   ŋú-tú'ŋá   kéce
      SEQ-mourn-PL   M/PL-people   their/ACC

      lù   à-túb-òr-i̱   kídíàmá.
      who   3PL-cut-ABL-RFL   above
      'They mourned for their people who were cut off [and remained] above.'

The typical characteristic for this type of "reflexive passive" is that the agent is never mentioned, which is the same as in normal passive constructions (see example (49b)). The reflexive in (55) is checked under [AGRo/AGRo'], as in the sentence structure of (52).

3.5 Applied and Direct Object

Baker (1988) points out that there are differences between languages with respect to how they treat direct and applied objects. The term "applied object" refers to all objects that are created through applicative morphemes, i.e., head-bearing morphemes like benefactive, instrumental, and causative (described in section 3.4.1 above). The applied object occurs in the accusative case and requires case-checking through the specifier-head relationship of its head-bearing morpheme.

I use the term "applied object" for objects caused by benefactive, instrumental, and causative morphemes, i.e., they are optional. Then there are inherently ditransitive roots like sell, give, buy, etc. They underlyingly require an indirect object (although this indirect object does not always become overt due to discourse constraints as can be seen in chapter 6), this indirect object is licensed (not created) through the benefactive morpheme *-okin* that also creates the applied benefactive object. So in Toposa there is a difference between an indirect and an applied object.

Toposa treats the applied object in the same way as the direct object, i.e., it marks both of them with accusative case. Both have the properties of direct objects. The properties of direct objects are the following: (1) direct objects follow the verb, as in (56a) below, (2) direct objects can drop out, as in (56b), and (3) direct objects can be passivised, as in (56c). All these properties are demonstrated in the following examples:

3.5 Applied and Direct Object

(56) a. È-mín-á   ŋá-kílê.³²
       3SG-love-RFL F/PL-milk/ACC
       'He loves milk.'

   b. È-mín-á.
      3SG-love-RFL
      'He loves [it].'

   c. È-mín-àè   ŋá-kílê.
      3PL-love-PAS F/PL-milk/ACC
      'Milk is loved.'

In Toposa the same properties apply to the applied object. Consider the following example with a benefactive construction:

(57)   À-lím-ókín-î   lò-káàtó   káŋ
       1SG-tell-BEN-IMP M/SG-brother/ACC my

       ŋá-kíʼró   ŋùnà.
       F/PL-matters/ACC these/ACC
       'I shall tell my brother about these matters.'

Note how the applied object follows the verb, which corresponds to property (1) of direct objects listed above. It is not possible to change the sequence of the direct and applied object:

(58)   *À-lím-ókín-î   ŋá-kíʼró   ŋùnà
        1SG-tell-BEN-IMP   F/PL-matter/ACC   these/ACC

        lò-káàtó   káŋ.
        M/SG-brother/ACC my
        'I shall tell my brother about these matters.'

The applied object can also drop out, corresponding to property (2) of direct objects:

(59)   À-lím-ókín-î   ŋá-kíʼró   ŋùnà.
       1SG-tell-BEN-IMP F/PL-matter/ACC   these/ACC
       'I shall tell [him] these things.'

---

³²In Toposa there are some emotional state verbs that always contain a reflexive suffix, but they can also be used transitively even though the reflexive suffix is present, for example, *gur* 'weep/weep over', *boly* 'relax/play', *mina* ~ *mina̱* 'like/love'.

Even both objects can be dropped:

(60) À-lím-ókín-î.
1SG-tell-BEN-IMP
'I shall tell [him] [about it].'

Finally, both arguments can be passivised, as required by property (3) of direct objects:

(61) a. À-lìm-òkìn-ó   ŋá-kí'ró   ŋùnà.
3SG-tell-BEN-PAS F/PL-matter/ACC these/ACC
'These matters were told [to him]/he was told about these matters.'

b. À-lìm-òkìn-ó   lò-káàtó   káŋ
3SG-tell-BEN-PAS M/SG-brother/ACC my

(ŋá-kí'ró   ŋùnà).
F/PL-matter/ACC these/ACC
'My brother was told (about these matters).'

As both arguments behave like direct objects, they show up as overt arguments and create a VOO construction. Consider the tree for (57):

3.5 Applied and Direct Object

(62)

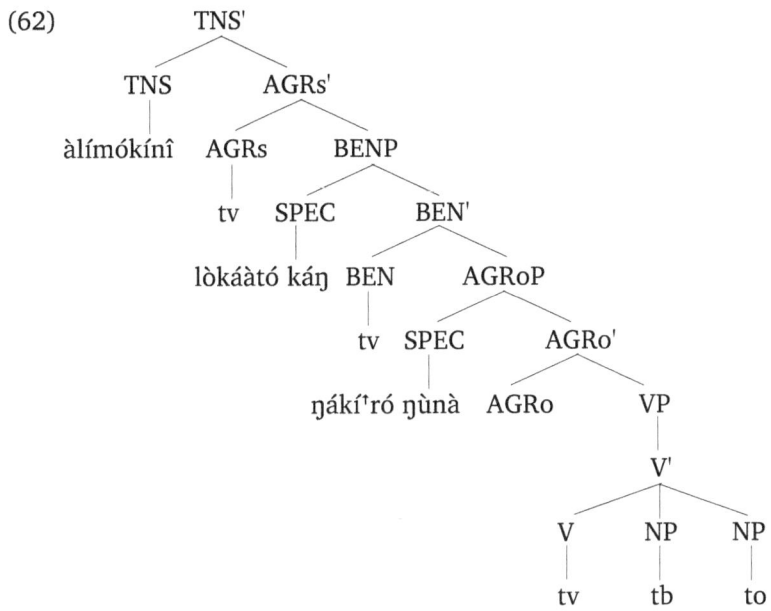

In a similar way, example (61b) also presents a double accusative VOO construction, because the passive subject has accusative-marking, (see section 3.4.2.1). This can be diagrammed in the following way:

(63)

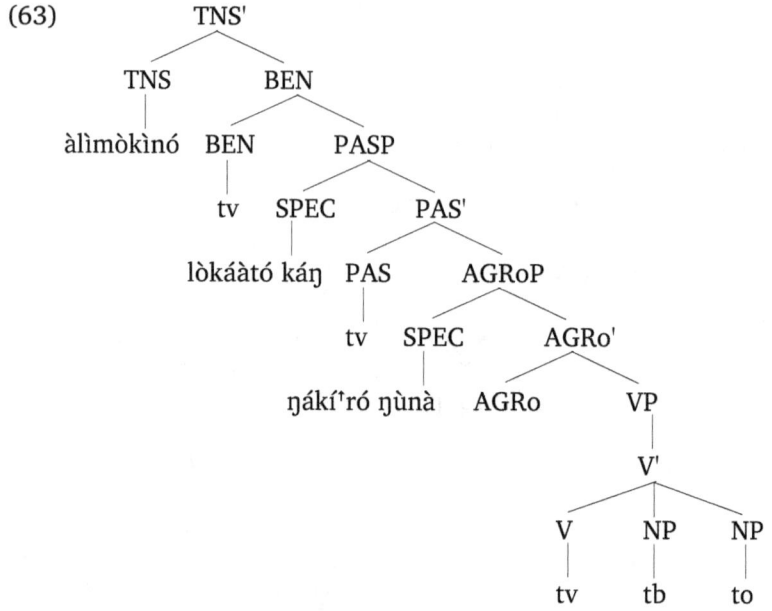

Note that the difference between the two representations is that the passive accusative-marking of the benefactive object in (61b) is checked under the specifier of the PAS head and not under the specifier of the BEN head, and that the AGRs head drops out.

3.6 Summary

This chapter showed the different morphological processes of the language and how the checking theory takes care of the case-bearing affixes and the case-assignment of the newly created arguments. The case-bearing affixes, such as applicative and causative, create new projections, so that every affix has its own head and its own specifier for case-checking. The checking theory of the Minimalist Program enables a clear demonstration of the morphological mechanisms of the language, because it is a morpho-syntactic approach and shows how the morphology directly influences the syntax. The morphological affixes have feature-carrying function. They are case-bearing units and the accusative case of the applied object is checked through the specifier-head relationship of each of these affixes. Since the affixes function as case-bearing units there is never any conflict of how to assign case in double object constructions,

3.6 Summary

for the case-assignment is clearly defined through the different case-bearing heads. The complicated system of UTAH (Baker 1988) becomes redundant and gives way to a much simpler checking process. It was also mentioned that the basic nominative-accusative case-marking is interrupted by ergative-absolutive case-marking in the passive.

The next chapter will show the interaction between rich morphology and word order in Toposa, because the co-occurrence of case-bearing suffixes creates new arguments which force the normal word order to be restructured.

4

Complex Verb Morphology and Word Order

The previous chapter discussed Toposa sentence structure in the context of verb morphology. It was shown that the morphology drives the structure-building processes, and that every affix receives its feature-bearing head. This chapter will discuss how the structure-building and the VSO/VOO word order are affected when the verb morphology combines several case-bearing affixes.

4.1 Co-occurrence of Argument-Increasing Devices

If the co-occurrence of argument-bearing suffixes creates more than one accusative argument after the verb, the obvious question that needs to be asked is how the basic sentence structure is affected by the increase in the number of arguments. As the Minimalist approach is feature-driven, each additional morphological argument-bearing head induces a new specifier-head relationship. Another question that arises at this point is how many affix heads and case-specifier relationships the basic sentence structure can tolerate.

Up to this point the discussion concentrated on each argument-decreasing or argument-increasing device individually, showing that all of these processes involve the split of IP into separate argument-increasing affix projections, which also provide the specifier-head relation for case-marking. Consequently, the co-occurrence of these affixes split the

IP into multiple head-bearing projections, so that theoretically Toposa might have one, two, three, or even four arguments following the verb, if the respective affixes are present in the verb to produce them. (For discussion of the interaction of co-occurring incorporation processes see Baker 1988:362 ff.)

In simple case-bearing processes, as shown in chapter three, the permitted maximal sentence structure is a double accusative construction. Thus, Toposa has two extended sentence patterns: VSO (a normal transitive sentence) and VOO (a double accusative construction that occurs with benefactive and instrumental, for example). Consider once more these two basic patterns:

(64) a. È-màs-í   nyí-kókù   ŋá-kílê.
     3SG/SUB-drink-IMP   D/SG-child/NOM   F/PL-milk/ACC
     'The child is drinking milk.'

   b. È-jà-kìn-í   Lòkálè   nyá-lírú.
     3SG-receive-BEN-IMP Lokale/ACC F/SG-spear/ACC
     'He receives the spear for Lokale.'

It is still possible for the subject to be overt in double accusative constructions like (64b), but this is somewhat awkward and hardly ever used:

(65) ?È-jà-kìn-í   nyé-kílè   Lòkálè   nyá-lírú.
      3SG-receive-BEN-IMP M/SG-man/NOM Lokale/ACC F/SG-spear/ACC
      'The man receives the spear for Lokale.'

As shown in chapter three, Toposa has three feature-bearing affixes that increase the number of arguments: causative, benefactive, and instrumental. All of these affixes co-occur in double combinations (causative-benefactive, causative-instrumental, and benefactive-instrumental), and even in a triple combination (causative-benefactive-instrumental).

If the causative[1] and the benefactive combine in a transitive verb root, it is to be expected that two extra arguments are created in addition to the direct object, i.e., a causative and a benefactive argument, which would yield the following:

---

[1]Recall causative constructions and how the intransitive sentence and the transitive sentence change their valence. The intransitive sentence becomes a transitive one, and the causer of the action moves into the S slot of the transitive sentence. The transitive sentence becomes a ditransitive one, where the causer occupies the S slot of the ditransitive sentence, and the S of the embedded transitive sentence occurs in the first accusative object of the new sentence. A ditransitive sentence has a double-object construction.

(66)   *È-tì-ìn-ákín-î   nyé-kìlé   nyá-béˈrú
       1SG-CAUS-give-BEN-IMP M/SG-man/ACC   F/SG-woman/ACC

   nyá-lírú.
   F/SG-spear/ACC
   'I cause the man to give the spear to the woman.'

There are three accusative arguments: *nyékìlé* 'man' is the causative argument, *nyábéˈrú* 'woman' is the benefactive object, and *nyálírú* 'spear' is the direct object. As usual, the succession of the arguments follows Baker's Mirror Principle (1988:13), reflecting the sequence of affixes in the verb (person agreement, causative, and benefactive):

(67)   È-tì-ìn-ákín-î.
       1SG-CAUS-root-BEN-IMP
       'I cause [somebody] to give [something].'

Example (66), however, is not grammatical. The only possible way of expressing the above sentence is to have two accusative objects after the verb, i.e., the number of arguments needs to be reduced by one, retaining either the benefactive argument, as in (68a), or the causative, as in (68b):

(68) a. È-tì-ìn-ákín-î   áyòŋ   nyá-béˈrú   nyá- lírú.²
       1SG-CAUS-give-BEN-IMP I/NOM   F/SG-woman/ACC   F/SG-spear/ACC
       'I cause [someone] to give the spear to the woman.'

   b. È-tì-ìn-ákín-î   nyé-kìlé   nyá-lírú.
      1SG-CAUS-give-BEN-IMP M/SG-man/ACC   F/SG-spear/ACC
      'I cause the man to give [someone] the spear.'

This means that, at least for underlying transitive sentences which are considered below, the language does not allow triple accusative arguments consisting of causative, benefactive, and direct object, suggested in the ungrammatical example (66).

---

²This sentence is grammatical only under the condition that the subject pronoun is overtly stated, because it is needed to differentiate between the agent and the causer. This function of pronouns, together with their focus function, will be discussed in section 5.1.1.
   Nevertheless, the sentence (68a) can be interpreted in two ways: (a) 'I cause [someone] to give the spear to the woman', or (b) 'I cause the woman to give the spear [to someone]'. The distinction between the benefactive object of option (a) and the causer in option (b) can only be made in the wider context of discourse, which will be shown in detail in section 5.1.

The reason for this restriction could be that the verb is inherently unable to case-mark three arguments, a scenario which was totally impossible under GB, but which is theoretically quite possible under the Minimalist Program, where each argument is checked under its morphological head, and case-marking takes place under the specifier-head relationship of each affix. In this way, the causative and benefactive affixes assign case to the causative and benefactive arguments, respectively, which would result in the following tree for sentence (66):

(69)

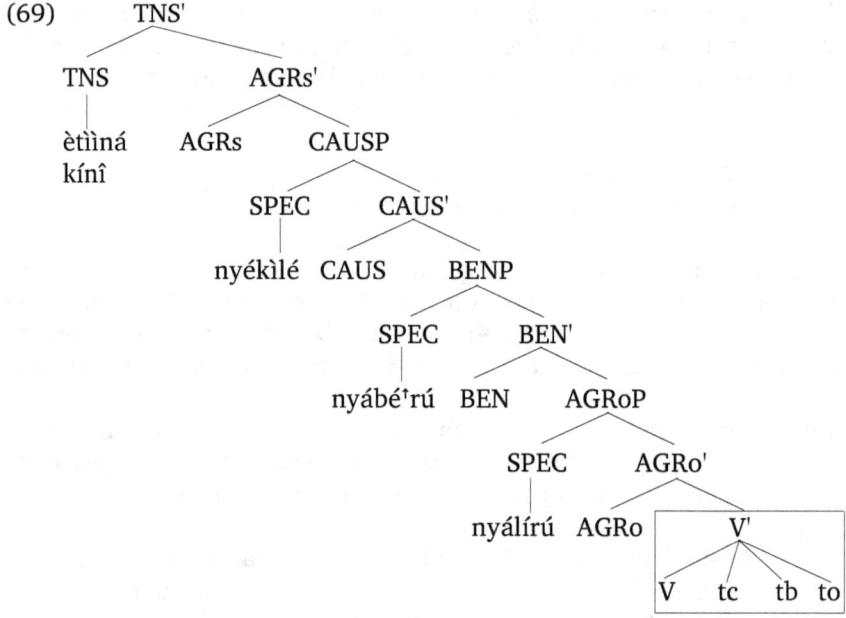

Case-marking is shifted to the specifiers of the respective heads, so no violation of verbal case-marking takes place, (which was the argument that was used under GB against complex case-assignment), nevertheless, example (66) is ungrammatical. Therefore, the reason for the ungrammaticality of triple accusative constructions might lie in the universal nature of the VP, i.e., the verb-complement relationship between verb and direct object.

Under GB, the verb-complement relationship was the following (Chomsky 1981):

4.1 Co-occurrence of Argument-Increasing Devices

(70)
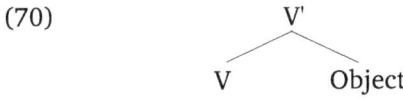

Recall that the lexicon contains all the lexical and morphosyntactic information for nouns and verbs. The bundles of morphosyntactic and lexical information are taken from the lexicon into the numeration, and are then transferred to the VP. The VP now contains the full sentence information: The subject is set in the specifier of VP, the V has three complements, causative, benefactive, and direct object (as presented in (69). The causative and benefactive objects are licensed by their respective affixes.

The question at this point is whether the standard head-complement relationship needs to be changed for Toposa into a head-complement relationship with two accusative objects, one of which would be either the incorporated causative or benefactive object, the other the direct object. For (68b) this might look as follows:

(71)
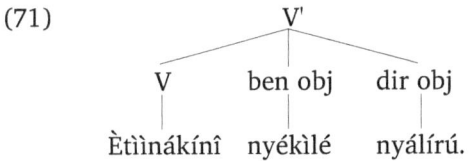

There is in fact structural evidence to support this suggestion, because in Toposa the verb-complement relationship with the direct object is not as narrow as required by (70). The verb and the direct object can be separated structurally in a number of ways: Firstly, the structural slot after the verb is reserved for the subject (see sentence (64a) for example). Second, this slot can be filled with adverbs such as *nàbó* 'again' and discourse markers such as *nàì* 'then' and *câ* 'so':

(72) a. Tà-tác   nàbó   ŋá-kírô,...
       SEQ-answer again   F/PL-matter
       'He addressed the matter again,...'

   b. Tà-tác   câ   ŋá-kírô,...
       SEQ-answer just   F/PL-matter
       'He just addressed the matter,...'

   c. Tà-tác   nàì   ŋá-kírô,...
       SEQ-answer then   F/PL-matter
       'He then addressed the matter,...'

The above structural conditions are syntactic information of the lexicon and determine for the computational process that either the subject or another X projection are allowed to move between the verb and the direct object. If the slot after the verb is filled with an X projection, the slot is occupied by the incorporated object, as in (64b). If more than one head-bearing affix occurs, the arguments of the case-bearing affixes, i.e., the incorporated objects, compete for their existence. See the following diagram for this structural restriction:

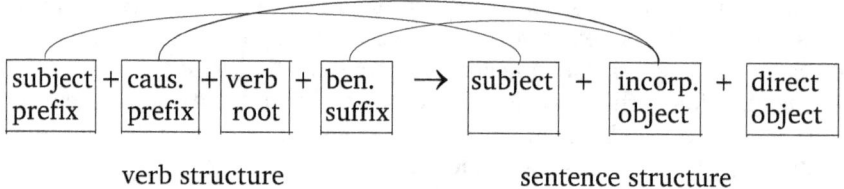

| subject prefix | + | caus. prefix | + | verb root | + | ben. suffix | → | subject | + | incorp. object | + | direct object |

    verb structure   sentence structure

Figure 4.1. Case-bearing affixes and argument structure

This diagram illustrates how co-occurring head-bearing affixes force the arguments to compete for the place of the incorporated object.

After having examined causative-benefactive constructions, causative-instrumental combinations will be considered next.

(73) a. Ì-tú-dúŋ-ì-ò   nyá-bérù   nyí-kòkú
       3SG-CAUS-cut-IMP-INS F/SG-woman/NOM   D/SG-child/ACC

    nyá-kírîŋ.
    F/SG-meat/ACC
    'The woman causes the child to cut the meat [with something].'

   b. Ì-tú-dúŋ-ì-ò   nyá-bérù   nyé-kí'léŋ
      3SG-CAUS-cut-IMP-INS F/SG-woman/NOM   M/SG-knife/ACC

    nyá-kírîŋ.
    F/SG-meat/ACC
    'The woman causes [him/her/it] to cut the meat with the knife.'

The causative-instrumental constructions operate under the same syntactic restrictions as the causative-benefactive constructions: only one incorporated object may occur. A choice needs to be made between the causative and the instrumental object.

4.1 Co-occurrence of Argument-Increasing Devices

Furthermore, triple object constructions with causative, instrumental, and direct object are avoided:

(74) *Ì-tú-dúŋ-ì-ò nyá-bérù nyí-kòkú
   3SG-CAUS-cut-IMP-INS F/SG-woman/NOM D/SG-child/ACC

   nyé-kí'léŋ nyá-kírîŋ.
   M/SG-knife/ACC F/SG-meat/ACC
   'The woman causes the child to cut the meat with a knife.'

The last combination of two co-occurring head-bearing suffixes is benefactive-instrumental. Consider the following examples:

(75) a. À-gùm-àkìn-é-á nyé-kìlé ŋá-ákôt.
   3SG-shoot-BEN-IMP-INS M/SG-man/ACC F/PL-blood/ACC
   'He shot (= drained) the blood for the man [with something].'

  b. À-gùm-àkìn-é-á nyé-màli ŋá-ákôt.
   3SG-shoot-BEN-IMP-INS F/SG-arrow/ACC M/SG-blood/ACC
   'He drained the blood [for someone] with an arrow.'

Again, the same syntactic restrictions apply as with the other double combinations: only one incorporated object may occur, either the benefactive object, as in (75a), or the instrumental object, as in (75b).

Likewise, triple accusative constructions with benefactive, instrumental, and direct object would be ungrammatical:

(76) *À-gùm-àkìn-é-á nyé-kìlé nyé-màli
   3SG-shoot-BEN-IMP-INS M/SG-man/ACC F/SG-arrow/ACC

   ŋá-ákôt.
   M/SG-blood/ACC
   'He drained the blood for the man with an arrow.'

Next, consider triple combinations with transitive verbs, where causative, instrumental, and benefactive co-occur, for example:

(77) a. Ì- tù-dùŋ-òkìn-í-ò   nyá-bérù   nyí-kòkú
    3SG-CAUS-cut-BEN-IMP-INS   F/SG-woman/NOM   D/SG-child/ACC

    nyá-kírîŋ.
    F/SG-meat/ACC
    'The woman causes the child to cut the meat [with a knife for someone].'

  b. Ì-tù-dùŋ-òkìn-í-ò   nyé-kí'léŋ   nyá- kírîŋ.
    3SG-CAUS-cut-BEN-IMP-INS   M/SG-knife/ACC   F/SG-meat/ACC
    'She causes [someone] to cut the meat with a knife [for someone].'

  c. Ì-tù-dùŋ-òkìn-í-ò   nyé-kìlé   nyá-kírîŋ.
    3SG-CAUS-cut-BEN-IMP-INS   M/SG-man/ACC   F/SG-meat/ACC
    'She causes [someone] to cut the meat [with something] for the man.'[3]

  d. *Ì-tù-dùŋ-òkìn-í-ò   (nyá-bérù   )nyí-kòkú
    3SG-CAUS-cut-BEN-IMP-INS   (F/SG-woman/NOM)   D/SG-CHILD/ACC

    nyé-kìlé   nyé-kí'léŋ   nyá-kírîŋ.
    M/SG-man/ACC   M/SG-knife/ACC   F/SG-meat/ACC
    'The woman causes the child to cut the meat with a knife for the man.'

Again, note how in (77c) the benefactive object is possible, however *nyékìlé* 'man' can also be understood to be the causative object in the same way as *nyíkòkú* 'child' in (77a) can only be interpreted as the causative object, not as the benefactive one. Here, as in the other combinations discussed above, causative takes precedence over benefactive. Ultimately, the correct interpretation between causative and benefactive arguments takes place in the wider context of discourse (as will be shown in the next chapter).

A sentence like (77d) has three incorporated arguments. Theoretically, a feature-based approach like the Minimalist Program could account for all these arguments, because they are all case-feature checked under the heads of the affixes, and the cases are checked under their respective heads, which could then be diagrammed as follows:

---

[3]Parallel to example (68a) earlier in this chapter, this sentence can only be interpreted correctly in context. The two meanings, of course, are (a) 'She causes [someone] to cut the meat with a knife for the man', and (b) 'She causes the man to cut the meat [with something]'.

4.1 Co-occurrence of Argument-Increasing Devices

(78)
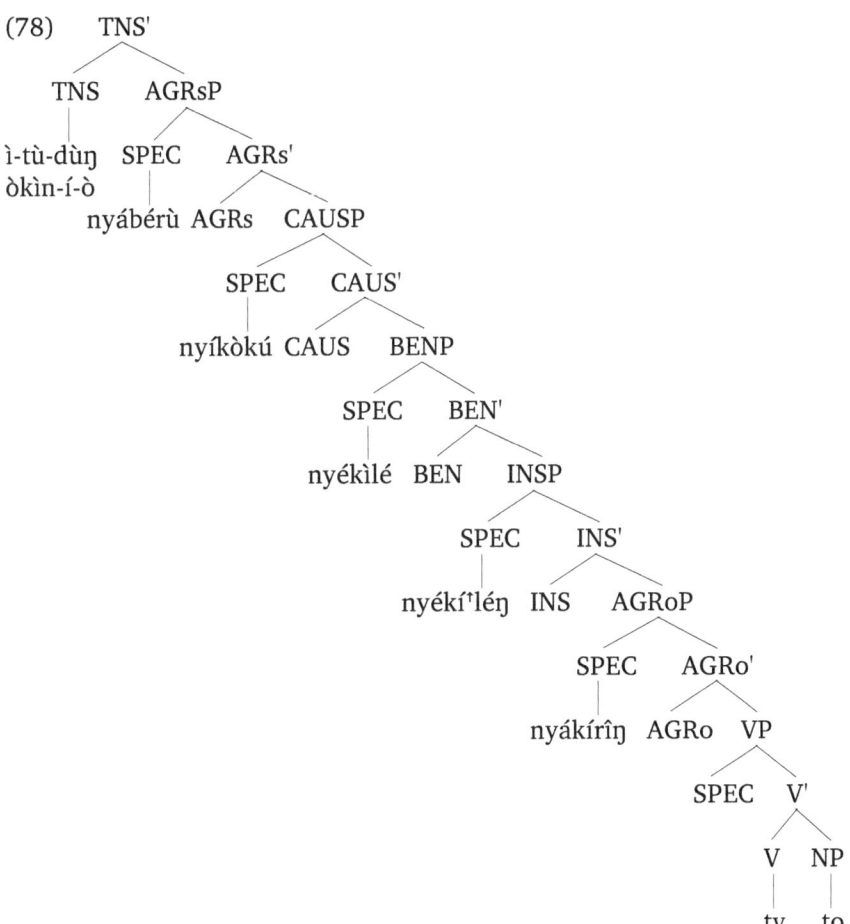

The verb and the complement relationship to the direct object in the VP, however, is violated. The syntax does not allow more than one incorporated argument after the verb (see 71).

As was shown above, when two arguments compete for the position of the incorporated object, only one incorporated argument is structurally permitted in addition to the direct object (figure 4.1). Apparently, Toposa has developed a preference hierarchy of incorporated arguments, where the causative construction takes precedence over the benefactive construction, and the benefactive construction takes precedence over the instrumental construction.

> causative > benefactive > instrumental

Figure 4.2. Preference hierarchy

Under these restrictions, a typical double accusative construction, as in (75a) and (75b), produces the following tree (using (75b) as an example):

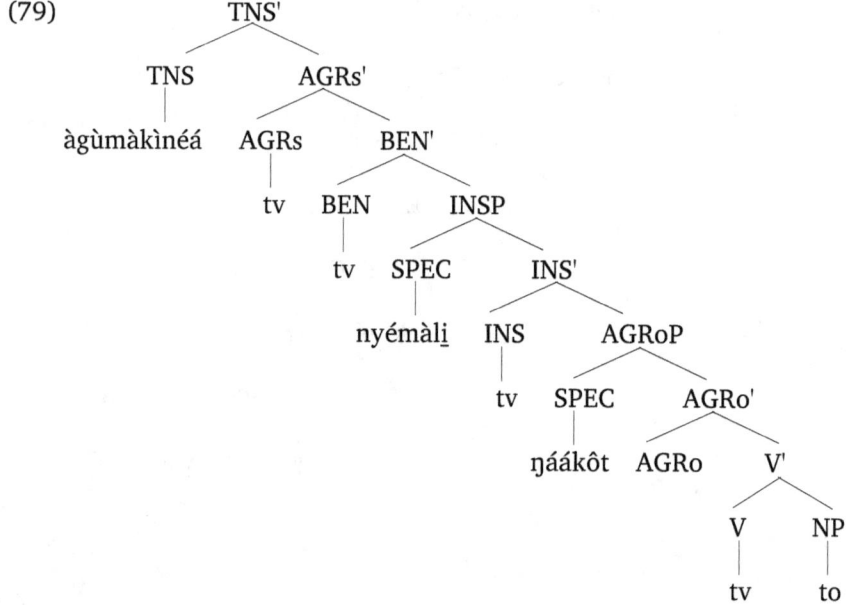

(79)

The tree has two case-bearing heads, BEN and INS. Only the specifier of the INS is occupied for case-checking because only the instrumental argument is overt. Analogously, in the tree for (75a), it is the specifier of BEN that is built.

In other words, standard double accusative constructions can never have more than one incorporated and one direct object, as presented in (75b).

One special feature of Toposa is that it allows both incorporated arguments to be dropped:

4.1 Co-occurrence of Argument-Increasing Devices 95

(80) À-gùm-àkìn-é-á.
 3SG-shoot-BEN-IMP-INS
 'He shot (= drained) [something for someone with something/for a purpose].'

This produces the following tree:

(81)

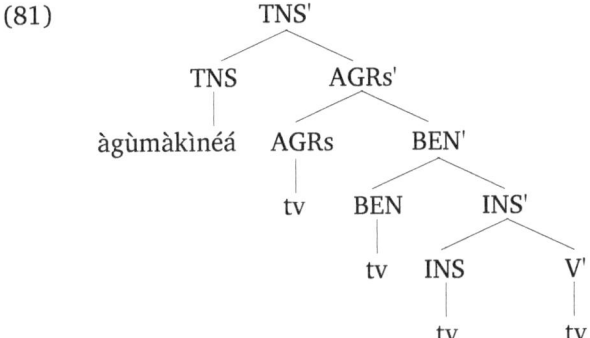

Note how both BEN and INS remain without specifier, for no case-checking takes place.

Note further, that a sentence like (81) cannot stand on its own, i.e., without wider context, because the question arises, where the referent for the benefactive or instrumental is located. In Minimalist terms, it needs to be determined where the case-checking takes place for the benefactive and instrumental arguments which are explicitly marked on the verb in a sentence like (81). These questions point to the fact that syntax is also embedded in discourse and that discourse considerations in turn determine the morphosyntactic sentence-building process in the lexicon. Due to these complex interconnections, all the case-bearing units like causative, benefactive, and instrumental need to be dealt with again in the context of discourse, which will be done in the next chapter.

So far only transitive roots have been considered. It is predictable that intransitive roots can license one additional incorporated argument for there is no direct object. This is the case, for example:

(82) É-tè-ryàŋ-àkìn-í nyá-bérù
 3SG-CAUS-be.afraid-BEN-IMP F/SG-woman/NOM

 nyí-kòkú   ŋí-kílyôk.
 D/SG-child/ACC M/PL-men/ACC
 'The woman caused the child to be afraid of the men.'

In this sentence the causative object fills the normal slot for the incorporated object, while the benefactive object takes the place reserved for the direct object in transitive constructions.

It is also predictable that an intransitive verb root with three incorporated arguments violates the Toposa verb phrase as it was presented in (71):

(83) *Ì-tì-jì-kìn-í-ò   ŋí-kí'lyók
        3SG-CAUS-fight-BEN-IMP-INS   M/PL-men/ACC

        ŋú-tú'ŋá   ŋá-kwààrási.[4]
        M/PL-people/ACC   F/SG-spears/ACC
        'He makes the men to fight for the people with spears.'

The only possible way to express this scenario is by reducing the number of arguments. In (84a) the benefactive object is overt, and in (84b) the causative is incorporated:

(84) a. Ì-tì-jì-kìn-í-ò   ŋú-tú'ŋá   ŋá-kwààrási.
        3SG-CAUS-fight-BEN-IMP-INS   M/PL-people/ACC   F/SG-spears/ACC
        'He makes [someone] to fight for the people with spears.'[5]

     b. Ì-tì-jì-kìn-í-ò   ŋí-kí'lyók   ŋá-kwààrási.
        3SG-CAUS-fight-BEN-IMP-INS   M/PL-men/ACC   F/SG-spears/ACC
        'He makes the men to fight [for someone/something] with spears.'

These data suggest that with intransitive verbs two incorporated objects are the structurally allowed maximum, even when there are three head-bearing affixes present in the verb.

To summarise: With transitive roots, only one incorporated argument can become overt as the other slot is occupied by the direct object. Constructions in which both incorporated arguments are expressed are only possible with intransitive verb roots.

The restriction of the choice of arguments is a grammatical feature of Toposa which reflects the morphosyntactic nature of the language. The

---

[4] The root *ji* 'fight' in Toposa is intransitive, 'to fight someone' is constructed with the preposition *ka* 'with': *nyjiere ka ŋimoe* 'fight with/against enemies', or the verb is causativised but has simple transitive meaning: *Kitijikisi Ŋitoposa Ŋibuya* 'the Toposa fought the Boya (lit., the Toposa caused the Boya to fight)'.

[5] Parallel to example (68a) earlier in this chapter, this sentence can only be interpreted correctly in context. The two meanings, of course, are (a) 'He makes [someone] to fight for the people with spears', and (b) 'He makes the people to fight [for someone] with spears'.

reduction to only one applied argument is determined in the lexicon as numeration begins.

4.2 Co-occurrence of Argument-Increasing and Argument-Decreasing Devices

The last section examined various combinations of those case-bearing affixes which, if they occur by themselves, license an additional argument in the structure-building process; and we explored the sentence structures these affix-combinations produce. This section will investigate what happens when argument-increasing and argument-decreasing affixes are combined. Passive will be considered first.

4.2.1 Combinations with passive

In chapter three the Toposa passive was analysed as the absolute subject of an intransitive sentence (cf. 3.4.2.1, also 3.3.1). Because of the accusative case-checking of the passive subject, the passive is conceptualised as a VP with a direct object. The subject of the passive intransitive sentence becomes the direct object of the verb, and the affix-bearing argument which occurs together with the passive morpheme creates an incorporated object. Based on this analysis, this section will examine what happens when one or two head-bearing affixes are added to the passive verb. First, consider a simple benefactive extension:

(85) É-pó-kín-ˈí ŋí-kíˈlyók nyá-kírîŋ.
3SG-cook-BEN-IMP M/PL-men/ACC F/PL-meat/ACC
'She cooked the meat for the men.'

The sentence has two objects, the direct object *nyákírîŋ* 'meat' and the indirect object *ŋíkíˈlyók* 'men'. Both objects can be passivised.

If the direct object is passivised, the sentence has two object arguments, the direct object *nyákírîŋ* becomes the absolutive subject, i.e., the passivised absolutive subject of the intransitive sentence, and the benefactive object *ŋíkíˈlyók* becomes the incorporated object:

(86) Kí-pó-kín-òè ŋí-kíly'ók nyá-kírîŋ.
3SG-cook-BEN-PAS M/PL-men/ACC F/PL-meat/ACC
'The food was cooked for the men.'

The VP of (86) has no specifier, for the passive sentence has no nominative subject but an absolutive subject with accusative case-marking. Thus, the VP has two accusative complements:

(87)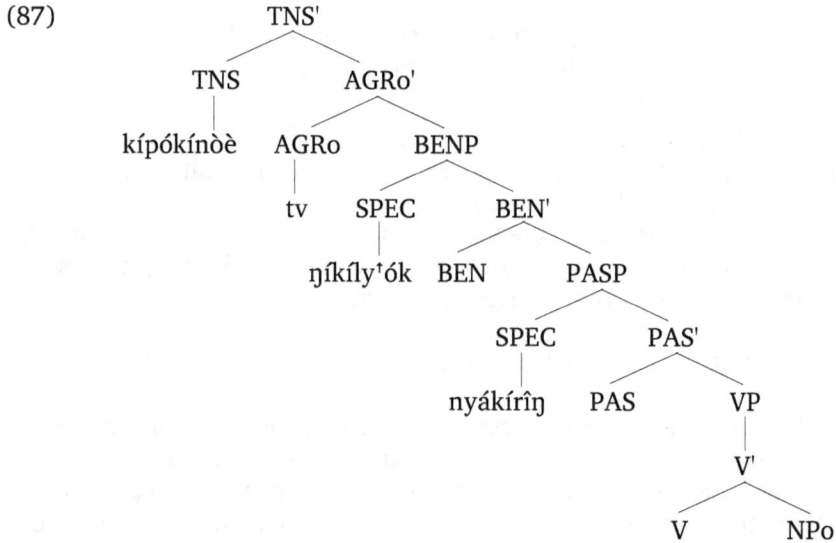

The absolutive subject of the transitive sentence takes the position of the direct object, and the benefactive object is the incorporated object. Consequently, both objects keep their normal position that they have in the non-passivised ditransitive VOO sentence of (85), i.e., in the passive construction the incorporated object directly follows the verb and precedes the passivised direct object.

If the indirect object is passivised, the direct object drops out, and the passivised object becomes the subject of the sentence. It is not possible to passivise the indirect object and to have the direct object staying *in situ*, as attempted in (88):

(88) *Kí-pó-kín-òè   nyá-kí'ríŋ   ŋí-kílyôk.
   SEQ-cook-BEN-PAS   F/SG-meat/ACC   M/PL-men/ACC
   'The men were cooked for, and it was meat.'

The correct version of (88) is:

(89) Kí-pó-kín-òè   ŋí-kílyôk.
   SEQ-cook-BEN-PAS   M/PL-men/ACC
   'The men were cooked for.'

4.2 Co-occurrence of Argument-Increasing and Argument-Decreasing Devices

This sentence has the following tree structure:

(90)

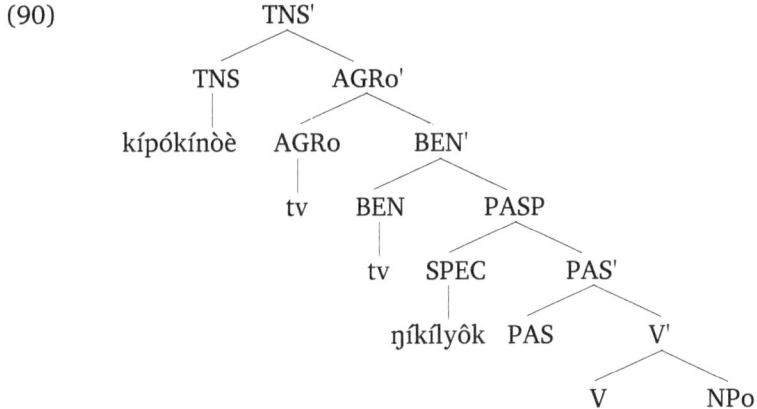

The diagram shows that (89) is logically an intransitive sentence, which has structurally been converted to a transitive one in which the subject has accusative-marking and appears in the VP as complement of the verb. Furthermore, agreement is with the object rather than the subject. Remember also that the agent is never mentioned in Toposa passive constructions.

The logical syntactic explanation for example (89), where the direct object does not appear in the passivised sentence, is the following: the incorporated object becomes the absolutive subject which so far has been interpreted as the complement of the verb, in the same way as the direct object. If the incorporated object is passivised, it becomes the absolutive subject of the sentence and it swaps places with the direct object, which then becomes the incorporated object. It is impossible for the direct object, however, to take the place of the incorporated object as in (88), because it is not licensed by a head-bearing affix, as incorporated objects normally are. Therefore, the only grammatically correct version of constructions where the indirect object is passivised, follows the pattern of (89), i.e., the direct object must drop out.

Benefactive-passive constructions can be extended by a further head-bearing affix, that is, by causative. However, causative-benefactive-passive combinations are only possible with intransitive verb roots, since only an intransitive verb root can add two incorporated arguments. Consider the following intransitive sentence with two incorporated objects:

(91) É-sí-mét-ókín-ˈî   ŋí-sòrók   ŋí-kàsùkówu̱.⁶
      3SG-CAUS-fight-BEN-IMP M/PL-yg.men/ACC   M/PL-elders/ACC
      'He/she caused the young men to fight the elders.'

When passivised, this produces a sentence in which the causative object becomes the passivised object and the benefactive object becomes the direct object:

(92) É-sí-mét-ókín-ˈó   ŋí-sòrók   ŋí-kàsùkówu̱.⁷
      3PL-CAUS-fight-BEN-PAS M/PL-yg.men/ACC   M/PL-elders/ACC
      'The young men were caused to fight the elders.'

Thus, sentence (92) with its two accusative objects has the following tree:

(93)

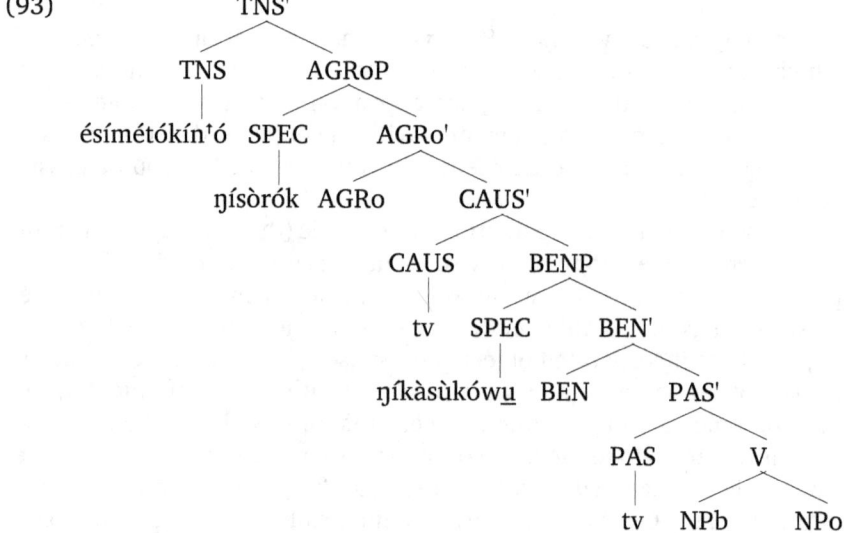

In this passive construction the complement relationship of the VP (as illustrated in (71)) is maintained, for the passivised absolutive subject takes the place of the direct object. The VP has no specifier, since the

---

⁶The root *met* 'intratribal fighting' really is intransitive in the Toposa lexicon. For a construction based on this root to be transitive, a causative prefix has to be added. (The root *ji* 'interpersonal fighting' works the same.

⁷This sentence was elicited in isolation. In connected discourse, the benefactive causative construction usually occurs without the accusative object. Further investigation may be needed here.

4.2 Co-occurrence of Argument-Increasing and Argument-Decreasing Devices

subject of the sentence is an absolutive object which becomes the complement of the VP. The benefactive NP checks its case-marking under the specifier of BEN, and the passivised causative checks its accusative features under the specifier of AGRoP, since it has become the absolutive object. The AGRo moves to the position of AGRs because in passive constructions object agreement takes place. As always, the succession of the affixes determines the order of the projections: AGRoP, CAUSP, BENP, PASP, according to the order of the affixes in the verb:

(94) É-sí-mét-ókín-ô.
AGRo-CAUS-root-BEN-PAS
'They were caused to fight.'

To summarize the findings,[8] a passive sentence with direct and indirect object is always VOO in those constructions where the direct object is passivised, as in (86), and where the verb has an intransitive root, as in (92). When the indirect object is passivised, only VO is possible, as in (89). Both resulting sentence constructions, VO and VOO, fit into the structure of the Toposa VP as defined in diagram (71).

4.2.2 Combinations with reflexive

The other argument-reducing construction that can be combined with various case-bearing affixes on the verb is the reflexive.
Recall that the Toposa reflexive VP is normally a VS construction:

(95) Tó-cák-ùn-i̱   nyá-bérù.[9]
SEQ-fall-ALL-RFL   F/SG-woman/NOM
'The woman fell down.'

The reflexive VP has an interface VS projection because the reflexive NP is incorporated in the verb as the reflexive pronoun -i̱. Logically, the sentence is transitive, as the reflexive pronoun is an incorporated accusative argument, but on interface level it is intransitive, because it has the nominative subject as its only constituent, situated in the specifier of VP and moved to the specifier of AGRs for case-checking, shown in the following tree:

---

[8]In this section only the benefactive and causative-benefactive have been considered. Causative-passive works in the same way as causative-benefactive. Instrument-passive and benefactive-instrumental-passive constructions also exist, but they had to be excluded from this discussion as they only occur in specific discourse contexts.

[9]The allative suffix -un is not case-bearing and does not need to be considered here.

(96)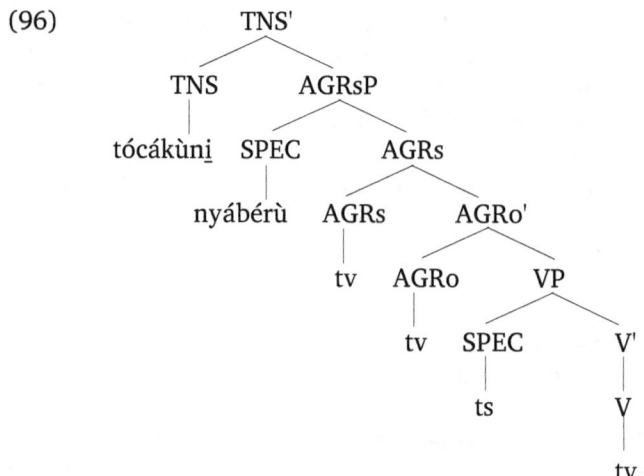

The problem with the Toposa reflexive is that the pronoun is integrated in the verb, which means that the verb undergoes a noun incorporation, but morphologically the pronoun is only a suffix and thus has a feature-checking head, but no specifier. The suffix checks its feature under the AGRo head. There is no need for a specifier, because no case-marking of the reflexive pronoun takes place.

Since no overt pronoun occurs, the morphological reflexive reduces the transitivity of the sentence by one argument. The tree structure of (96) represents an intransitive sentence which is logically transitive. In a feature-based approach the logical transitivity of the reflexive is not reflected in the tree structure, for the interface is the only level of interpretation, in this case the intransitive sentence. The Minimalist Program does not say any more about the logical connection between underlying forms and surface forms, which under GB had been demonstrated for phenomena such as relative constructions, passive, morphological reflexives, etc. Under the Minimalist Program these forms become mere 'taxonomics' (Chomsky 1993:4).

The Toposa reflexive combines with head-bearing affixes like benefactive and instrumental. Reflexive-causative combinations have not been found.

If the reflexive combines with the benefactive, the BEN and the RFL both receive heads for feature-checking in the structure-building process:

4.2 Co-occurrence of Argument-Increasing and Argument-Decreasing Devices 103

(97) a. Tó-ryáŋ-àkìn-ó-si̱   Ŋí-túkòì.
SEQ-frighten-BEN-RFL-PL   M/PL-zebras/NOM
'The [members of the] Zebras [generation set] became very afraid.'

b. Kí-bóy-ìkìn-ó-si̱   ŋú-túŋà.
SEQ-sit-BEN-RFL-PL   M/PL-people/NOM
'The people settled down.'

Note the logical syntactic process that takes place with intransitive roots like 'fear/be afraid'. The verb root is originally intransitive, it is extended syntactically by the benefactive to a transitive sentence and by the reflexive to a ditransitive sentence, but on interface level it is merely intransitive, because the benefactive constituent is not overt, and the reflexive is a morphological suffix that again reduces the transitivity:

(98)
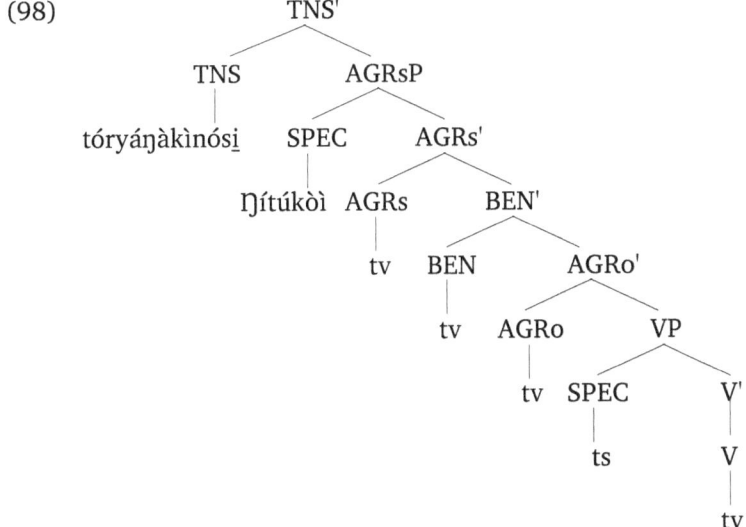

The movement of the verb is as follows: it moves from V to [AGRo/AGRo'] for reflexive feature-checking, then to [BEN/BEN'] to check the benefactive features, further to [AGRs/AGRs'] for agreement-checking, and finally to [TNS/TNS'] to have the tense features checked. The nominative subject moves from the [SPEC/VP] to [SPEC/AGRsP] for nominative case-checking.

If the reflexive-benefactive construction occurs with a transitive verb root, the interface representation of the sentence is transitive, i.e., the basic VSO sentence. The logical sentence structure, however, has four arguments: the subject, the implicit benefactive argument, the incorporated reflexive pronoun, and the direct object:

(99) Tò-rwá-kìn-i   nyá-bérù   nyá-únò.
      SEQ-clasp-BEN-RFL   F/SG-woman/NOM   F/SG-rope/ACC
      'The woman clasped the rope.'[10]

Note that in the above construction the logical argument of the reflexive can only be the benefactive object, because the sentence has already the direct object as its logical accusative argument. The incorporated reflexive argument might be regarded as the benefactive object. In order to distinguish between the RFL as the object pronoun suffix and the benefactive pronoun suffix (as in (97a) and (97b)), the benefactive-reflexive feature has the [BEN-RFL] head, shown in (100):

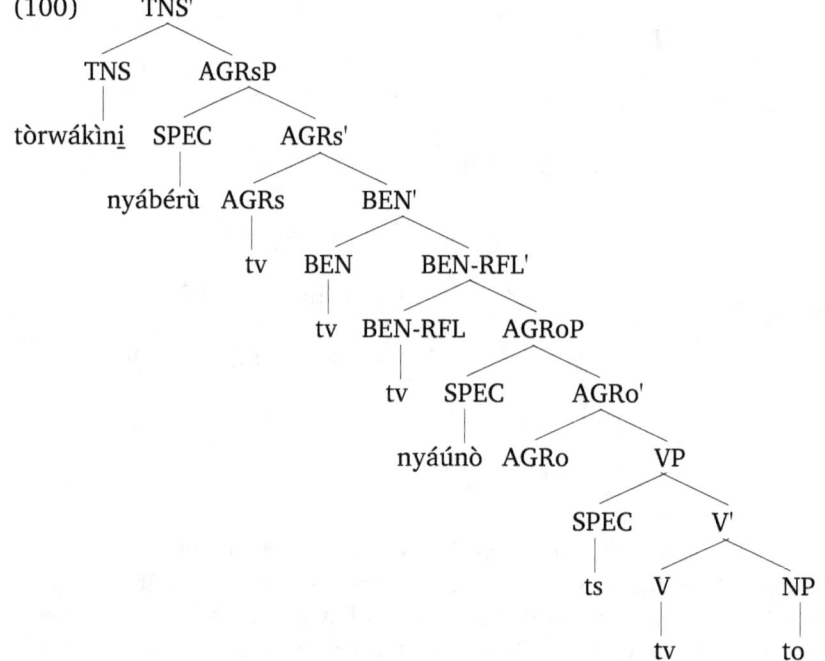

The movements of the verb are the following: it checks its pronominal benefactive features under [BEN-RFL/BEN-RFL'], its benefactive features

---

[10]The verb 'clasp' is inherently reflexive in Toposa.

4.2 Co-occurrence of Argument-Increasing and Argument-Decreasing Devices

under [BEN/BEN'], its agreement features under [AGRs/AGRs'], and its tense features under [TNS/TNS']. The direct object moves from its complement position in the verb to the specifier of AGRoP, and the subject checks its case-marking features under the specifier of AGRsP.

Combinations of the reflexive with instrumental operate in the same way as reflexive-benefactive, for example:

(101) ...ná   á-bál-átò-ri̱   ŋí-jìyé,...
      ...when 3PL-speak-PER-INS/RFL M/PL-Jiye/NOM
      '...when the Jiye said,...'

So far it has been shown that the co-occurrence of one argument-bearing suffix with the reflexive does not change the intransitive VP. Even in a triple combination of benefactive, instrumental, and reflexive, the VP remains intransitive, because the arguments are not overt. See the following example:

(102) ...ná   é-cúm-ákín-ótò-ri̱   ŋí-mòè
      ...when 3PL-spear-BEN-PER-INS/RFL M/PL-enemies/NOM
      '...when the enemies speared each other [with something for a reason/purpose].'

A sentence construction in which the benefactive argument (103a), or the instrumental argument (103b) surfaces, is ungrammatical:

(103)a. *...ná   é-cúm-ákín-ótò-ri̱   ŋí-mòè
        ...when 3PL-spear-BEN-PER-INS/RFL M/PL-enemies/NOM

        nyá-ryáŋ
        F/SG-government/ACC
        '...when the enemies speared each other [with something] for the government.'

    b. *...ná   é-cúm-ákín-ótò-ri̱   ŋí-mòè
        ...when 3PL-spear-BEN-PER-INS/RFL M/PL-enemies/NOM

        ŋá-kwààrási̱
        F/PL-spears/ACC
        '...when the enemies speared each other with spears [for a reason/purpose].'

The spell-out representation of a sentence with the triple combination benefactive-instrumental-reflexive as in (102) is as follows:

(104)

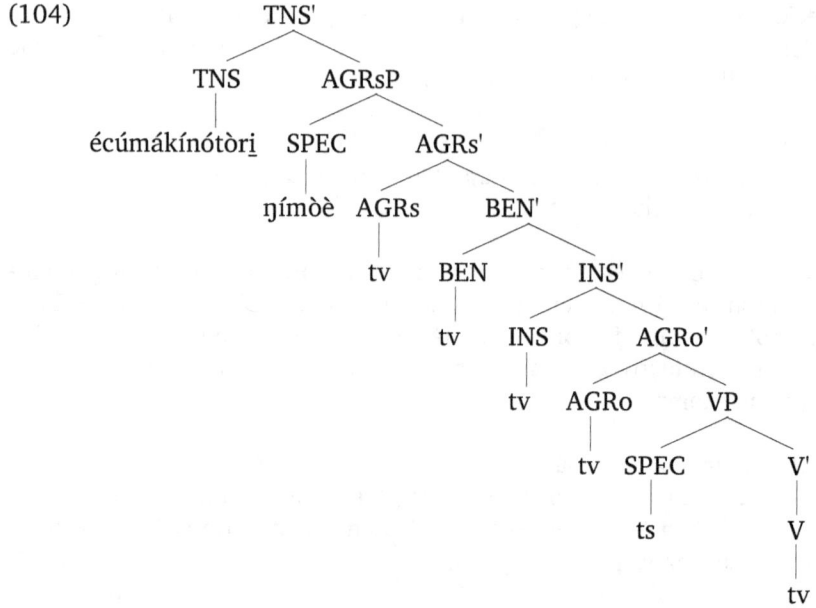

The verb moves from the VP to [AGRo/AGRo'] to check its reflexive features, to [INS/INS'] to check its instrumental features, to [BEN/BEN'] to have the benefactive features checked, and to [AGRs/AGRs'] for agreement feature-checking. The subject moves to the specifier of AGRsP for nominative case feature-checking. The representation of (104) has no specifier relationship in the benefactive and instrumental, because no case-checking takes place, since the benefactive and instrumental arguments are not explicit.

4.3 Alternatives to the Double Object Construction

Since Toposa syntax is restricted to VOO constructions, it is natural that the language looks for alternatives to express more than two accusative arguments. Three accusative arguments are either expressed using a PP construction, or in two separate sentences.

The PP construction allows one of the three arguments to occur in a prepositional phrase, employing prepositions like *kotere* 'for' and *ka* 'with'. In the instrumental sense only *kà* 'with' requires the nominative case. Examples (105a) and (105b) demonstrate this with the applicative and the causative, respectively:

(105) a. Á-tú-dúŋ-ákín-ˈí   nyá-béˈrú   nyá-kíˈríŋ.
3SG-CAUS-cut-BEN-IMP   F/SG-woman/ACC   F/SG-meat/ACC

kà   nyé-kìlêŋ.
with   M/SG-knife/NOM
'He caused the woman to cut the meat with the knife.'

b. È-dúŋ-ì-ò   nyé-kíˈléŋ   nyá-kíˈríŋ
3SG-cut-IMP-INS   M/SG-knife/ACC   F/SG-meat/ACC

kòtèré nyà-bèrû.[11]
for   F/SG-woman/ACC
'He cuts the meat with a knife for the woman.'

In example (105a) the instrumental argument and in (105b) the benefactive argument is pushed into the PP construction.

It is also possible to construct a sentence in which both the benefactive and the prepositional object appear in PP constructions:

(106)   È-dúŋ-ì-ò   nyá-kíˈríŋ   kà   nyé-kìlêŋ
3SG-cut-IMP-INS   F/SG-meat/ACC   with   M/SG-knife/NOM

kòtèré nyà-bèrû.
for   F/SG-woman/NOM
'He cuts the meat with a knife for the woman.'

Another way of expressing three object arguments is to split the sentence into two separate ones, which is demonstrated in (107) with a causative-benefactive construction:

---

[11] After *kotere* the gender prefix which is always H is lowered and *nyaberu* changes from HLF to LLF, probably due to a floating tone: *kotere'*.

(107) É-tíŋ-ákín-ˈí   nyá-béˈrú,   tò-lìm-óki̱
       3SG-force-BEN-IMP   F/SG-woman/ACC   SEQ-tell-BEN

       lò-káàtó   káŋ   ŋá-kíˈró   ŋùnà.
       M/SG-brother/ACC   my   F/PL-maters/ACC   these/ACC
       'He forced the woman to tell these matters to my brother (Lit., He forced the woman, [she] told these matters to my brother).'

4.4 Summary

This chapter adduced evidence that the rich morphology of Toposa influences its sentence structure, as each affix receives its head projection. Although the rich morphology of Toposa suggests a theoretical accumulation of up to four accusative arguments, namely three incorporated objects and one direct object, the maximum permitted number of arguments is two, one incorporated object in addition to the direct object. The sentence structure of V(S)OO, discussed in chapter three is thus never expanded. The reason for this restriction to two accusative arguments lies in the nature of the VP which determines that the head-complement relationship of verb and direct object cannot be violated, an obviously universal feature (Chomsky 1981). Thus, one indirect or incorporated object is the only possible interference between the verb and the direct object.

The next chapter shows how the choice between which argument is implicit and which argument becomes explicit in verbal extensions is a matter of discourse antecedent relationships.

5
Complex Verb Morphology in Discourse

The previous chapter showed how complex combinations of case-bearing affixes never resulted in more than a V(S)OO word order, because the nature of the VP only allows one argument between the verb and its complement. It also hinted at the fact that the selection of arguments that occur in complex verbal processes is related to discourse. (See Schiffrin (1994) on approaches to discourses.)

Generative Grammar has dealt with discourse phenomena mainly in terms of topic and focus. The standard generative approach suggests checking these under the specifier of CP (Chomsky 1993:12). This chapter will depart from this point of view and treat discourse concepts as feature-initiated and in relation to verbal morphology.

This chapter will show that the head-bearing affixes of the verbal morphology have a discourse referent which determines the occurrence and non-occurrence of constituents and affects constituent order.

When the investigation shifts from isolated sentences to connected discourse, the sentence structures found are rarely VOO but more frequently VO, even when there are argument-producing verbal affixes that would allow more incorporated objects to occur.

(108)   ...ná   é-cúm-ákín-ótò-re   ŋí-móê,...
        when   3PL-spear-BEN-PER-INS   M/PL-enemies/ACC
        '...when [they] speared the enemies [with something for a reason/purpose],...'

This sentence has neither an explicit instrumental nor an explicit benefactive argument, but only an accusative object.

The question that immediately arises is this: if there are no overt arguments, what licenses the benefactive and instrumental-marking on the verb?

The answer is: The benefactive and instrumental-marking of the verb relate to a referent outside the matrix sentence. This referent is properly case-checked and spelled-out in the sentence in which it occurs. Consequently, a VO construction results, because the argument of the case-bearing affix does not occur in the basic sentence structure, but is only marked on the verb. The next section will attempt to formalise the relationship between the outside referent and the marking on the verb by suggesting the introduction of a new principle: the Principle of Reference.

5.1 The Principle of Reference

The Principle of Reference is fundamental for the morphosyntactic processes on discourse level in Toposa. It describes the relationship between an antecedent and its subsequent morphological marking. The principle has the following properties:

α is an antecedent for β if and only if
(a) α is a referring expression (nominal category)
(b) α is a checked nominal category
(c) α licenses the checking domain for β.

In other words, this Principle of Reference establishes the relationship between an antecedent, a noun or an NP, and its morphological marking on the verb in subsequent sentence structure. The relationship functions in the following way: After the overtly realized antecedent has gone through proper case-checking, it licenses the morphological marking on subsequent verbs.

The Principle of Reference involves two checking domains: one of the NP (a), and one of the morphological feature (b) on the subsequent verb. In this way a connection is created between the checking domain of the NP and the feature-checking head of the morphological reference feature.

The Principle of Reference is supported by the Principles of Economy and Full Interpretation (FI). For example, if a noun has a subsequent referent in discourse, either the same noun, or a personal pronoun, the

5.1 The Principle of Reference

Principle of FI filters out the phonological and logical repetition of that overt noun in the subsequent sentence. If the overt noun is not phonologically licensed in the sentence, there has to be morphological marking on the verb. Additionally, the Principle of Economy guarantees that no redundant step takes place in derivation, i.e., no structure is built for the case-checking in the sentence where there is affix-marking on the verb. The affixes then receive feature heads, but no specifiers.

The relationship between the Principle of Reference and the reference-marking on the verb will now be demonstrated with personal pronouns (5.1.1), causative, applicative, and complex verbal processes (5.1.2).

5.1.1 Subject and object pronouns in discourse

In a complex sentence structure, the licensing of the subject prefix on the verb is triggered by the case-checking of the referent in the first sentence. Consider the following example:

(109) S1 [Ani   i-ir-ar-i   Locikio ŋa-kiro
            when   3SG-hear-ABL-IMP   Locikio F/PL-matter

        ka   nya-ate,]   S2   [ta-nap-un-i̠,]
        of   F/SG-cow   SEQ-charge-ALL-RFL

     S3 [ku-cum   nya-ate,]   S4   [ta-ar   jik.]¹
         SEQ-spear   F/SG-cow   SEQ-kill   completely
     'When Locikio heard the matters (= words) of the cow, he charged, he speared the cow, he killed [it] completely.'

The subject prefixes[2] of the verbs in S2–S4 refer back to the nominative subject *Locikio* of S1 that went through nominative case-checking. The case-checking of the antecedent in S1 then triggers the dropping of the nominative subject in S2, S3, and S4. The complex sentence structure of (109) can be represented in the tree diagram in (110) (omitting S4):

---

[1] Note that the subject prefix occurs in two different sets, depending on the nature of the verb. Non-sequential verbs occur with the person agreement prefixes *a- e- i-* the underlying forms for 1st/2nd/3rd person, while narrative-sequential verbs use the prefixes *to- ~ ta-* (for TO-class verbs) and *ki- ~ ku-* (for KI-class verbs).

[2] The subject prefix is an affix that has the status of a subject. It is treated in the Minimalist Program as a piece of morphology that licenses a head and a specifier-head relationship for case-checking.

(110)

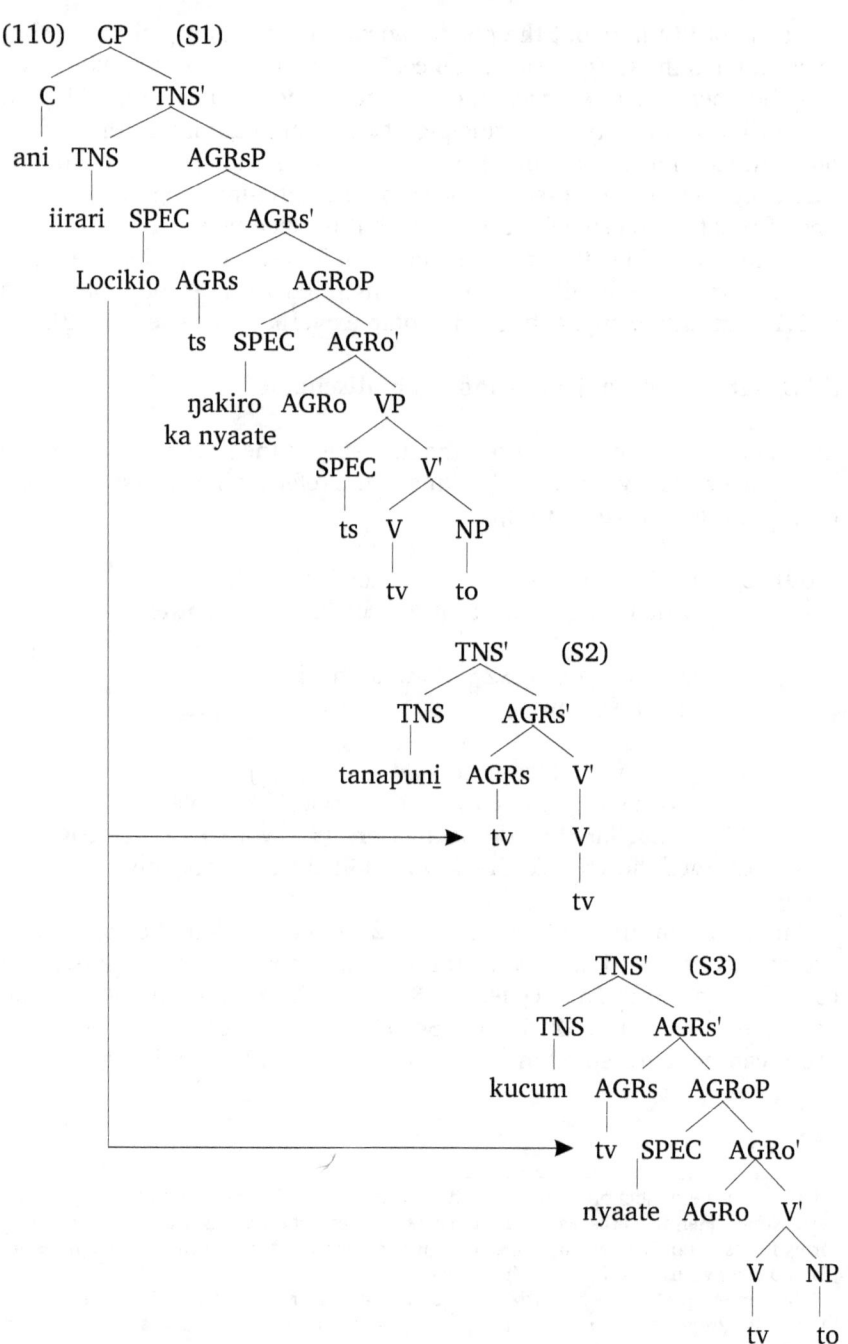

5.1 The Principle of Reference

The verb in S1 moves for checking procedures to [AGRs/AGRs'] and to [TNS/TNS']. The subject of the sentence moves to [SPEC/AGRsP] for nominative case-checking, and the object to [SPEC/AGRoP] for accusative case-checking.

The verb in S2 moves to [AGRs/AGRs'] and to [TNS/TNS']. There are no specifiers as no overt arguments appear.

The verb in S3 moves for checking procedures to [AGRs/AGRs'] and [TNS/TNS']. The accusative object moves to the specifier of AGRoP for case-checking. The specifier of AGRsP is missing because the agreement prefix is licensed by the nominative constituent of S1. Note also that the VP has no specifier, as no overt subject occurs in S3.

The Principle of FI filters out the phonological and logical repetition of the subject in S2 and S3, because after spell-out it appears at PF and LF in form of a verbal prefix, licensed through the antecedent subject in S1. Since the Principle of Economy guarantees that no redundant step takes place in derivation, no redundant structure is built, the specifiers of AGRsP in S2 and S3 are not licensed. Therefore, no movement for nominative case-checking takes place in S2 and S3. Thus the Principle of Economy and FI make sure that S1 has an outcome of VSO, and the subsequent sentence structures are changed to V in S2 and to VO in S3.

The relationship between the antecedent and the references of the morphological subject prefixes can be diagrammed as shown in (111). The diagram shows that the phonological and logical realisations of the subject prefix in S2, S3, and S4 are licensed by the proper case-checking and spell-out of the overt NP of S1 into PF and LF (represented by the lines with arrows). Consequently, the subject NPs (or personal pronouns) in sentences S2, S3, and S4 are absent. Note that the phrasal projection of the subject in sentence S1 licenses that the agreement head and the VPs in S2 and S3 receive no specifier.

(111)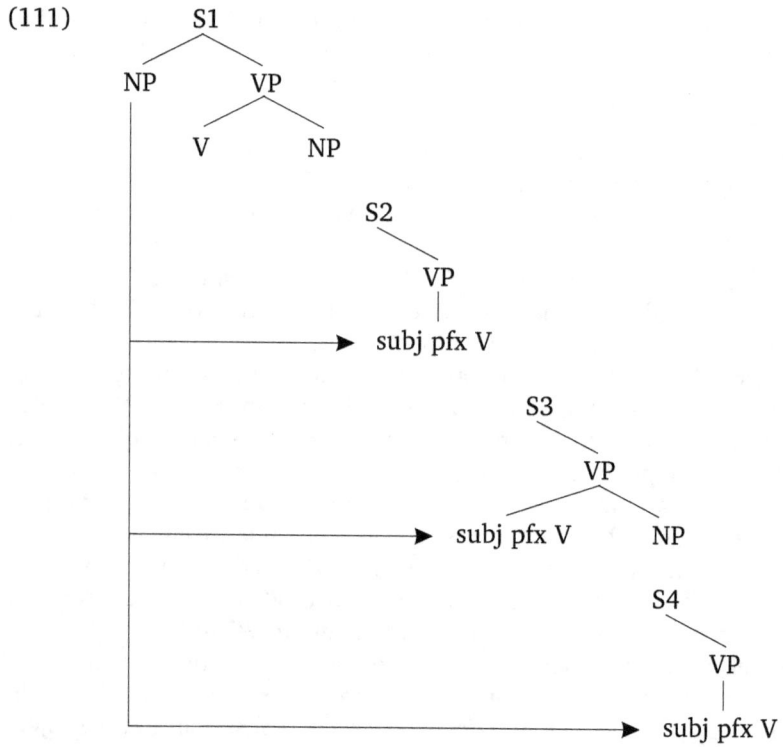

The Principles of Economy and FI and the Principle of Reference also eliminate the object in embedded sentences, if it has an antecedent in the matrix sentence. The object, however, is not marked on the verb as verbal affix in the subsequent sentence. Consider the following example:

(112) S1 [To-lom-a   kwee   na-koomwa,]
         SEQ-enter-ABL jackal F/SG-mound

     S2 [ki-por-o   nai   nye-ŋatuny.]
         SEQ-miss-ABL then   M/SG-lion
     'Jackal entered a termite mound, so Lion missed [him].'

The normal procedure is to have a nominative subject antecedent go through phonological feature and case-checking and then be referenced on the verb in the following sentence. However, the drop of the pronoun is not referenced on the verb in S2. The object pronoun is dropped without being marked on the verb. The representation of sentence (112) is as follows:

5.1 The Principle of Reference   115

(113)

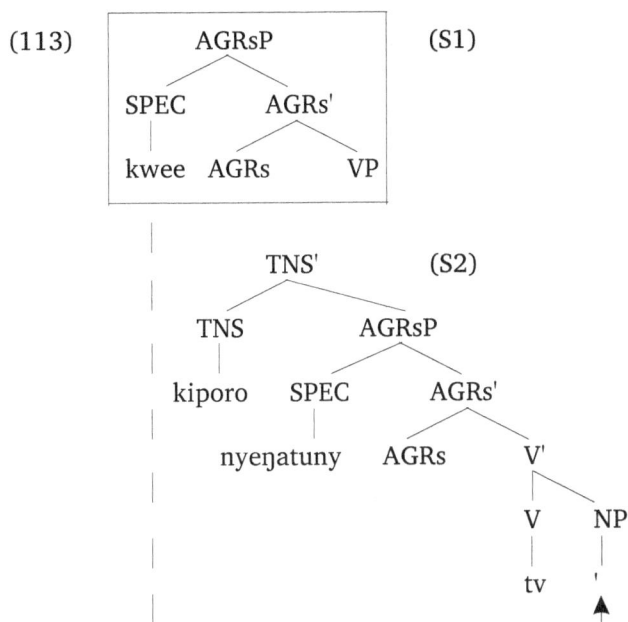

Note that the VP of S2 consists of a verb only, as in an intransitive sentence. The NP in the box[3] represents the designated element that licenses the elision of the object. The diagram does not show any indication of a transitive construction in S2 whatsoever. The reason for this lack of indication lies in the nature of the Minimalist Program. Since it is a feature-based approach and the dropped object does not occur at PF and LF, there is no structure built for the pronoun, and the representation of S2 looks like an intransitive sentence.

In some sentence constructions the subject prefix, which is normally licensed through a nominative noun, is licensed through the accusative case-checking of an object in the previous sentence, as in (114).

(114) S1 [To-ryam-u̱   nye-sapat,]
        SEQ-sleep-ALL M/SG-boy

   S2 [e-per-i   lo-kale̱.]
       3SG-sleep-IMP   M/LOC-home
   'He found the boy sleeping at home.'

---

[3]From here on, boxing will be used to present the antecedent without diagramming the entire sentence it occurs in.

The designated element that licenses the dropping of the NP in S2 is the object *nyesapat* 'boy' of S1. The subject prefix of the verb in S2 refers to the object NP of S1 and at the same time also licenses the absence of the subject in S2.

5.1.2 Causative and applicative in discourse

The Principle of Reference, in conjunction with the Principles of Economy and FI, dominates the applicative and causative constructions also and regulates the absence of the incorporated arguments. The references on the verb are ensured through an antecedent, as (115) with a causative construction will demonstrate.

(115) S1 ["Ani moi na e-bun-o nya- ryaŋ
        if tommorrow when 3SG-come-RFL F/SG-government

        na-kop kusi̱,] S2 [ki-ta-any-ik̲i ŋi-borekeya lu."]
        F/LOC-land yours IV-CAUS-see-BEN M/PL-things these
        'When the government comes to your (pl.) land one day, cause [them] to see (= show them) these things.'

The embedded S2 has a causative prefix on the verb, but the causative argument *nyaryaŋ* 'government' is missing, as it had already been mentioned in the previous sentence:

(116) To-lim-ok̲i nya-ryaŋ Lotunyeny, tem-a̱,
        SEQ-tell-BEN F/PL-government Lotunyeny said-RFL

        "To-tiŋ nya-perewa na ka nya-woru na
        IMP-keep F/SG-sheet this and F/SG-cloth this

        lo-ka-jok-on̲i."
        M/SG-DER-good-SG
        'The government told Lotunyeny and said, "Keep this sheet (= document) and this cloth (= flag) well."'

Here the overt noun *nyaryaŋ* is morphologically licensed and formally case-checked for nominative and appears properly at PF and LF. Consequently, it does not appear in the successive sentence (115) in form of an overt noun, instead, it is licensed as causative prefix on the verb. Because the referent is properly case-checked, the Principle of FI makes sure that

5.1 The Principle of Reference

no superfluous element appears at PF and LF in (115). Since the prefix on the verb is sufficient and grammatically correct, no overt noun occurs. The structure of S2 in (115) is VO instead of VOO, due to the Principle of Economy, which blocks structure-building for an overt causative noun. This structure-building and spell-out process works similarly to diagram (111), which shows the occurrence of subject prefixes related to an antecedent.

The Principle of Reference is confirmed by applicative constructions which work in the same way as causative. For example, there are many sentences in Toposa discourse where the benefactive extension is suffixed to the verb, but the constituent does not occur:

(117) Na   e-lep-un-o   ite   keŋe   ŋa-kile,   e-a-u,
       when 3SG-milk-ALL-RFL mother his   F/PL-milk 3SG-bring-ALL

       to-buk-okị   na-dere   na-ka-polo-nị   ŋina
       SEQ-pour-BEN   F/LOC-calabash   F/SG-DER-big -SG   which

       sek   e-buk-on-okin-o   ŋa-kile   ŋu-rwa   daanị.
       always 3PL-pour-HAB-BEN-?   F/PL-milk   M/PL-days   all

'When his mother had milked the milk, she brought [the milk], she poured [it] into a big calabash into which she always poured [her] milk.'

The discourse referent for the benefactive construction *tobukokị* 'she poured for someone' is found in (118) from a previous sentence:

(118) A-bu   nai   ki-do-u   nyi-koku   ni-sapat.
       3SG-come   then   SEQ-drop-ALL   D/SG-child   D/SG-boy
       'Then [she] came and gave birth to a baby boy.'

In (118), the benefactive object *nyikoku nisapat* 'boy-child' appears and is properly case-checked for accusative. Sentence (119) has no specifier-head relationship in the benefactive extension, as no case-checking takes place under the benefactive head.

The instrumental works analogously to the benefactive, in that it, too, has its referent in discourse. Consider example (119) with the verb *eperitotore* 'where they slept':

(119) S1 [Ta-any-u-tu̱   nye-kitoe   lo-ti-ka-polo-ni̱
           SEQ-see-ALL-PL   M/SG-tree   M/SG-very-DER-big-SG

    lo-ti-ko-oy-eni̱,]   S2 [ŋolo   e-ra-i   nye- tyama̱]
    M/SG-very-DER-tall-SG   which   3SG-be-SG   M/SG-place

    S3 [ŋolo   e-per-ito-to-re̱   ɲi-kilyok   ka
        which   3PL-sleep-PER-PL-INS   M/SG-men   of

    nya-kop   ka   ɲina.]
    F/SG-land   of   that
    'They saw a very big and a very tall tree, which was the meeting-place [where] the men of that country slept.'

The instrumental extension -*re̱* of the verb 'sleep' refers to the tree, which has properly been case-checked for accusative case in S1.

Any head that carries nominative case-marking, as in example (117), or accusative case-marking, as in example (119), serves as a feature-based referent in discourse.

To summarise, all argument-increasing affixes and the subject prefix have the same type of relationship to a licensed constituent. The case-checking through the specifier of the respective constituent in previous discourse units determines that it can be dropped after it is marked on the verb, so it does not appear at PF and LF. In other words, the Principle of FI eliminates these superfluous elements at PF and LF, and the Principle of Economy prohibits that any specifier is built.

It is predictable that complex verbal processes work in the same way as the causative and applicative. As shown in chapter 3, head-bearing affixes co-occur, but no extra constituent becomes overt. The same holds for combined affix processes in discourse, as (120) will show for benefactive-instrumental.

(120) S1 [...a-ryaŋ-akin-oto-re̱,]   S2 [tem-a-si
          3PL-fear-BEN-PER-INS/RFL   said-RFL-PL

    "Too   to-rem-oe,   ya-u   nya-lyel   na-kop."]
     let   SEQ-spear-PAS   bring-ALL   F/SG-grave   F/LOC-land
    '...[when] they had became frightened of him and had said "Let him be speared [so that] he will bring his grave home." '

5.1 The Principle of Reference

The verb *aryaŋakinotore̱* '[when] they became frightened [because of him]' is a verb that has the benefactive extension *-akin*, followed by perfect aspect *-oto* and the instrumental suffix *-re̱*. These verbal extensions have their referents in a previous sentence. The benefactive refers to Teko, and the instrumental to the time, i.e., the 'day of oil'. According to the Principle of Economy, the benefactive suffix and the instrumental suffix occur without respective specifier and indicate that case-checking for the benefactive and instrumental took place elsewhere, i.e., in the preceding sentence construction (121), in which the respective referents for the benefactive and instrumental suffixes occur:

(121) S1 [To-rem-oe   Teko   nya-kou,]   S2   [ku-wok-o
         SEQ-spear-PAS   Teko   F/SG-head   SEQ-carry-ABL

      nya-kwara,]   S3   [to-dol-un-o   lo-re,]
      F/SG-spear   SEQ-arrive-ALL-?   M/LOC-village

      S4   [kotere   e-lam-it-o   ta-apa   keŋe̱
            as   3PL-curse-PER-PL   PL-fathers his

      ka   na-paaran   ka   nya-kimyet,...]
      on   F/LOC-day   of   F/SG-oil

'Teko was speared in the head, he carried the spear [in his head], he reached the settlement, just as his fathers had cursed him on the day of oil (= that day when he drank the oil)...'

Note also that temporal PP constructions can serve as antecedent, cf. S4 of (121). Case-checking of the NP in such cases takes place under the SPEC of PP.

Sentence (120) is best diagrammed in the following way:

(122)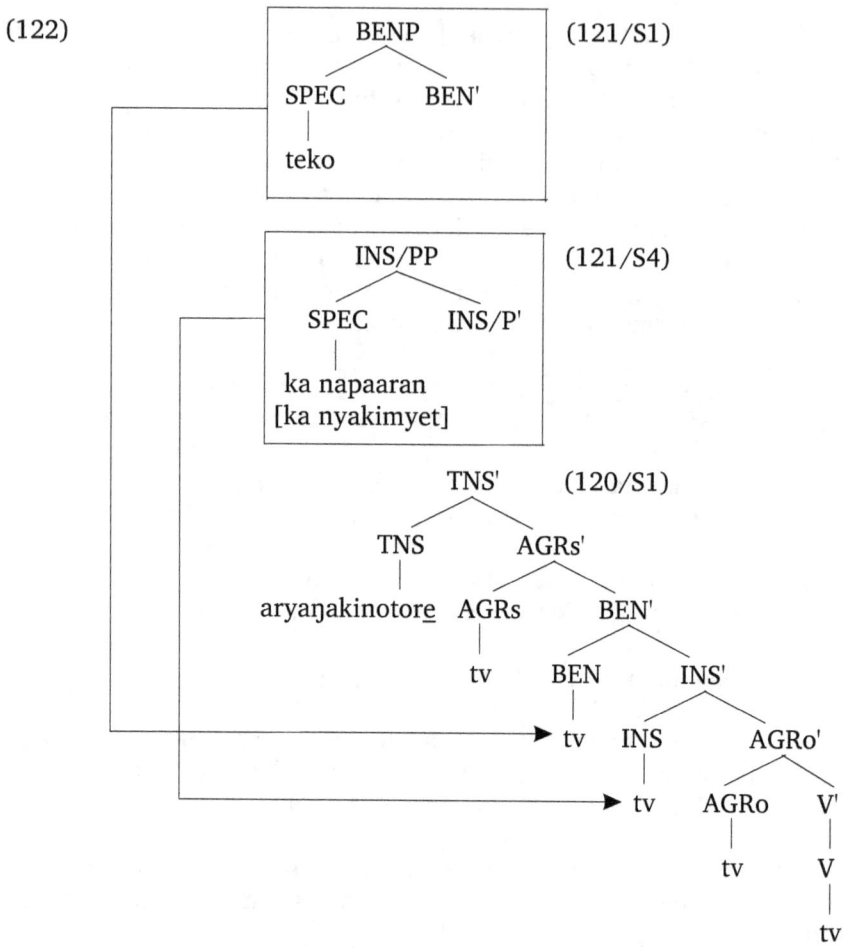

Sentence (120) consists of one verb, so the tree representation has only heads and no specifier, because the specifiers are not licensed and no structure is built for them, due to the Economy Principle.

The verb moves for checking procedures to the [BEN/BEN'], to the [INS/INS'], to [AGRs/AGRs'], and to [TNS/TNS']. The phrasal projections in the boxes show the benefactive and instrumental antecedents of the verbal sentence. Consequently, (120) is a sentence with three empty categories (see Bouchard 1984).

In the old system of GB the benefactive, the causative, and the instrumental would have been interpreted as pros, which have their antecedent in discourse. Since the Minimalist Program is feature based, it no longer relies on Chomsky's typology of empty categories.

5.2 The Principle of Focus

As shown in the last section, affixes without arguments have antecedents in discourse. It also happens that arguments occur after antecedent-checking, and if they do so, they are in focus.

Toposa differentiates structurally between focus by identification (assertive focus) and contrastive focus. This differentiation has been borrowed from functional approaches to focus, especially Wiesemann 1996 and Watters 1976.

This study however, takes a syntactic approach to focus, remaining in line with the Minimalist Program.[4] I suggest to set up a relationship between the focus by identification and the morphology of the verb by putting the focus inside the VP. Focus has to be understood as a complex process that involves the Principle of Reference and the Principles of Economy and FI, which work together to spell out focus in the following way: The Principle of Reference ensures that an antecedent licenses the reference of the subject, causative, or applicative on the verb, and after referencing on the verb it licenses the absence of the respective constituents on sentence level. If, however, an argument occurs, after going through the process of the Principle of Reference, the constituent carries the extra feature [+ focus]. When it is in focus, it is syntactically an incorporated complement of the verb, internal to the VP, and semantically it carries the feature [+focus]. This complex process is typical for focus by identification in Toposa.

In general, focus by identification presupposes information, either explicit or implicit (Wiesemann 1996:124). In Toposa, the implicit information is syntactically marked on the verb as causative, benefactive, or instrumental affixes, and as subject prefix. If the arguments occur in addition to the syntactic marking on the verb, they identify an expression by focusing it. The focal arguments have a functional focus head domain, under which the [+ focus] feature is checked. The focus head heads the respective AGRs, CAUS, BEN, or INS, because it is licensed by the presence of subject, causative, or applicative affix. The relationship between the morphological heads AGRs, BEN, INS, and CAUS and the focus head creates a typical Form Chain in the structure-building process (Chomsky 1993:15), with short successive cyclic movements. The Focus-Form Chain, a feature-based concept of the Minimalist Program, replaces GB's focus operator interpretation of focus-oriented languages, whereby the

---

[4]Toposa focus is interpreted in the framework of propositional focus (cf. 2.4), where focus represents the informative part of the sentence, and the open proposition is the anchoring part of the sentence. (This approach was also the one adopted by GB.)

scope operator of GB is mostly situated in an A-bar position, if it is verb-internal.[5]

As mentioned before, focus basically was interpreted in GB (Chomsky 1981) as an operator which is situated at the specifier of CP and that attracts movement of the NP to the specifier of the CP. Sentence (123) is an example from English.

(123) Apples, I want.

The fronting of the accusative NP is reflected in the following tree:

(124)

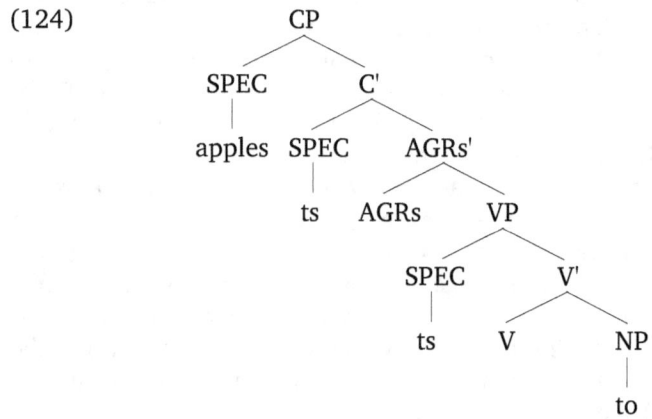

The problem with this interpretation is that all instances of focus are interpreted by fronting the constituents. Kiss (1995:23) was one of those who broke with that tradition and presented a discourse-semantic approach in which focus-oriented languages have a parametric variation of focus interpretation (see section 2.4). This study also departs from the mainstream interpretation by proposing a new Focus Principle.

Because the Principles of Economy and FI do not completely explain the focus operation, and because focus by identification is integrated into the morphological checking process, a Focus Principle has to be formulated that explains and guides the process of licensing (FI) and the structure-building in the focus process. This Focus Principle explains the relationship between the antecedent, the marking on the verb, and the occurrence of the focus constituent if it carries a [+ focus] feature. The Principle of Focus has the following properties:

---

[5]The correct landing site of the Focus Movement depends on the parametric variations such as [SPEC/VP], [SPEC/IP], [SPEC/FP], [SPEC. CP], etc/ (Kiss 1995:23).

5.2 The Principle of Focus

ß has a focus-checking domain if and only if
(a) α is a referring expression to ß
(b) α is a checked nominal category
(c) α licenses the morphological checking domain for ß
(d) ß is overt.

In other words, if an NP has an antecedent in discourse, and has been properly case-checked and morphologically marked and occurs in spite of the proper case-checking and marking of the verb, it carries an extra [+ focus] feature. This focus feature of the NP is checked in its focus-checking domain.

The following section examines how the Focus Principle works in conjunction with personal pronouns, causative, and applicative.

5.2.1 Personal pronouns and focus

The Principle of Focus guides the occurrence of personal pronouns in discourse in the following way: Because the subject pronouns are marked on the verb as prefixes after they have been properly case-checked with a referent, the Principles of Economy and FI regulate that an element is allowed to appear at PF and LF only once in order to be grammatical.[6] Since the pronominal subject appears as prefix at PF and LF according to the Principle of Reference, it cannot appear again at PF and LF, unless it carries an extra feature, i.e., as soon as the pronoun appears in addition to the subject prefix, it carries the extra feature [+focus], for example:

(125)   S1 [Nya-ce   paaran   ki-la-a   nye-ŋatuny
           F/SG-another   day   SEQ-walk-ABL   M/SG-lion/NOM

        na-moni,   nya-ki-rap   ŋa-kee-moogwa,]   S2 [ku- rum
        F/LOC-bush   F/SG-DER-search   F/PL-his-food/ACC   SEQ-catch

        iŋesi   nya -koli.]   S3 [Ki-petepet-aki   iŋesi,]   bala
        him/ACC   F/SG-trap/NOM   SEQ-kick.hard-BEN   he/NOM   saying

---

[6]Chomsky (1986a:98) states: "The Principle of FI requires that every element at PF and LF, taken to the interface of syntax with systems of Language use, must receive an appropriate interpretation—must be licensed." In other words, the feature-based approach takes care of the elements in projecting them into feature-carrying heads.

"A-to-pud!"
1SG-SEQ-escape
'One day [when] Lion walked through the bush to search for his food, a trap caught him. He kicked very hard saying, "Let me get out!" '

Note the occurrence of the third-person singular pronoun in S3 of the complex sentence structure. The nominative subject *nyeŋatuny* 'lion' of S1 is properly case-checked and marked as subject prefix on the verb in S3. However, since the personal pronoun *iŋesi* occurs in S3, it carries the [+focus] feature. The referent 'lion' is identified again. Because the personal pronoun carries the [+focus] feature, a focus head is built for the focus to be feature-checked, and a specifier for the AGRsP, because the pronoun occurs in subject position, and the VP also has a specifier, because the third sentence has an overt subject. See tree diagram in (126), which represents example (125) and shows the relationship between the antecedent of S1 and the personal pronoun subject of S3.

Recall that the characteristic of focus by identification or assertive focus (Wiesemann 1996) is that it presupposes information, either explicit or implicit. The implicit information, then, is identified through focus. In the case of Toposa pronouns this means that the subject prefix on the verb carries the implicit information in S3, and the implicit information is focalised through the occurrence of the third-person pronoun.

Kiss (1995) points out that focus can be either VP-internal or VP-external, i.e., either the structural focus position is related to the VP, or it occurs outside the VP. In this sense Toposa focus operates verb-internally, which is demonstrated by the fact that the specifier of VP is occupied with the focused subject argument, and because focus is related to verbal morphology.

5.2 The Principle of Focus

(126)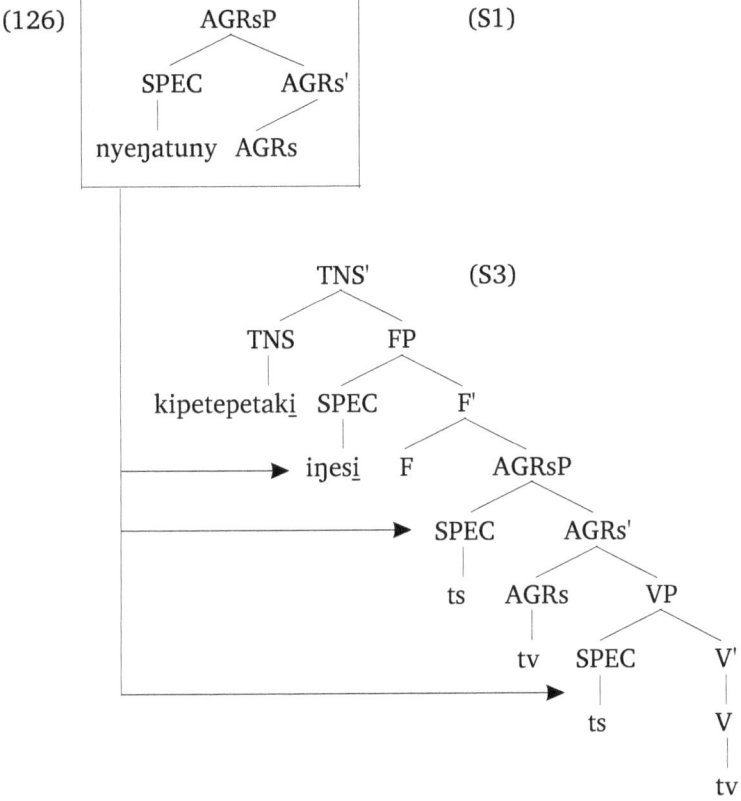

5.2.2 Causative/applicative and focus

As in the case of pronouns, causative and applicative constructions also have a [+focus] feature when their arguments are fully expressed in discourse. Usually, according to the Principles of Economy and FI, the causative and applicative have a morphological marker on the verb, as shown in chapter three. In the [+focus] version of the causative and applicative construction, the arguments are fully expressed and occur in addition to the marking on the verb, and in relation to the Principle of Reference. Thus they are licensed through the [+focus] feature, as in the following examples with causative (127) and benefactive (128):

(127) S1 [Ta-ŋa-u-tu̱   ka   na-bore̱,]
        SEQ-open-ALL-PL from F/LOC-back

   S2 [ki-ti-ji-ki-si̱   ŋi-bokoi,] S3 [to- rem-o,]
      SEQ-CAUS-fight-BEN-PL   M/PL-Bokoi   SEQ-spear-PL

   S4 [ta-ar-a,]   S5 [to-ron-er   nai   nya-kop   jik.]
      SEQ-kill-PL   SEQ-bad-RES   so   F/SG-land completely

'They opened (= attacked) from behind, they caused the [members of the] Bokoi [generation-set] to fight, they speared [them], they killed [them], the land (= the situation) became completely bad.'

The causative prefix in the verb *kitijikisi̱* 'they caused to fight' creates an extra accusative argument. The incorporated object *ŋibokoi* is overt, thus it is mentioned twice, first as prefix on the verb, and then as fully expressed argument. Therefore, the fully expressed argument is in focus and occurs at LF with the [+focus] feature.

The antecedent, which is referenced as a causative prefix in (127), and which occurs as a causative object in focus in (127), was fully expressed two sentences before:

(128) S1 [To-rub-aki̱   nye-meto   jiik,]
        SEQ-go.on-BEN   M/SG-fight always

   S2 [tani̱   e-lili-e-te   ŋi-bokoi,]
      until   3PL-angry-IMP-PL   M/PL-Bokoi

   S3 [to-lom-a-si   ikesi̱   daŋ   lo-meto.]
      SEQ-enter-ABL-PL   they   also   M/LOC-fighting

'The fight continued always, until [the members of the] Bokoi [generation-set] were angry, they also entered into the fighting.'

In the construction in (129), it is the benefactive object *ŋikilyok* 'men' that is fully expressed in order to identify the agent of the discourse:

(129) S1 [Ani   e-ra-i   nya- ate   na-ka   nye-tale̱,]
        if   3SG-was-SG   F/SG-cow   F/SG-of   M/SG-s.custom

   S2 [ki-to-rop-un-oe   nya-ropio,]
      SEQ-CAUS-cut-ALL-PAS   F/SG-HLTT

5.2 The Principle of Focus

    S3 [ki-po-kin-ae   ŋi-kilyok.]
         SEQ-cook-BEN-PAS M/PL-men
'If a cow was one of sacred custom [i.e., it was sacrificed/ritually killed], the HLTT [i.e., the heart/lungs/throat/tongue all attached to each other as one part] is cut [and] is cooked for the men.'

The antecedent to the benefactive construction, the *ŋikilyok* 'men' of (129) were already expressed in the preceding sentence (130/S4):

(130) S1 [Nya-ate kode nye-moŋ e-twan-i,]
         F/SG-cow or   M/SG-ox   3SG-die-IMP

      S2 [ŋa-ber<u>u</u>   e-yeŋ-e-te,]   S3 [ki- nero-to
          F/PL-women 3PL-skin-IMP-PL   SEQ-divide-PL

      ŋi-nerin   kec<u>e</u>, ŋa-ber<u>u</u>   ka nya-pei teker ka
      M/PL-parts their M/PL-women of F/SG-one clan and

      ŋa-pesur kec<u>e</u>,] S4 [to-pe-o   ŋi-kilyok
      F/PL-girls their   SEQ-roast-PL M/PL-men

      nya-kou, ŋi-syepyon, ŋi-molokony.]
      F/PL-head M/PL-sides   M/PL-feet
'[If] a cow or an ox dies, it is the women [who] skin [the animal] and divide their parts, women of one clan and their girls. The men roast the head, the sides, the feet.'

In both causative and benefactive constructions, the syntactic representations require a functional [+focus] head, similar to the personal pronoun construction. The focus feature triggers the building of a focus head and the building of the specifier of the benefactive where the benefactive object receives its accusative case features. In the normal construction the specifier of the benefactive (130) or of the causative construction (128) is not occupied, because the causative or benefactive has its antecedent beyond the basic sentence. A focus head is created so that the focus features can be checked. The verb of (127/S2) has a focused causative argument that is checked under the specifier-head relationship of the focus head, because it is licensed by the focus feature.

The causative-benefactive construction in (127) has the following representation in which the causative object is in focus, thus the focus phrase heads the causative phrase:

(131)

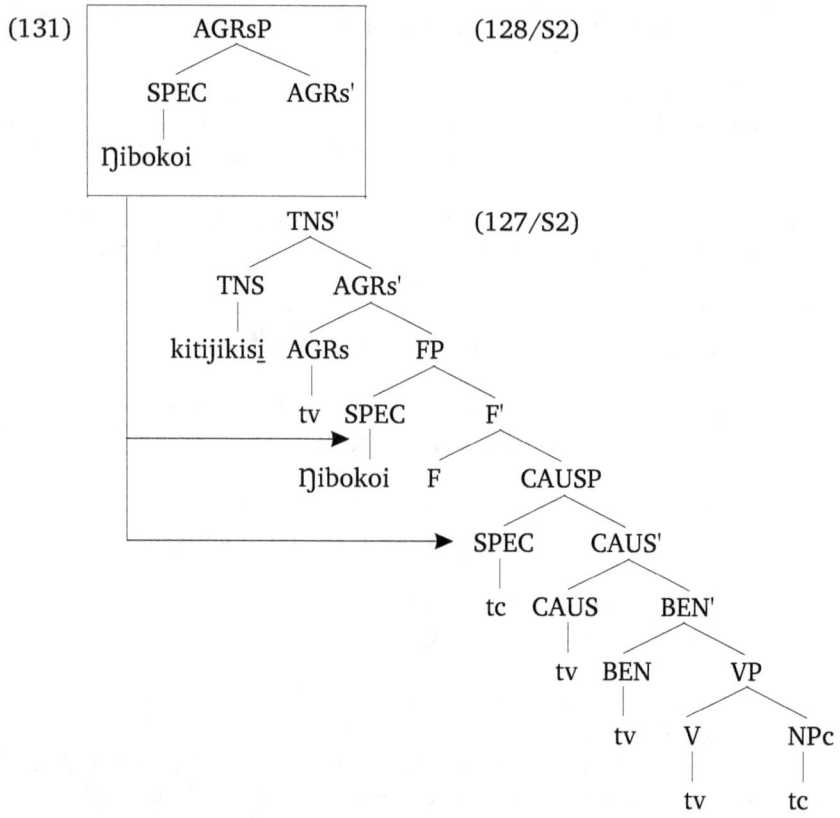

The verb moves to have its benefactive features checked under [BEN/BEN'], then to [CAUS/CAUS'] for causative feature-checking, to [AGRs/AGRs'] for agreement-checking, and to [TNS/TNS'] to have the TNS features checked. The causative object moves to the specifier of CAUSP for case-checking and to the specifier of FP for focus-checking. The boxed NP refers to the antecedent of (128) that licenses the morphological feature head CAUSP and the focused causative argument which checks its focus features under the focus head of (127), but is case-checked under the specifier-head relationship of CAUSP.

The instrumental construction also has a focus variant. First of all, it has an unmarked and a marked version. The unmarked version is constructed with the instrumental suffix and no extra instrumental argument, see the shortened repetition of (119):

5.2 The Principle of Focus

(132) ...ŋolo   e-per-ito-to-re
       which   3PL-sleep-PER-PL-INS

   ŋi-kilyok   ka   nya-kop   ka   ŋina.
   M/SG-men   of   F/SG-land   of   that
   '[a tree...under] which the men of that country slept.'

The marked version has two variants. One variant is constructed with the instrumental suffix and the accusative focused argument, as shown in (133a). The second marked version is constructed with the preposition *ka* 'with' in a PP and has an additional [+contrast] feature and heads the VP as follows:

(133) a. I-des -e-a   nya-kulit   nya-ate.
         3SG-beat-IMP-INS   F/SG-stick/ACC   F/SG-cow/ACC
         'He is beating the cow with a stick.'

   b. I-des-i   nya-ate   ka   nya-kulit.
      3SG-beat-IMP   F/SG-cow/ACC   with   F/SG-stick/NOM
      'He is beating the cow with a stick.'

As the instrumental argument of (133a) carries the feature [+focus], it is constructed with a focus head in the same way as (131).

The construction of (133b) has an additional feature [+contrast]. Note that Baker mentions that some languages have both constructions, the prepositional and the incorporated one, and others have only the prepositional version (like English), or only the verbal applicative form (like Kinyarwanda). Languages with double constructions as shown in (133a) and (133b) enable Baker to develop his prepositional incorporation theory. With these two constructions he is able to demonstrate that the instrumental suffix is incorporated into the verb and leaves the object of the PP behind, which then functions as the applied object (1988:229ff.).

Notice that the [+focus] feature in construction (133b) is not attached to the NP of PP only, but to the whole PP phrase. Note that in (133a) the instrumental suffix creates an extra argument. However, if the instrumental suffix is missing, as in (133b), the occurrence of the focused PP is licensed. In order to express that the PP is focused, the structure-building process demands a focus domain, to which the PP then moves. This focus phrase heads the VP as in (134).

(134)

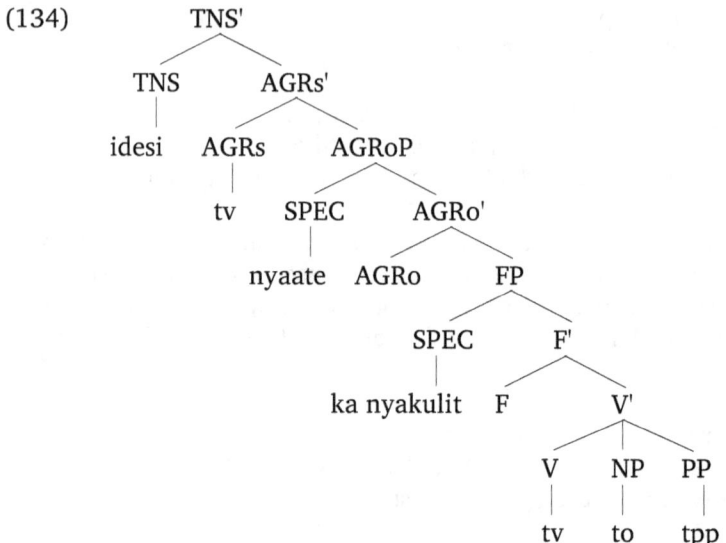

The verb moves from its base position in the VP to [AGRs/AGRs'] to have its agreement features checked and to [TNS/TNS'] for TNS feature-checking. The NP object moves to the specifier of AGRo for case-checking, and the PP moves to the specifier of FP to have its [+ focus] feature checked. Note that a phrase is moved to the specifier of FP, because the whole PP is in focus, and not just the NP of the PP.

5.3 Contrastive Focus

Focus in Toposa distinguishes between assertive focus, which is interpreted in its predicate domain and related to verb morphology, and contrastive focus, which needs to be structurally interpreted because it has a structural position. Focus by contrast (or selective focus), in general, presupposes a choice of information out of known information (Wiesemann 1996:125). The only new information is the result of the choice, that is why the selection is exhaustive (Watters 1976:177).

The strategy for Toposa's contrastive focus is that the contrastive constituent moves to the front of the sentence, i.e., into a contrastive position. Any argument or PP can move into a contrastive focus position and move in front of the verb. The following examples will show how the subject of an intransitive sentence, the subject of a transitive sentence, the

5.3 Contrastive Focus

object of a transitive sentence, and the locative and time PP move to the front of the sentence, when they are in focus:

(135) a. ...e-syeme-ki̱, nye-muno̱ e-ak-ar-i.
　　　　1SG-look-BEN M/SG-snake/ACC 3SG-leave-ABL-IMP
　　　　'...I looked, [it really was] <u>a snake</u> [that] left.'

　　b. Nya- kuju̱ e-yen-i daani̱ na pa
　　　　F/PL-God/ACC 3SG-know-IMP all which not

　　　　ny-a-yen-i ayoŋ.
　　　　NEG-1SG-know-IMP I
　　　　'<u>God</u> [alone] knows everything that I don't know.'

　　c. Ŋuna daani̱ e-rwor-o nye-tau
　　　　these all/ACC 3SG-speak-RFL M/SG-heart

　　　　a-riŋa a-ya-i kidiama.
　　　　1SG-be.still 1SG-be-SG up/above
　　　　'My heart spoke <u>all that</u> while I was still up [in the air].'

　　d. Nya-kwaare̱ ka nya-paaran e-tep-i nya-kuru.
　　　　F/SG-night and F/SG-day 3SG-rain-IMP F/SG-rain
　　　　'<u>Night and day</u> it rained rain.'

　　e. Na-kipi e-per-i.
　　　　F/LOC-water 3SG-sleep-IMP
　　　　'He slept in the <u>water</u> (and not in a dry place).'

These fronted focus constructions create the word order patterns SV (135a), SVO (135b), OVS (135c), PPVS (135d), PPV (135e). The contrastive position in front of the verb is also the place where wh-words move to, for example, the question words *ŋai* 'who?' and *nyo* 'what?' move from the argument position in the VP to the front of the sentence. Consider the questions in (136):

(136) a. Ŋai e-los-i lo-kale̱?
　　　　who 3SG-go-IMP M/LOC-home
　　　　'Who is going to the home?'

b. Nyo   i-muj-i   nya-beru?
   what   3SG-eat-IMP   F/SG-woman
   'What is the woman eating?'

This agrees with Kiss's observation that in all languages which display surface structure Focus Movement into the scope position, foci share the landing site with wh-phrases (1995:24).

In generative syntax this kind of focus is known as "narrow focus" and was treated as a focus operator that moved into the structural CP-focus position of the sentence at surface structure. Since Minimalist theory has eliminated the deep and surface structure division of syntax, the elements which trigger the focus movement are now morphological operators that require feature-checking.

As Toposa makes a distinction between focus by identification and contrastive focus, it employs two different strategies: Focus by identification is focus *in situ* and requires feature-checking under FP, whereas contrastive focus moves to the specifier of CP and implicitly carries the additional feature [+ contrast].

The above constructions (135a–135e), (136a), and (136b) have in common that the focus feature is placed in the specifier of the CP, because the normal structural position of CP in the sentence is in front of the verb. In order to receive focus, the focus constituent moves out of its base position to the specifier of CP to have its contrastive focus features checked.

It is important to note that the nominative subject constituents of (135a) and (135b) lose their case-marking features when they are moved in front of the verb, for all fronted constituents have accusative case-marking.

Since the checking theory states that all elements which have a morphological feature have a head that carries the bundles of features, the theory runs into problems at this point. The change in case-marking from nominative to accusative in (135a) and (135b) has to be accounted for in the feature-checking process.

If the subject constituent moves from the specifier of the AGRs position into the CP position, no recording takes place for the change from nominative to accusative case-marking. This is why all the focused constructions with subject nominative-marking (like (135a) and (135b)) have to pass through the specifier-head relationship of a focus head, where they pick up accusative marking before they move into the specifier of CP. The responsible head will be called 'focus-case-marking' (FCM). The introduction of this head is necessary to indicate that a change from nominative to accusative takes place; see the tree in (137) for example (135a).

5.3 Contrastive Focus

(137)
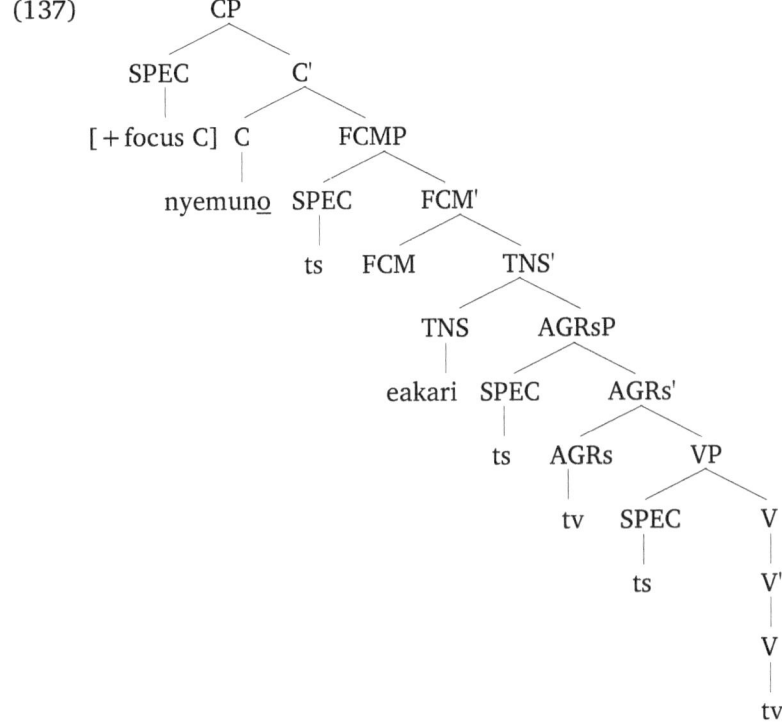

In the usual way, the verb visits all places like [AGRs/AGRs'] and [TNS/TNS'] for feature-checking. The nominative subject moves from [SPEC/VP] to [SPEC/AGRsP] to check its nominative features, then to [SPEC/FCMP] to check its accusative features, and then to [SPEC/CP] to have its focus features checked.

Now consider diagram (138) of the transitive sentence (135b), where the nominative subject moves to the front. The structure-building process requires an extra FCMP head to accomplish the change to accusative because the focus feature triggers the change in case-marking:

(138)
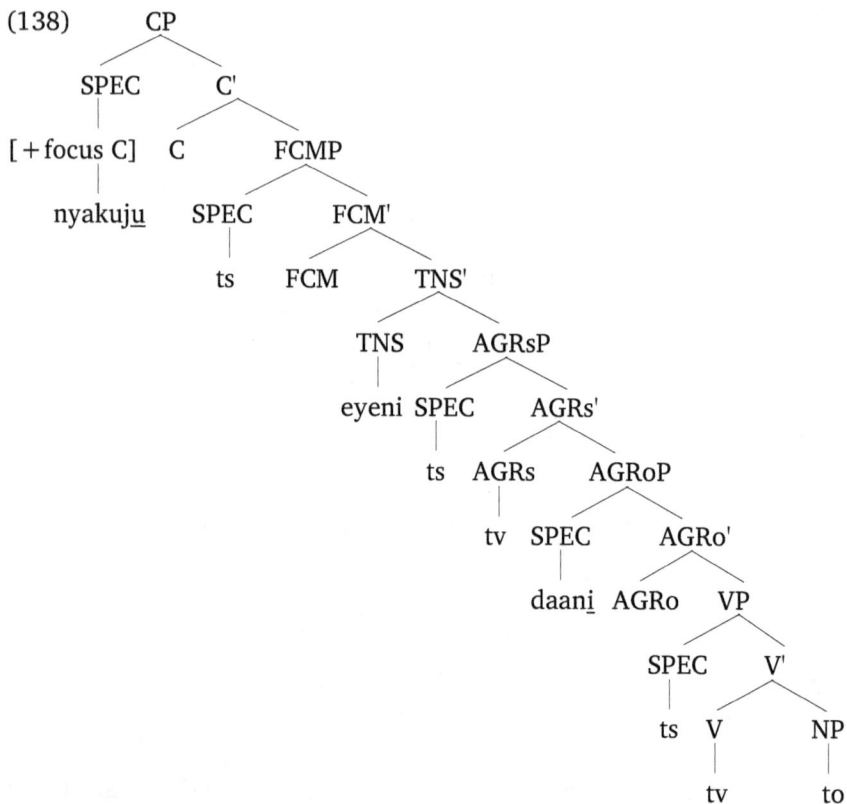

In the usual manner, the verb has to visit all places like [AGRs/AGRs'] and [TNS/TNS'] for feature-checking. The nominative subject moves from [SPEC/VP] to [SPEC/AGRsP] to check its nominative features, then to [SPEC/FCMP] to check its accusative feature, and then to [SPEC/CP] to have its focus features checked. The accusative object moves to [SPEC/AGRo] to have its case features checked.

In the next diagram, the FCMP is deleted because no change of case-marking takes place. For example, since the accusative object of (135c) is focused, it simply moves to the front of the sentence and to the specifier of CP:

5.3 Contrastive Focus

(139)
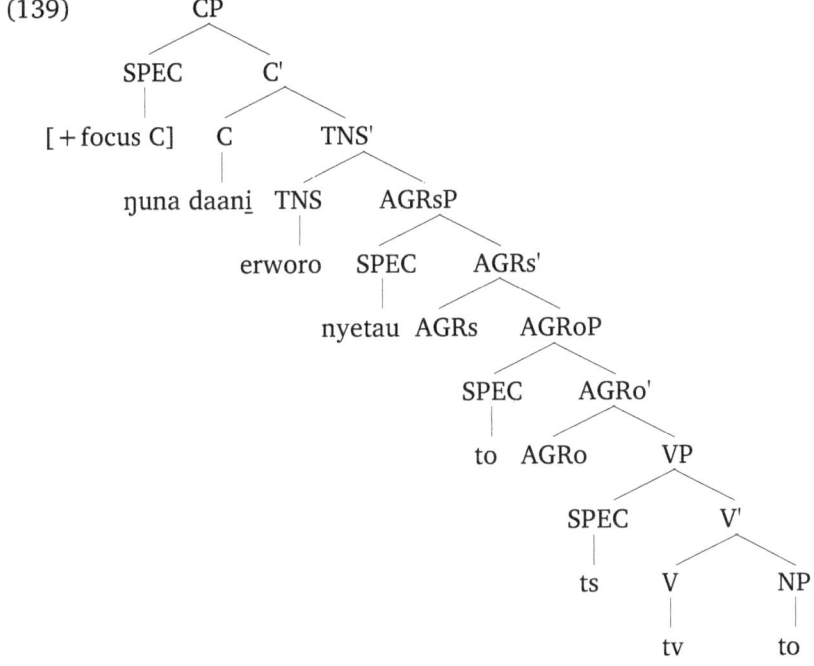

The verb moves to [AGRs/AGRs'], [TNS/TNS'] for feature-checking. The accusative object moves from inside the verb to [SPEC/AGRoP] to check its accusative features and then to [SPEC/CP] to have the focus features checked. The nominative subject moves from the [SPEC/VP] to the [SPEC/AGRsP] to have its nominative features checked.

There is no problem of case-marking with the movement of the PPs because they already have accusative-marking, so no extra FCMP head is needed, see the trees in (140) and (141) for examples (135d) and (135e):

(140)

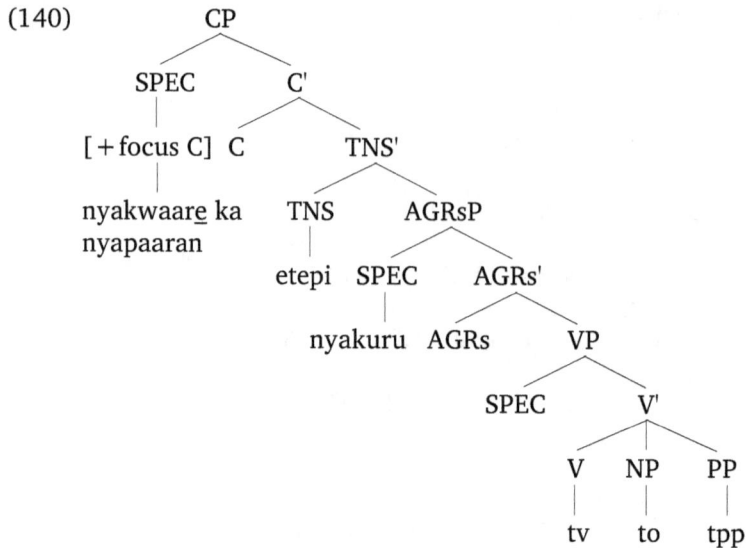

The normal procedure for the verb takes place. It visits all places like [AGRs/AGRs'], [TNS/TNS'] for feature-checking. The accusative object moves from inside the verb to [SPEC/AGRoP] to check its accusative features. The PP moves from inside the verb to [SPEC/CP] to have its contrastive focus features checked. The nominative subject moves from the [SPEC/VP] to the [SPEC/AGRsP] to have its nominative features checked.

(141)

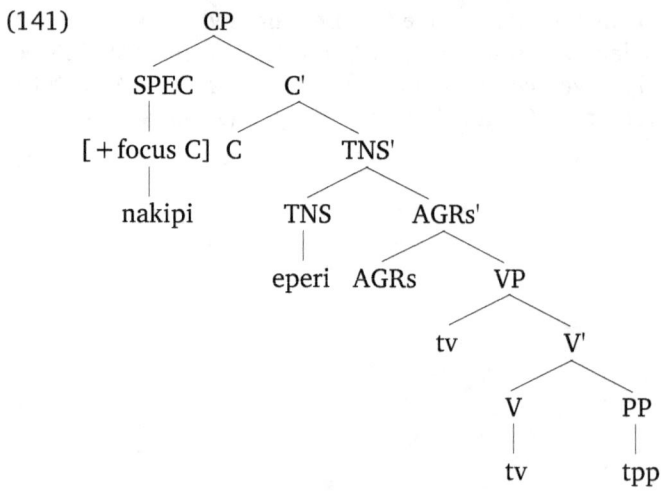

5.3 Contrastive Focus

Again, the verb visits the [AGRs/AGRs'], [TNS/TNS'] for feature-checking. The PP moves from inside the verb to [SPEC/CP] to check its contrastive focus features.

As pointed out above, wh-question words are fronted in the same way as happens with contrastive focus. The structural representation of the two wh-questions (136a) and (136b) after movement are therefore as follows:

(142)

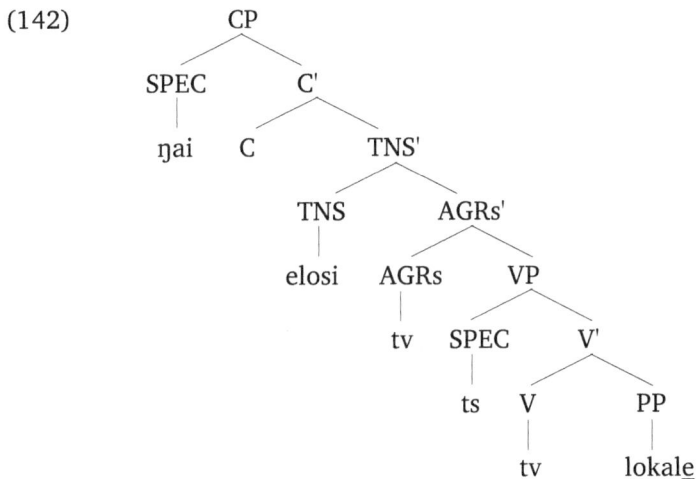

The verb moves to [AGRs/AGRs'], [TNS/TNS'] for feature-checking. The question word *ŋai* moves from inside the verb to [SPEC/CP]. The PP stays *in situ* as no case-checking takes place.

(143)
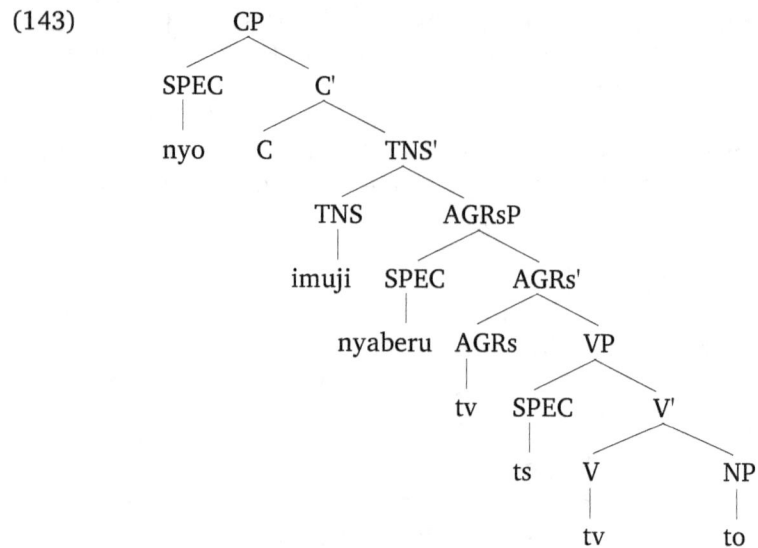

The verb visits the [AGRs/AGRs'], [TNS/TNS'] for feature-checking. The question word *nyo* moves from inside the verb to [SPEC/CP], but differently from (142), the nominative subject moves to [SPEC/AGRsP] for case-checking.

Based on the observation that contrastive focus elements and wh-words choose the same landing site, Wiesemann has suggested that wh-questions carry inherent focus (1996:123), a conclusion that seems justified by the Toposa data.

5.4 Defocalised Information

Another modification in sentence structure takes place in defocalising constructions. The language expresses defocalised information, new or known, at the end of the sentence by postposing the constituents, also referred to as 'tail' or 'afterthought'. (For a detailed functional description of postposed constituents see Dooley and Levinsohn 2000.) Defocalised information distracts the attention of the hearer, away from the main information. Thus, defocalising constructions have the opposite effect of focus.

There are two grammatical ways of expressing the afterthought in Toposa, either it is added by nominalisation, as in (144a), or the

5.4 Defocalised Information

afterthought adds another noun that is specified by a relative construction as in (144b):

(144) a. Ki-met-oki-si̱   nai   ŋi-kaitotoi   ŋulu,
     SEQ-quarrel-BEN-PL then   M/PL-siblings these

   Ŋu-wana   ka   Ŋi-moru̱.
   M/PL-wana/ACC   and   M/PL-stones/ACC
   'So these siblings quarrelled, the Wana [generation-set] and the Stones [generation-set].'

b. Bu   nya-pei   Siŋaita, iŋesi̱   na
   come   F/SG-one   Siŋaita, it/ACC   which

   e-bee-i   Mosiŋo.
   3SG-is.called-IMP   Mosingo
   'One [section] came to [the river] Singaita, that one is called Mosingo.'

Note that the structural place for the defocalised constituent is the end of the sentence. The tail information in both examples of (144) is placed in relation to the nominative of the sentence. The subject moves to the SPEC of AGRsP to receive its case-marking, while the tail information carries accusative marking since the unmarked case in the Toposa system is the accusative. Therefore, tail information moves to the SPEC of AGRoP to check its accusative features, as shown for (144a):

(145)

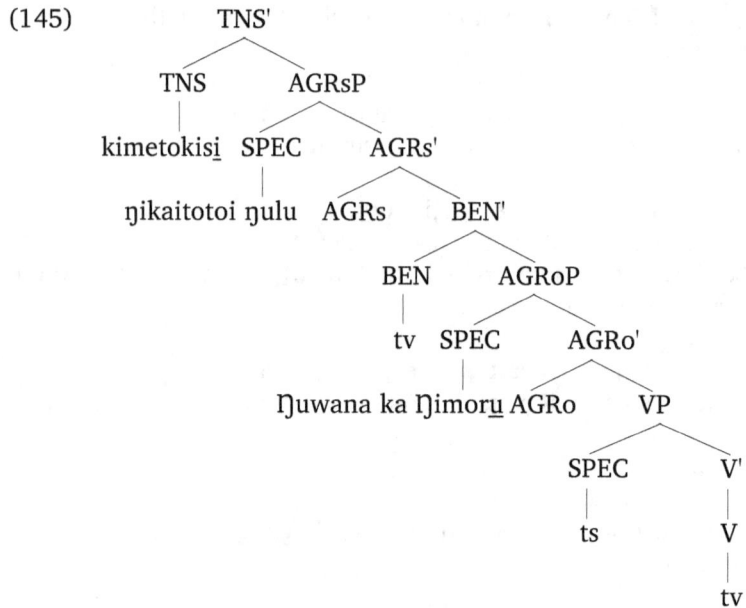

The verb moves from its base to [BEN/BEN'] to have the benefactive features checked, to [AGRs/AGRs'] to check its agreement features, and to [TNS/TNS'] for tense feature-checking. The subject NP moves to [SPEC/AGRsP] for nominative case-checking, and the tail information moves to [SPEC/AGRoP] to check its accusative features.

Even though defocalised expressions are not really accusative objects, the specifier of the object can conveniently be used as landing site in order to be able to accommodate the required case-marking.

5.5 Inherent Focus

Besides focus by identification, contrastive focus, and defocalized elements, the language has two inherent focus devices, negatives and yes/no questions. According to Wiesemann, they can be regarded as inherent focus, because they emphasize more than simple affirmations (1996:123):

(146) a. E-los-i   nye-kile   lo-kal<u>e</u>.
       3SG-go-IMP   M/SG-man   M/LOC-home
       'The man goes home.'

5.5 Inherent Focus

b. Ny-e-los-i   nye-kile   lo-kal<u>e</u>.
   NEG-3SG-go-IMP M/SG-man   M/LOC-home
   'The man does not go home.'

c. E-los-i   nye-kile   lo-kale-a?
   3SG-go-IMP M/SG-man   M/LOC-home-QUE
   'Does the man go home?'

The negative in Toposa is expressed by a prefix which heads the subject prefix of the verb. The negation prefix requires an extra head because of feature-checking:

(147)
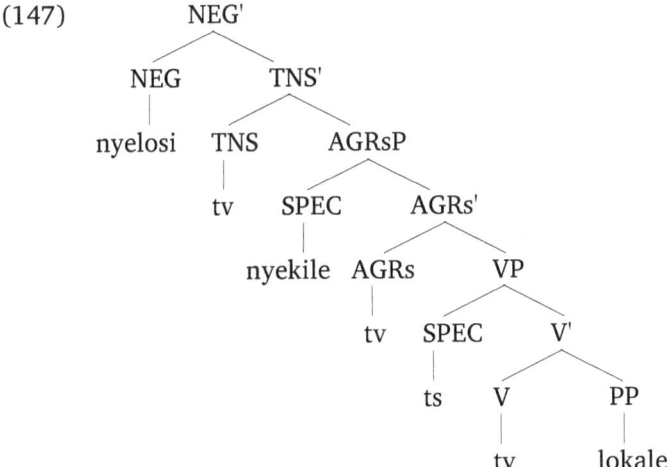

The verb moves to [AGRs/AGRs'], to [TNS/TNS'] for agreement-checking and tense-checking, and to [NEG/NEG'] to have the negation prefix checked. The nominative NP *nyekile* 'man' moves to SPEC of AGRsP for case-checking. Note that the negative prefix alters the verb structure, but not the sentence structure.

The question particle *-a* of (146c) could be regarded as a focus particle, in that it changes the normal sentence to an inherently [+focus] sentence. This question-particle receives its own focus head, which results in the following structure:

(148)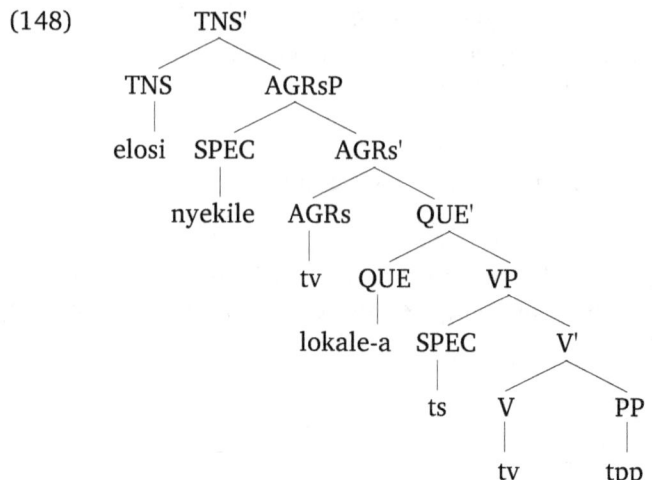

Note that even though the question particle is attached to the last word of the sentence, it has scope over the whole sentence. As the Minimalist Program is morphologically driven, all the morphological features undergo feature-checking, thus the question particle also has to be checked. For this purpose, a head [QUE] is created to ensure the feature-checking of the particle, so the PP needs to move to [QUE/QUE'] for feature-checking.

5.6 Summary

This chapter showed how the Toposa verbal morphology functions in discourse. The morphological marking of subject prefixes, causative, and applicative affixes rely on antecedent relationships in discourse and are licensed through a referent that has gone through a specifier-head relationship, i.e., through nominative or accusative case-checking beyond the minimal sentence. Since the antecedent licenses the marking on the verb, the structure-building process does not license an extra argument in the minimal sentence, so the standard sentence structure in discourse is VO. If a personal pronoun, or an applicative, or a causative argument are made explicit in discourse, they are in focus and carry an extra focus feature.

The type of focus which is linked to verbal morphology is focus by identification. It is feature-based and requires a focus-head domain for feature-checking. The other type of focus, contrastive focus, is also feature-based, but differs from assertive focus in that it additionally triggers movement of

5.6 Summary

the focused constituent into the specifier of CP. However, during this movement on the way to the landing site, the nominative argument loses its case-marking, as all fronted constituents carry accusative case. This change in case-marking is accounted for by a separate feature-carrying head.

The chapter concluded the description of focus phenomena with defocalized constructions and two inherent foci, negatives and yes/no questions. While defocalized constructions and yes/no questions modify the sentence structure, negatives only affect the structure of the verb.

The next chapter will conclude this investigation of Toposa word order by examining how a referent-based interpretation of applicative, causative, and personal pronouns leads to a dominant VS/VO sentence structure in discourse.

6
The VS/VO Ergative Word Order

The previous chapter showed that the Principle of Economy, the Principle of FI, and the Principle of Reference constrain the morphological processes of head-bearing affixes in discourse to form sentences with only one accusative object, where the subject of VSO is mostly dropped, or, if it occurs, is situated in the specifier of the VP. This is possible since the incorporated argument does not appear in the matrix sentence because it has been case-checked before but appears marked on the verb. As shown in section 5.2, the incorporated argument only occurs if it is in focus. The problem that arises at this point is the difficulty of explaining that Toposa word order not only prefers VO sentences in discourse, but that there is also a clear predominance of VS sentences over VSO sentences.

A simple frequency count[1] of Toposa sentence types in discourse across different genres (narrative, procedural, hortatory) shows that VO/VS constructions outnumber VSO sentences by far.[2] According to this count, the VSO variant reaches an occurrence of less than 10 percent in narrative and about 20 percent in hortatory text, and hardly appears in procedural material at all. Thus, VSO needs to be considered highly marked. The V

---

[1]Although frequency counts do not always reflect the real constituent ordering, it is still the most widely used method to determine the main word order in a language (Dixon 1994:5, Matthews 1992:4ff., Comrie 1989:8).

[2]The VO/VS basic word order is also found in subordinate clauses in Toposa. The observation is important with respect to Philippaki-Warburton's suggestion that the basic word order is often not found in independent clauses, but in subordinated ones (1985:114–115).

construction, where S or O remain implicit is less frequent,[3] but far more common than the VSO construction.[4]

This yields the following word order parameter:

Basic word order in discourse	VO VS V
Marked discourse word order	VSO (VOO)

Figure 6.1. Overview of Toposa word order

The question that arises here is why discourse shows a constellation of predominantly VS/VO structures instead of VS/VSO ones. Evidently, there are language-specific mechanisms at work which produce this VS/VO discourse order, which will be investigated now.

6.1 The Principle of Reference in Complex Sentences

This section (and the following ones) will show how the Principle of Reference in complex sentence structures promotes VO or V constructions in subsequent sentences, after the first sentence has begun the structure with VS. This will be demonstrated with the omission of subjects, direct objects, and applied and causative objects.

As shown in section 5.1.1, the subject and object pronouns are both dropped in complex sentence structures if the referent has occurred in a previous sentence, has gone through nominative case-checking, and is marked on the verb. Recall the following example with VS in S1, V in S2, and VO in S3:

(149) S1 [Ki-sya-u   nai nye-tome,]   S2 [to-nyo-u,]
      SEQ-begin-ALL   the M/SG-elephant   SEQ-rise-ALL

---

[3]The simple V construction (see diagram (122) in section 5.1.2), represents an amalgamation of heads, where through the Principle of Reference, the Principle of Economy and FI, the arguments do not appear in the matrix sentence, because they have been case-checked before and have been spelled out into PF and LF, but leave their affix-marking on the verb.

[4]One narrative text, for example, *Nyepido* 'The Assembly' has 33 VS sentences, 17 VO sentences, 20 V sentences, and 10 VSO sentences (see appendix B). One procedural text, *Nyemoŋ Lominat* 'The Beloved Ox', yielded 22 VS sentences, 24 VO sentences, 22 V sentences, and 2 VSO sentences.

6.1 The Principle of Reference in Complex Sentences

S3 [ta-tac ŋa-kiro.]
    SEQ-answer F/PL-matter
'So then Elephant began, he rose, he answered the matter (= addressed the issue).'

In (149) the nominative subject of the first sentence leaves the subject marked on the verb in S2 and S3. Consider how the occurrence of a pronoun in S2 and S3 changes the meaning of the sentence, because it is a focus construction:

(150) F {S1 [Ki-sya-u   nai nye-tome̱,]   S2 [to-nyo-u
         SEQ-begin-ALL the M/SG-elephant   SEQ-rise-ALL

iŋesi̱,] S3 [ta-tac   iŋesi̱ ŋa-kiro.]}[5]
he   SEQ-answer he   F/PL-matter
'So then Elephant began, it was he who rose, it was he who answered the matter (= addressed the issue).'

Example (150) is not acceptable as a basic structure. As soon as the pronoun occurs, it has a [+focus] feature, and a focus head is established in the tree (cf. 5.2.1). The meaning of the sentence changes as the pronouns are in focus.

If the applicative object in complex sentence constructions is implicit because it has a referent in a preceding sentence of the sentence structure, a V (or VPP) construction is the normal result:

(151) S1 [Na   e-lep-un-o   ite   keŋe̱ ŋa-kile,]
         when 3SG-milk-ALL-INS   mother his   F/PL-milk

S2 [e-a-u,]   S3 [to-buk-oki̱   na-dere
    3SG-bring-ALL   SEQ-pour-BEN   F/LOC-calabash

na-ka-polo-ni̱   ŋina.]
F/LOC-DER-big-SG   into which
'When his mother had milked the milk, she brought [it], she poured [it] into that big calabash.'

In S3 in (151) neither the subject pronoun, nor the object pronoun, nor the benefactive object are overtly mentioned in the VPP construction. The subject and the benefactive, however, are marked on the verb *tobukoki̱*

---

[5]Note that "*F*" in front of a sentence marks it as a focused structure, parallel to "*" for ungrammatical constructions, and "?" for awkward ones.

'she poured [for someone]'. The antecedent for the subject is the nominative subject ite *keŋe* 'his mother' in S1, the antecedent for the object is the accusative object *ŋakile* 'milk' in S1, and the antecedent for the benefactive is *nyikoku nisapat* 'boy-child' which has been checked outside the matrix sentence (cf. examples (117) and (118) in chapter 5).

Reconsider also example (152) with a causative construction:

(152) S1 ["Ani moi   na   e-bun-o   nya-ryaŋ
      if   tomorrow when 3SG-come-RFL F/SG-government

        na-kop   kusi̱,] S2 [ki-ta-any-iki̱   ŋi-borekeya lu."]
        F/LOC-land yours   IV-CAUS-see-BEN M/PL-things these
     'When the government comes to your (pl.) land one day, cause [it] to see (= show [it]) these things.'

In spite of its causative construction, S2 is merely VO (rather than VOO), because the referent *nyaryaŋ* 'government' for the causative is case-checked in S1 and does not occur overtly in S2. Therefore, the normal sentence structure of subsequent sentences is VO. As shown in chapter five, the applied object only occurs with the direct object in the same sentence if it is in focus (see section 5.2).

In all Toposa sentence constructions examined so far it is the S of a prior VS which serves as nominative referent, never the S of a preceding VSO.

Since the Economy Principle, the Principle of Reference, and the Principle of FI control the explicitness of constituents in discourse, the preferable word order pattern of complex sentence structures is VO, as in (152/S2), or V, as in (151/S2 + S3), no matter how many head-bearing affixes the verb has.

A prominence of VO or V sentences in complex sentence structures, however, does not explain why it is the S of a VS sentence construction which mainly serves as a nominative referent for subsequent VO/V constructions, rather than the S of a VSO sentence. To explain this preference, the following section will analyse whether there are any restrictions on the combination of transitive and intransitive constructions in the structure of complex sentences.

6.2 Ergative Tendencies in Complex Sentences

In a nominative-accusative system with a basic VSO sentence structure, theoretically any kind of combination of transitive and intransitive

6.2 Ergative Tendencies in Complex Sentences

sentences should be possible, like VSO-VO-V, VS-VO-V, or VS-VSO-VSO. However, besides all the principles that work in the morphological processes described in chapter five, Toposa has restrictions on how transitive and intransitive sentences are allowed to combine in discourse structure, as the following data will demonstrate.

For example, the VO sentence pattern only combines with preceding VS constructions, as in example (152), but apparently never with VSO ones. This is true of both coordinated sentence combinations as in (153a), or subordinated ones as in (153b):

(153) a. S1 [Ki-sya-u   nai   nye-tome̱,]   S2 [to-nyo-u,]
         SEQ-begin-ALL then   M/SG-elephant   SEQ-rise-ALL

   S3 [ta-tac   ŋa-kiro.]
        SEQ-answer F/PL-matter
   'So then Elephant began, he rose, he answered the matter (= addressed the issue).'

b. S1 [Ani   e-dol-i   kwee   lo-kale̱,]
       when   3SG-reach-IMP   jackal M/LOC-home

   S2 [to-ryamu̱-   ite   keŋe̱]
        SEQ-find-ALL   mother   his

   S3 [e-per-i   lo-ka-ron-oni̱.]
        3SG-sleep-IMP   M/LOC-DER-bad(ly)-SG
   'When Jackal reached home, he found his mother fast asleep.'

As in (153a) the nominative subject *nyetome̱* 'elephant' is not overt in S2 and S3, the result is a VS-V-VO pattern. Similarly, in (153b) there is no overt subject in S2, as *kwee* 'jackal' was already mentioned in S1, resulting in a VSPP-VO-V construction.

A VS-VSO-VPP pattern, where the subjects are overt in both S1 and S2, whether as NPs or as personal pronouns, would be a highly focused structure:

(154) F {S1 [Ani   e-dol-i   kwee   lo-kale̱,]
           when   3SG-reach-IMP   jackal M/LOC-home

   S2 [to-ryam-u̱   iŋesi̱   ite   keŋe̱]
        SEQ-find-ALL   he   mother   his

S3 [e-per-i   lo-ka-ron-oni.]}
      3SG-sleep-IMP   M/LOC-DER-bad(ly)-SG
   'When Jackal reached home, it was he who found his mother fast asleep.'

In nominative-accusative VSO word order systems, one expects that even when the Principle of Economy does not allow the personal pronoun to become overt, VSO constructions combine freely with VO ones. However, in Toposa, such combinations are rare and awkward, as the following example shows:

(155) ?{S1 [To-tuk   nye-bu   ŋa-kile,]
           SEQ-take   M/SG-hyena   F/PL-milk

      S2 [ki-ŋit   nabo   kwee,...]}
         SEQ-ask   again jackal
      'Hyena took a mouthful of milk, he asked Jackal again,...'

Sentence (155) is grammatically not very acceptable. If VSO and VO sentences follow each other in Toposa, the normal discourse pattern is to separate them into independent sentences, as (156a) and (156b) demonstrate. The period in (156a) marks a potential pause:

(156) a. To-tuk   nye-bu   ŋa-kile.
         SEQ-take M/SG-hyena   F/PL-milk
         'Hyena took a mouthful of milk'

      b. Ki-ŋit   nabo   kwee,...
         SEQ-ask again jackal
         'He asked Jackal again.'

Obviously, VSO-VS combinations are rare and focused whenever they occur, while VSO-VO combinations are completely awkward, whereas VS and VO combine freely.

The explanations for these tendencies are found in discourse. For example, in Toposa narrative discourse the participants are always introduced in a VS sentence, never a VSO one. The VS sentence then is usually followed by a VO construction (or V), because the subject is not overt. Consider how the main participant is introduced at the beginning of a typical narrative:

6.2 Ergative Tendencies in Complex Sentences

(157) S1 [Bee   koloŋ nuwan   to-lot   nye-bu
         it.is.said time   long.ago SEQ-went   M/SG-hyena

      nya-ce   paaran na-moni   nya-ki-dep
      F/SG-some   day   F/LOC-bush F/SG-DER-search

      ŋa-kee-moogwa,] S2 [to-ryam-u̱   nya-ate
      F/PL-his-food   SEQ-found-ALL F/SG-cow

      ka na-moni,]   S3 [ki-gelegele-u lo-re   keṉe.]
      in F/LOC-bush   SEQ-drive-ALL   M/LOC-village his
'It is said that long ago one day (= once upon a time) Hyena went into the bush to collect his food, he found a cow in the bush, he drove [it] to his village.'

Note how in S1 the subject in the VSPP construction stages the main participant *nyebu* 'hyena', while the following sentence is a VO construction in which the object introduces *nyaate,* 'a cow' as a prop.[6]

This demonstrates nicely how the S of the intransitive sentence and the O of the transitive sentence typically introduce new information, a strategy apparently not restricted to Toposa discourse (cf. Du Bois 1987).

Even in coordinated and subordinated sentence structures which have independent subjects, the preferable combinations are VS-VS, or VSO-VSO, but not VSO-VS:

(158) a. S1 [To-ron-er   nye-karu,] S2 [ny-e-do   nya-kuru
            SEQ-bad-RES   M/SG-year   NEG-3SG-fall F/SG-rain

         ŋi-lapyo   lu   sek   e-do-ito-rẹ.]
         M/PL-months   which usually 3SG-fall-PER-INS
'The year became bad, the rain did not fall the months [during] which it normally falls.'

   b. S1 [Ki-pak-ak-i̱   nye-bu   ŋa-kile
         SEQ-splash-BEN-RFL M/SG-hyena   F/PL-milk

         lo-reet   ka kwee,]   S2 [ta-nap-akin-i̱,]
         M/LOC-face   of jackal   SEQ-charge-BEN-RFL

---

[6]Props (in contrast to major and minor participants) have only a passive role in the story; they never do anything significant (Grimes 1975:43ff).

S3 [ku-ruk-okin-i̱,]   S4 [ki- lany   kwee   nye-bu.]
   SEQ-chase-BEN-RFL   SEQ-escape jackal M/SG-hyena
'Hyena splashed the milk into the face of Jackal, he (= Hyena) charged at [Jackal], he chased [him], Jackal escaped Hyena.'

c. S1 [E-min-a-si   Ŋii-toposa   ŋi-baren   looi,
       3PL-love-RFL-PL M/PL-toposa   M/PL-livestock very

   S2 [kotere i-rum-it-o   ŋi-baren   nya-kumuj
       because 3PL-hold-PER-PL   M/PL-livestock F/SG-food

   kece̱   na-ka-jok-oni̱   daani̱, ŋa-kile,
   their   F/SG-DER-good-SG   all   F/PL-milk

   nya-kimyet, nya-kiriŋ.]
   F/SG-fat   F/SG-meat
'The Toposa love [their] livestock very much, because the livestock has (= provides) all their good food, milk, fat, meat.'

Sentence (158a) shows a VS-VS combination, (158b) a coordinate VSO-VSO construction, and (158c) a subordinate VSO-VSO sentence construction.

If a mixed pattern VS-VSO (or a VSO-VS, as in (156a) and (156b)) occurs in Toposa discourse, it normally does so in two separate sentences:

(159) a. To-lom-a   nye- kunyuk   na-dui   pir.
         SEQ-enter-ABL   M/SG-squirrel   F/LOC-hole   ideo
         'Squirrel entered *pir* into a hole.'

   b. To-kur   nye-ŋatuny nya-dui.
      SEQ-scratch M/SG-lion   F/SG-hole
      'Lion scratched the hole (= started to dig).'

Examples (158a–158c), (159a), and (159b) confirm the VS/VO pattern, since in embedded sentences with two overt subjects the preferred structure is VS-VS versus VSO-VSO, because the combinations VSO-VS and VS-VSO tend to be split into separate sentences.

This section demonstrated how in complex sentences in discourse the preferred combination of word order patterns is VS-VO. Based on this

6.3 Argument-Reducing Processes

finding, Toposa is best analysed as a language with ergative VS/VO word order pattern on discourse level.[7]

6.3 Argument-Reducing Processes

In addition to the interclausal relationships just considered, the argument-reducing processes like passive (sections 3.4.2.1 and 4.2.1) and reflexive (sections 3.4.2.2 and 4.2.2) also work naturally towards the established VS/VO order, because passives produce VO sentences, while reflexives form VS ones.

The passive construction is always an intransitive sentence with the subject bearing accusative-marking. The agent is never expressed. The procedural text in (160) illustrates this very clearly:

(160) S1 [To-gum-un-ae   nai   ŋa-akot,]   S2 [ki-maar-ae
      SEQ-shoot-ALL-PAS   then   F/PL-blood   SEQ-melt-PAS

      nya-turuno,]   S3 [to-lep-un-oe   ŋa-kile
      F/SG-butter/ACC   SEQ-milk-ALL-PAS   F/PL-milk/ACC

      na-lepan,] S4 [to-buk-okin-ae   daani   na-tubwa.]
      F/SG-fresh   SEQ-pour-BEN-PAS   all   F/LOC-trough
      'Blood is shot (= drained from a cow), butter is melted, fresh milk is milked, all is poured into a trough.'

This sentence construction is a string of VO-VO-VO-VPP constructions.[8]

The reflexive is naturally a VS sentence, because the reflexive object is integrated into the verb as a suffix:

(161) I-gur-o   nyi- koku.
      3SG-weep-RFL   D/SG-child
      'The child is weeping.'

---

[7]Dixon (1994:152ff.) shows that syntactic ergativity is shown either by constraints on the combination of clauses or the omission of coreferential constituents. Toposa does not coreferentially combine the object of the transitive clause with the subject of the intransitive clause, but it coreferences the subject of the transitive and intransitive clause. Thus, its ergative syntactic features extend only to the combination of sentences.

[8]The passive construction marks event-line progression in procedural texts, whereas in narrative texts it marks background information.

Almost all combinations of case-bearing arguments in combination with the reflexive in discourse have been found to have a typical VS word order:

(162) To-ryaŋ-akin-o-si̱   Ŋi-tukoi.
      SEQ-fear-BEN-RFL-PL M/PL-zebras
      'The [members of the] Zebras [generation-set] became very afraid.'

In this way, reflexive VS constructions contribute naturally to the VS/VO word order pattern in Toposa discourse.

6.4 Syntactic Ergatives

Even on sentence level, where the basic word order was analysed as VSO (section 3.1), there are two exceptions where the word order follows an ergative pattern. Normally, if a basic sentence is relativised, a relative clause can follow the subject of the intransitive sentence, as in (163a), or it follows the object of the transitive sentence, as in (163b), and both of them follow the verb:

(163) a. Ki-lip-u-tu̱   ŋi-moŋin   lu   moi
         SEQ-beg-ALL-PL   M/PL-oxen   which   later

         a-ar-akin-i-o   ŋu-tuŋa   lu-ke-syem-ok
         3PL-kill-BEN-IMP-PAS   M/PL-people   M/PL-DER-watching-PL

         nya-kidamadam.
         F/SG-war.dance
         'They beg oxen which will later be killed for the people watching the dance.'

      b. Ku-put-ar-o-si̱   nai   ŋu-tuŋa   lu   koloŋ
         SEQ-smear-ABL-RFL-PL   then   M/PL-people   who   long.ago

         e-ya   na-ki- do-un-et   ka   nyi-koku.
         3PL-be   F/LOC-DER-birth-ALL-INST   of   D/SG-child
         'Then the people who were present at the birth of the child anoint themselves.'

6.4 Syntactic Ergatives

Example (163a) has a VO (rel.pron.-VO) sentence construction; (163b) is a reflexive intransitive sentence that has a VS (rel.pron.-VPP) sentence construction.

If, however, the relative clause is linked to the subject of a transitive sentence, the word order changes so that the subject precedes the verb:

(164) Ŋu-tuŋa   daani̱ lu   e-sapan-e-te
      M/PL-people   all   who   3PL-initiate-IMP-PL

  i-toropy-e-te   ŋi-baren   kec̱e   daani̱.
  3PL-cut-IMP-PL   M/PL-cattle   their all

  'All people who have been initiated cut the HLTT [i.e., the heart/lungs/throat/tongue of their cattle (= they do not kill by cutting the throat).'

This S (rel.pron.-V) VO structure shows clearly how the syntax changes to an ergative pattern in that the word order becomes now a marked SVO construction.

Thus, the following word order relation is established for basic sentences with embedded relative clauses:

VO	relative clause	
VS	relative clause	
S	relative clause	VO

Figure 6.2. Word order in embedded relative clauses

In other words, if relative clauses follow the object of a transitive clause or the subject of an intransitive clause, the head constituent and the relative clause follow the verb, while transitive VSO sentences where the relative clause refers to the subject, are treated differently. In VSO constructions, the S and the relative clause are moved to the front of the sentence, resulting in an SVO order. Thus, in VS/VO constructions the relative clause is treated in the same way, while in VSO constructions it is fronted, revealing an ergative pattern (cf. figure 2.1).

As shown in section 3.3.2, the same ergative word order also occurs in basic sentences, if the subject slot of the transitive sentence is occupied by a noun and the object slot by a pronoun. If the pronoun is first or second person, the word order then changes from VSO to VOS, and the ergative marker *k-* occurs on the verb:

(165)　K-a-lim-okin-i　　　　ayoŋ　　lo-kaato　　　　　kaŋ.
　　　　ERG-1SG-tell-BEN-IMP　me/ACC　M/SG-brother/ACC　my
　　　　'My brother will tell me.'

All this shows that not only on the intraclausal level, but even more so on the interclausal level Toposa shows ergative features, and is thus best analysed as an "ergative-discourse" language.

In chapter 3 the basic sentence structure for Toposa was first laid down as VSO. Then chapters 3 and 4 showed how this basic sentence structure needed to be modified to VOO because of argument-bearing affixes. Chapter 5 discussed the argument-bearing affixes in discourse and demonstrated how the Principle of Reference logically results in a strong VO word order system. And the current chapter has argued for an ergative VS/VO word order in discourse, where not only VO is prevalent, but also the combination of VS-VO.

These results require that the basic sentence structure of Toposa be revised as VS/VO, rather than VSO (cf. 3.1), which will be the final task of this study.

Since the Minimalist Program is based on the structure-building process and morphological necessity, rather than on the dichotomy between deep structure and surface structure, the syntactic representation of a VS/VO pattern varies between the three basic syntactic representations, VS and VO and VSO, which will now be reconsidered in that order.

The VS set leaves out the object and the AGRoP projection, but has a full agreement S projection. Consider once more the following example:

(166)　E-ker-i　　　　nyi-koku.
　　　　3SG-run-IMP　D/SG-child
　　　　'The child is running.'

The representation of this sentence needs to be revised in the following way:

6.4 Syntactic Ergatives

(167)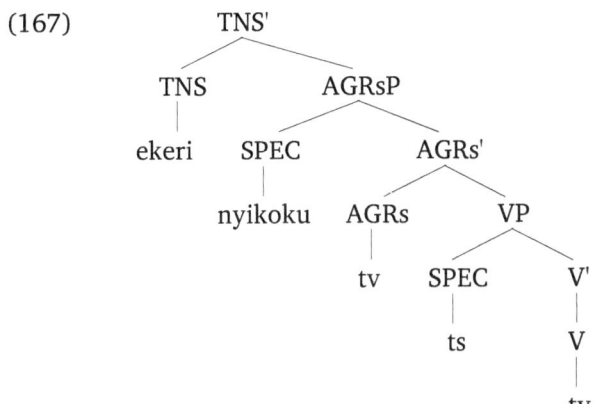

The VO set now leaves out the specifier of AGRsP and the specifier of VP, because no overt subject occurs, and no nominative checking takes place:

(168) E-mas-i ŋa-kile.
 3SG-drink-IMP F/PL-milk
 'He is drinking milk.'

The representation of this sentence needs to be revised as follows:

(169)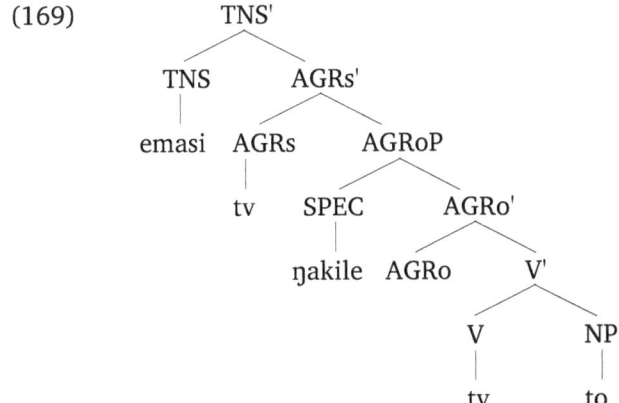

The VSO set has the full projections of AGRsP and AGRoP and a specifier in the VP. Recall the following sentence:

(170) E-mas-i   nyi-koku   ŋa-kile.
      3SG-drink-IMP D/SG-child F/PL-milk
      'The child is drinking milk.'

The representation of this sentence remains the same as diagram (22) in section 3.1:

(171)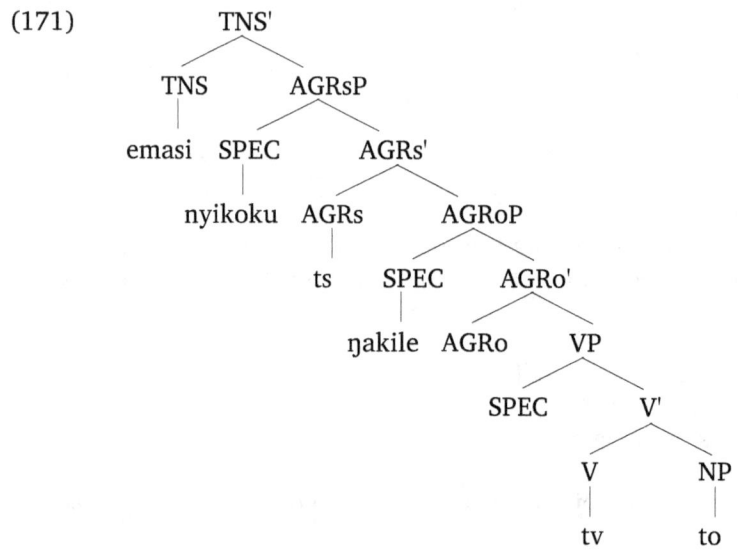

The last representation of Toposa word order is the rare VOS construction in which the object slot is occupied by a pronoun and the subject slot by a noun. This construction changes the order of projections. As the structure-building process, directed by morphology, guides the building of the tree, it is possible to change the order of projections. In this case the AGRoP follows TNS, and the AGRsP heads the VP. Remember the following example:

(172) K-a-lim-okin-i   ayoŋ   lo-kaato   kaŋ.
      ERG-1SG-tell-BEN-IMP me/ACC M/SG-brother/NOM   my
      'My brother will tell me.'

The resulting tree for this sentence (already presented under (38) in section 3.3.2) is:

6.4 Syntactic Ergatives

(173)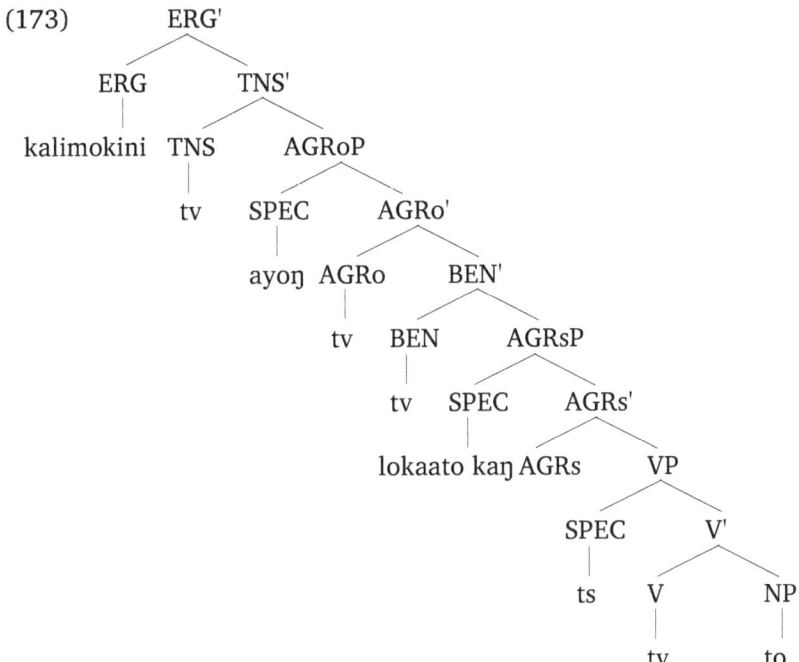

The verb moves from inside the VP to [AGRo/AGRo'] to check the accusative cross-reference features, to [BEN/BEN'] to check the benefactive features, to [TNS/TNS'] to check the tense features, and to [ERG/ERG'] to check the ergative-marking features. The accusative pronoun moves to the specifier of AGRoP to check its accusative case-marking, and the subject moves from the specifier of VP to the specifier of AGRsP to check its nominative case-marking. The ergative word order is preserved because the AGRoP heads AGRsP.

Finally, the syntactic representation of co-occurring affixes needs to be considered. These are syntactically represented by creating projections for each one. These projections are created out of morphological necessity so that the morphological features can be checked before spell-out. See the following instrumental-benefactive example as a representative for all co-occurrences of morphological affixes:

(174)   A-duŋ-akin-i-o   nya-kiriŋ.
        3SG-cut-BEN-IMP-INS M/SG-meat
        'He cut the meat [for someone with something].'

The syntactic representation of the above sentence has a benefactive head and an instrumental head representation, but no specifier in the benefactive and instrumental projections, because the benefactive and instrumental have no overt constituents:

(175)
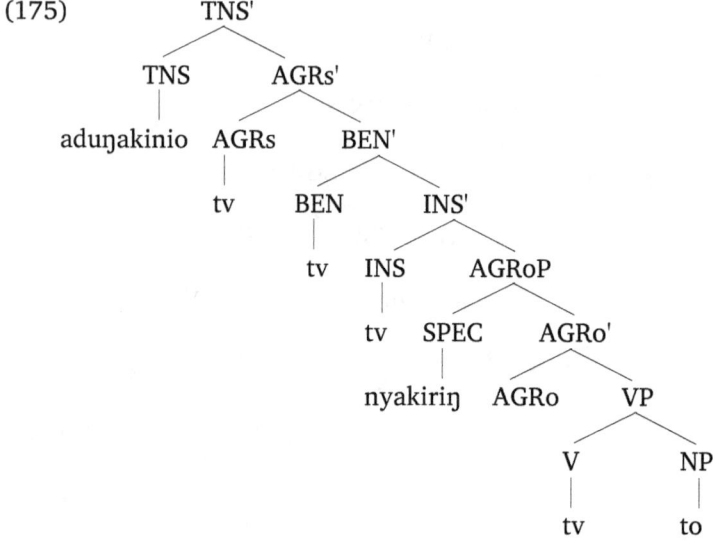

The verb moves from its position in the verb to [INS/INS'] to have its instrumental features checked, to [BEN/BEN'] to check the benefactive features, to [AGRs/AGRs'] to check the subject agreement features, and to [TNS/TNS'] to have its tense features checked. The direct object *nyakiriŋ* moves from the VP to the specifier of AGRoP to have its accusative features checked.

This concludes the presentation and revisions of Toposa's basic sentence types.

6.5 Summary

This chapter showed that Toposa has an ergative VS/VO discourse word order which is supported by morphosyntactic processes of subject prefixes, object pronoun constructions, causatives, and applicatives, all of which drop their respective constituents, so that a VO word order pattern emerges. There is an ergative restriction in sentence structure that joins VS/VO over against VSO/VS and VSO/VO.

There is also an ergative pattern in relative clauses in that the subject of the intransitive clause and the object of the transitive clause have the same relative construction, i.e., in both instances the head and the relative construction follow the verb. The subject of the transitive clause, however, is treated differently in that it is fronted together with the relative clause and produces an SVO word order.

In sentences that have an NP and a first- or second-person pronoun in object position, a VOS construction, which fits into the ergative VS/VO pattern, is prevalent.

Finally, the argument-reducing processes of passive and reflexive work naturally towards a VS/VO word order, in that the reflexive always produces a VS word order while the passive results in VO.

6.6 Conclusion

This study presented a feature-checking approach to sentence structure, discourse, and language typology within the generative framework, based on Chomsky's Minimalist Program. The data presented were supplied from Toposa, a highly inflectional Eastern Nilotic language of Southern Sudan.

The Minimalist Program's concept of feature-checking is based on the idea that all morphological features of the verb like subject, applicative, causative, passive, and reflexive have their source in the lexicon. These features enter into argument-bearing heads and build a specifier-head relationship for case checking. The verbs and nouns then move for checking purposes to their respective heads and specifiers.

The concept of feature-checking, together with the Principle of FI and the Principle of Economy, allowed me to explain the ergative discourse word-order of Toposa. This word order is the result of several morphosyntactic relationships that do not work as a hierarchical system of morphology, syntax, and discourse. Instead, they function as interdependent processes of morphosyntactic and discourse features.

Fundamental to this integration approach is the Principle of Reference. First, the Principle of Reference makes sure that an antecedent relationship leaves affix marking on the verb in the form of subject prefix, causative affix, and applicative suffixes. Second, it explains the absence of sentential arguments like overt subject, overt object, causative, and applicative arguments. Finally, it produces one component of the ergative word order: the predominance of VO in complex sentence constructions. The other component of the ergative VO/VS word order, the predominance of VS constructions, is due to a restriction on sentence combinations. On intersentence level, Toposa only combines VS-VO, never VSO-VO.

On sentence level, passive and reflexive constructions support the established VS/VO word order, since passive sentences are always VO, and reflexive ones are always VS, even if they co-occur with other argument-bearing affixes.

Relative clauses also work on an ergative sentence basis in that the relative clause related to the subject of the transitive clause precedes the verb, whereas the relative clause related to the object of the transitive clause and the subject of the intransitive clause both follow the verb.

Consequently, this study suggests that Toposa be analyzed as an "ergative discourse" language. Besides its ergative features on syntax and discourse levels, Toposa also shows traces of morphological ergativity in its cross-reference system and in passive constructions.

The focus system of Toposa, too, is a logical consequence of the processes of the Principle of Reference. The Principle of Reference produces focus by identification, if the antecedent is present, after being marked on the verb. In order to formalise the relationship between an antecedent and explicit NPs in subsequent sentences, an additional Focus Principle had to be introduced.

One side effect of the Principle of Reference is that in isolated sentences not all constituents can be expressed, in spite of the presence of several head-bearing affixes, because the Principle of Reference filters out disallowed arguments. The filtering process is threefold: either a choice needs to be made between competing arguments, arguments are relegated to the PP position, or the language forms two separate sentences.

Since Toposa is interpreted as an ergative discourse language with a complex interplay between morphology, syntax, discourse, and focus, it fits into the category of discourse-configurational languages in a broader sense (Kiss 1995). The reason is that discourse considerations like focus and referential relationships have a bearing on word order, and on morphosyntactic processes. However, Toposa cannot be interpreted in terms of focus prominence, following Kiss's suggestions because focus in Toposa is only one component in a complex process.

The feature-checking approach to sentence and discourse structure employed here has several theoretical implications. Word order typology is no longer determined by the theoretical considerations of whether syntax works independently of pragmatic mechanisms or whether pragmatic considerations dominate the principle of order. It was necessary to conclude first for Toposa (and possibly for other languages as well) that

6.6 Conclusion

syntax and pragmatics interrelate. (Note that the term "pragmatic" here refers to discourse phenomena). Word order typology then becomes a matter of multiple feature-checking, rather than a collection of isolated syntactic processes.

This interconnection of morphology, syntax, and discourse mediated through the feature-checking concept is new. It might help to account more adequately for the typological differences between languages on the continuum between highly inflectional and isolating languages. This means that the typological differences between languages lie first and foremost in their morphology, a tenet which will have to be tested against the background of a variety of other languages.

Appendix A

From Lexicon to Interface

Under the Minimalist Program, the cognitive system for each language consists of a lexicon and a computational system. The lexicon contains lexical word categories (verb, noun, adjective, etc.), the functional categories such as (tense, complementizer, agreement, etc.), and the grammatical features of the language for nouns and verbs. The word categories are universal but their phonological form is language specific. Some functional items are universal like tense, others are language-specific like agreement. The specific grammatical language features for Toposa nouns and verbs are the following:

> Nouns occur in singular and plural form; in the singular masculine, feminine, or diminutive noun prefix occurs; in the plural the gender contrast is masculine or feminine.
>
> Nouns take nominative and accusative case marking.
>
> Verbs have agreement, tonal tense marking, and morphological aspect marking.
>
> Toposa is a VSO language.

Consider now the sentence in (176).

(176) È-màs-í   nyí-kókù   ŋá-kílê.
       3SG/SUB-drink-IMP D/SG-child/NOM F/PL-milk/ACC
       'The child is drinking milk.'

The entry in the lexicon for the verb form èmàsí 'he is drinking' is -mas [v/tr] 'drink', the entry for nyíkókù is -koku [n] 'child' and for ŋákílê it is -kile [n] 'milk'.
The words occur in their root forms.
The numeration now picks the verb root -mas and the noun roots -koku and -kile. First, the word roots merge with their grammatical features. For nouns the grammatical features of gender, number, and case are attached to the root, and for verbs the inflectional features of person agreement, tonal tense marking, and imperfect aspect marking merge with the root. Next, the fully merged words are built into a sentence structure motivated by the grammatical features of the VSO word order required by Toposa. This fully constructed sentence is then transported into the VP.

(177)
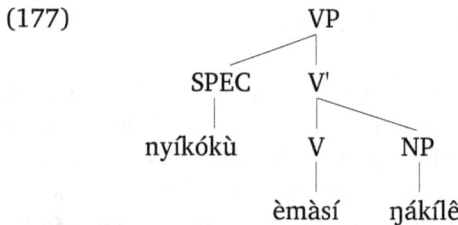

Then the computational process builds heads and partial trees, according to the evidence of lexical and grammatical features.
So the heads for subject agreement, for tense and aspect, and object agreement are built. The specifiers for the subject and object agreement are constructed because the sentence has an overt noun phrase subject and object. The case marking for each has to be checked under their respective specifiers. The tree for (178) then looks as follows:

From Lexicon to Interface 167

(178)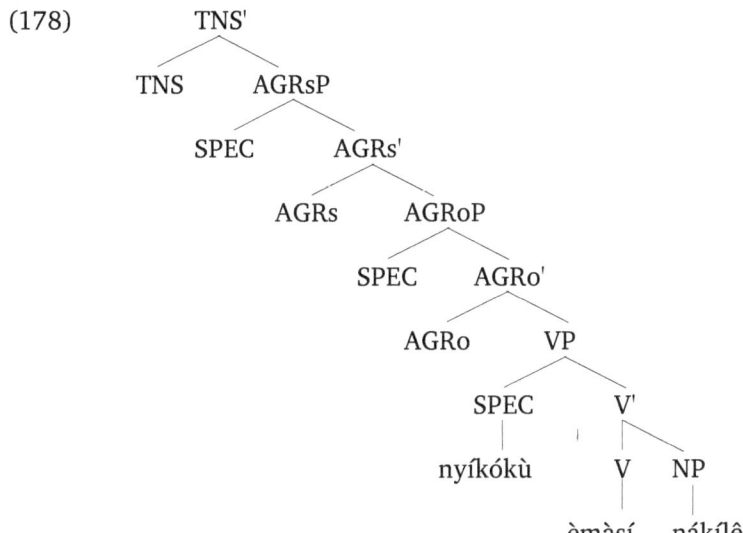

Now the words with their morphosyntactic features are moved to their respective heads and specifiers for checking purposes. Grammatical features of tense/aspect and agreement force the verb to move to the agreement subject and the tense heads. The NP object moves from the VP to the specifier of agreement object head for accusative case-checking, and the subject moves from the specifier of the VP to the specifier of subject agreement head for nominative case-checking. So after feature-checking is completed, the tree looks in spell-out as in (180).

(179)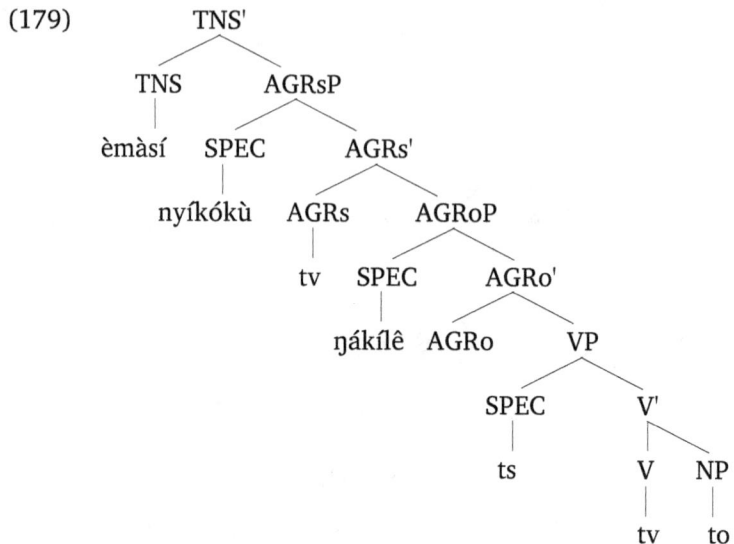

The above-described process also takes place for all the valence-increasing and valence-decreasing morphemes. Head-building morphemes like causative and applicative, passive and reflexive are first of all part of the grammatical features of the lexicon. Then in numeration and merge they are transformed through structure-building into heads and specifiers according to lexical and morphosyntactic evidence.

To illustrate this further, let us first consider the benefactive as a valence-increasing process, then the reflexive as a valence-decreasing process.

The benefactive morpheme is part of the grammatical features of the lexicon. It is a verbal extension that increases the valence of the transitive or intransitive verb in that it requires an extra object.

Consider the following sentence:

(180) À-lím-ókín-î   lò-káàtó-káŋ
      1SG-tell-BEN-IMP   M/SG-brother-my/ACC

   ŋá-kí⁺ró   ŋùnà.
   F/PL-matters/ACC   these/ACC
   'I shall tell my brother about these matters.'

From Lexicon to Interface 169

First, the numeration picks the verb root *-lim* and the benefactive suffix *-okin,* together with the compound noun root *-kaato,*[1] the noun root *-kiro* and the demonstrative root *ŋuna*. Then merge into words takes place. The verb root merges with agreement, tense, and aspect marking to form the verb, and the noun roots merge with their inflectional features of gender, number, and case into nouns, while the demonstrative merges with its case feature. All these words then build the sentence structure according to VSO word order which is captured in the VP as follows:

(181)

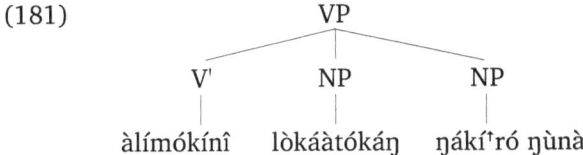

The computational process "merge" then builds heads and partial trees, according to the evidence of the lexical and grammatical features.

So the heads for subject agreement, for tense and aspect, and object agreement are built. Also the head for the benefactive is constructed. A specifier for the subject is not built because the sentence has no overt subject, but the specifier for the object is built under object agreement because the sentence has an overt object. The benefactive head also has a specifier because the benefactive morpheme licenses an extra object, whose case features are checked under the specifier of the benefactive head.

After structure-building the tree for (182) looks as in (183):

---

[1]The compound root *-kaato* is underlyingly *-ka-ito* 'of-mother'. The Toposa term for brother is literally 'one of [the same] mother'.

(182)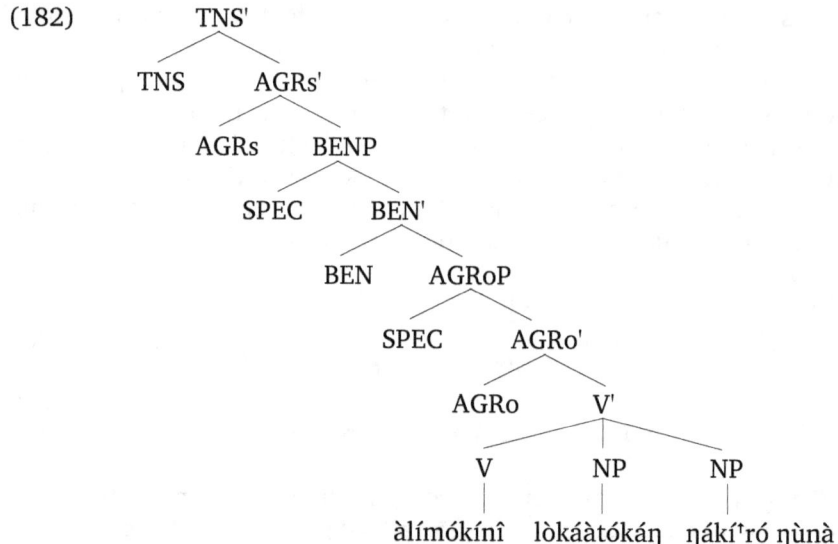

Finally, the words with their morphosyntactic features are moved to their respective heads and specifiers for checking purposes. The grammatical features of tense/aspect, agreement and benefactive of the verb force the verb to move to the benefactive, subject agreement and tense heads. The benefactive NP moves from the VP to the specifier of the benefactive head for accusative case-checking, the object NP moves from the VP to the specifier of object agreement for accusative case-checking. So after structure-building and feature-checking, the spell-out of (183) is as follows:

(183)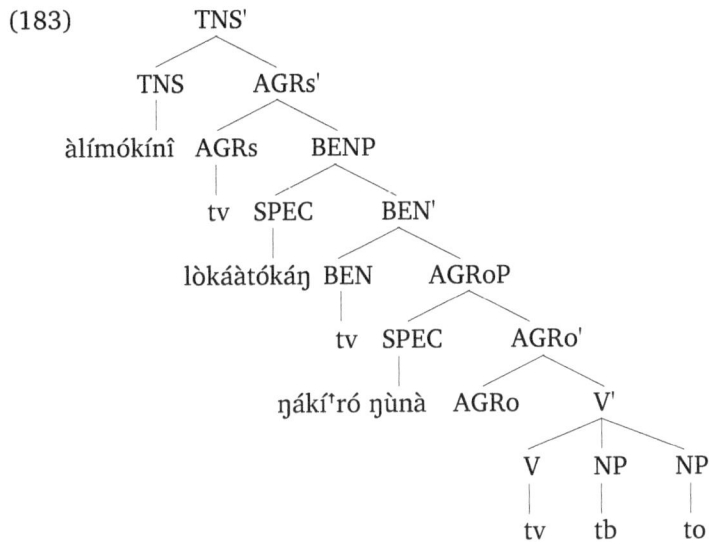

To show how a valence-decreasing process works, consider the following reflexive construction:

(184) Ì-dét-à nyá-bérù.
3SG-beat-RFL F/SG-woman/NOM
'The woman is beating herself.'

First, the numeration picks up the roots *-det* for the verb and *-beru* for the noun from the lexicon, together with the grammatical features of the reflexive and of verb agreement, tense, and aspect, as well as the grammatical features of gender, number, and case for the noun. The lexical and grammtical features are merged into words which are then built into the VSO sentence structure, which in turn is transported into the VP:

(185)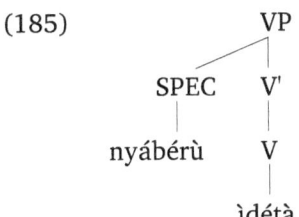

The computational process now builds heads and partial trees according to the lexical and morphological evidence. The grammatical features of the verb force the construction to build two agreement heads and one tense head. The specifier of the subject agreement head is built because the NP subject has to check its nominative case-features there.

Note that no extra feature head is built for the reflexive because the grammatical reflexive in Toposa is realized as a morphological feature that can be checked under the object agreement head, since it represents the integrated object morpheme of the sentence. The resulting structure is:

(186)

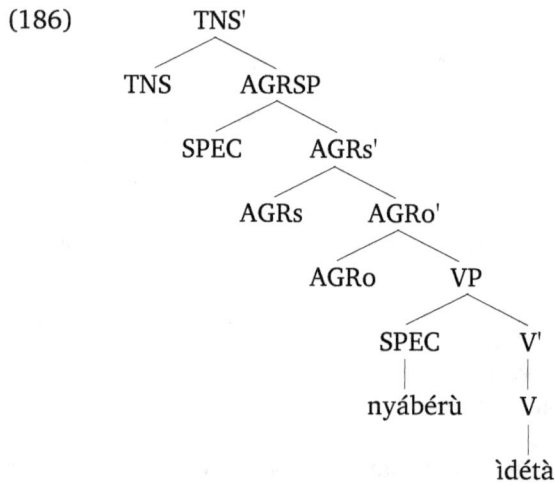

After structure-building movement and feature-checking take place, the verb checks its reflexive, agreement, and tense features, and the noun has to move to the specifier of the subject agreement head in order to have its case-features checked.

The resulting spell-out looks as follows:

(187)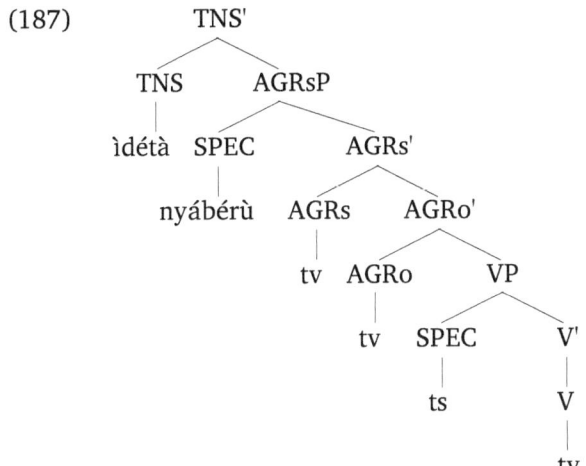

Appendix B

Nyepido * Nyekegiran Paulo Lopyem
The Assembly * Author Paulo Lopyem

1   Bee   koloŋ   nuwan   to-lot   Nye-bu   nya-ce
    is.said time   long.ago   SEQ-went   M/SG-hyena   F/SG-other
    it.is said.that.long.ago   he.went   Hyena   some

    paaran   na-moni   nya-ki-dep   ŋa-kee-moogwa,
    day   F/LOC-bush   F/SG-DER-collect   F/PL-his-food
    day   into.bush   to.collect   his.food

    to-ryam-u   nya-ate   ka   na-moni,   ki-gelegele-u
    SEQ-found-ALL   F/SG-cow   at   F/LOC-bush   SEQ-drive-ALL
    he.found   a.cow   in.the.bush   he.drove

    lo-reke-keŋe.
    M/SG-village-his
    to.his.village

'Once upon a time Hyena went into the bush to collect his food, found a cow in the bush, and drove [it] to his village.'

2 Ki-ryam-a   ka   Nye-ŋatuny   lo-rot,   ta-nyar-a
   SEQ-meet-PL with M/SG-lion   M/LOC-road   SEQ-call-ABL
   he.met   with Lion   on.the.road   he.called

   Nye-ŋatuny   Nye-bu,   "Na-yapa-koto!"
   M/SG-lion   M/SG-hyena   F/VOC-chop-rugged
   lion   hyena   Rugged.Chopper

   'He met with Lion on the road, Lion called Hyena, "Nayapakoto!"
   (= Rugged Chopper, i.e., nickname of Hyena)'

3 Ki-yi   Nye-bu,   "Ee,   Na-giri-nyaŋa!"
   SEQ-say.yes   M/SG-hyena   yes   F/VOC-stripe-yellow
   he.answered   Hyena   yes   Yellow.Stripes

   'Hyena said, "Yes, Nagirinyang!" (= Yellow Stripes, i.e., nickname
   of Lion)

4 Tem-a   Nye-ŋatuny,   "O   iyoo   lo,   i-ram-un-i
   say-ABL   M/SG-lion   ideo   you   this   2SG-drive-ALL-IMP
   he.said   Lion   hey.you.there you.are.driving

   nya-ate   ka   ai?"
   M/SG-cow   from   where?
   cow   from   where

   'Lion said, "Hey, you there, where are you driving the cow from
   (= where did you get this cow)?"'

5 Ta-tac   Nye-bu   tem-a,   "E-kiy-akin-i
   SEQ-answer   M/SG-hyena   say-ABL   1SG-go.early-BEN-IMP
   he.answered   Hyena   he.said   I.went.early

   ta   aaŋ   nya-ki-rim   nya-kop   e-war-i
   just   I   F/SG-DER-circle F/SG-ground   1SG-search-IMP
   just   I   circling   the.ground   I.was.searching

   ŋa-kaa-moogwa,   a-to-ryam-u   nai   nya-ate   na
   F/PL-my-food   1SG-SEQ-find-ALL then   F/SG-cow   this
   my.food   I.found   then   this.cow

	ka	na-moni."			
	in	F/SG-bush			
	in.the.bush				

'Hyena answered. He said, "I just went out early to circle the ground (= go around) in order to look for my food, then I found this cow in the bush." '

6 Tem-a   Nye-ŋatuny,   "Aye,   i-ram-ar-i
   say-ABL M/SG-lion   ideo   2SG-drive-ABL-IMP
   he.said Lion   well   you.drive.[it]

   nai   lo-re."
   then M/SG-village
   then to.village

'Lion said, "Ah [so is that], well, drive it to [your] village then." '

7 Tem-a   Nye-bu,   "Ee."
   say-ABL M/SG-hyena   yes
   he.said Hyena   yes

'Hyena said, "Yes." '

8 Tem-a   Nye-ŋatuny,   "Awaa,   ka-pan-a
   say-ABL M/SG-lion   ideo   IV-go-PL
   he.said Lion   ah yes   lets.go

   robo   e-dok-okin-i,   a-los-it   ta   aaŋ
   well   1PL-go.jointly-BEN-RFL   1SG-set.out-IMP   just I
   well.lets.go.together   I.had.set.out

   daŋ   nya-ki-rap   nya- kop,   nya-boŋ-un
   also F/SG-DER-cover   F/SG-ground   F/SG-return-ALL
   also to.cover   the.ground   returning

   nai   kaŋ nyi-bore   eeni."
   then my   D/SG-thing   this
   and.this.thing.mine

'Lion said, "Ah yes, let us go then, well, let us go together. I have also just gone to cover the ground (= to find food), this cow is my return (= reward, lit.: this thing is my returning)." '

9   Ta-ram-a-si   nai   ikes<u>i</u>   nya-ate   ka   a-pei,
    SEQ-drive-ABL-PL   so   they   F/SG-cow   with   ?-one
    so.they.drove   cow   together

      ani   e-dol-e-te   lo-re,   a-bu   Nye-ŋatuny
      when   3PL-reach-IMP-PL M/SG-village 3SG-came M/SG-lion
      when   they.reached   to.the.village he.came   Lion

      tem-<u>a</u>,   "Nya-kaŋ   nya-ate   na."
      say-ABL   F/SG-my   F/SG-cow   this
      he.said   it.is.mine   this.cow
    'They drove the cow together and when they reached the settlement, Lion came and said, "This cow is mine."'

10 Ta-marya-ta   Nye- bu   ka   Nye-ŋatuny nya-ate.
    SEQ-quarrel-PL M/SG-hyena amd M/SG-lion   F/SG-cow
    they.quarreled Hyena   with Lion   over.cow
    'Hyena and Lion quarreled over the cow.'

11 Ki-ir-a-si   nai   ŋi-tyaŋ   daan<u>i</u>   nya-tem-ar-<u>i</u>
    SEQ-hear-ABL-PL then M/PL-animals all   F/SG-say-ABL-RFL
    they.heard   then all.the.animals   that

      e-ŋolop-a-si   Nye-bu   ka   Nye-ŋatuny,
      3PL-brawl-ABL-PL M/SG-hyena with M/SG-lion
      they-brawled   Hyena   with   Lion

      e-marya-a-te   nya-ate.
      3PL-quarrel-IMP-PL F/SG-cow
      they.quarreled   over.cow
    'All the animals heard that Hyena and Lion were brawling, [that] they were quarreling over the cow.'

12 Ku-ud-un-<u>i</u>   nai   ŋi-tyaŋ   daan<u>i</u>
    SEQ-gather-ALL-RFL so   M/SG-animals all
    they.gathered   so   all.the.animals

Nyepido

```
          lo-pido            nya-ki-tyak      Nye-bu         ka    Nye-ŋatuny.
          M/LOC-assembly     F/SG-DER-judge   M/SG-hyena     and   M/SG-lion
          in.an.assembly     to.judge         Hyena          and   Lion
```
'All the animals gathered in an assembly to judge between Hyena and Lion.'

13
```
     To-dip-akin-i            ŋi-tyaŋ          ni-ti-etyaama,
     SEQ-sit.down-BEN-RFL     M/PL-animals     place-very-wide.circle
     they.sat.down            the.animals      in.a.very.wide.circle

          ki-liliŋ            nya-kop          cek.
          SEQ-quiet           F/SG-ground      ideo
          it.was.quiet        the.ground       completely
```
'The animals sat down in a wide circle. The ground (= everyone) was completely quiet.'

14
```
     Ki-sya-u             nai      Nye-tome,         to-nyo-u,
     SEQ-begin-ALL        then     M/SG-elephant     SEQ-rise-ALL
     he.began             then     Elephant          he.rose

          ta-tac             ŋa-kiro.
          SEQ-answer         F/PL-matter
          he.answered        the.matter
```
'Then Elephant began. He rose and answered the matter (= addressed the issue).'

15
```
     Tem-a,     "Ba-si      mono     eesi,        kon-i          nya-ate     ai?
     say-ABL    say-PL      just     you/PL       be.how-IMP     F/SG-cow    QUE
     he.said    you.say              you          how.is.it      cow         ?
```
'He said, "You are saying [what]? How is the cow (= what is the matter)?"'

16
```
     To-lim-okin-ae          nai,     tem-ar-ae          e-marya-a-te
     SEQ-tell-BEN-PAS        so       say-ABL-PAS        3PL-quarrel-IMP-PL
     it.is.told              so       it.is.said         they.quarreled

          Nye-bu            ka      Nye-ŋatuny       nya-ate.
          M/SG-hyena        and     M/SG-lion        F/SG-cow
          Hyena             and     Lion             over.cow
```
'So it is told (or: tell me), it is said [that] Hyena and Lion quarreled over a cow.'

17 A-los-iti   koloŋ   Nye-bu   nya-ki-rap
    3SG-go-PER   time   M/SG-hyena   F/SG-DER-find
    he.has.gone   some.time.ago   Hyena   to.find

    ŋa-kee-moogwa,   ki-rap-u   nya-ate   na,
    F/PL-his-food   SEQ-find-ALL   F/SG-cow   this
    his.food   he.found   this.cow

    ta-ram-u   nai,   ani   e-dol-i   lo-rot,
    SEQ-drive-ALL   so   when   3SG-reach-IMP   M/LOC-road
    he.drove.home   so   when   he.reached   the.road

    ki-ryam-a   ka   Nye-ŋatuny,   ku-ruk-u-tu
    SEQ-meet-ABL   with   M/SG-lion   SEQ-go.jointly-ALL-PL
    he.met   with   Lion   they.went.together

    nai, ani   e-dol-un-e-te   lo-re,   tem-a
    so   when 3PL-reach-ALL-IMP-PL   M/LOC-village   say-ABL
    so   when they.reached   to.village   he.said

    Nye-ŋatuny   nya-keŋe   nya-ate."
    M/SG-lion   M/SG-his   F/SG-cow
    Lion   his   the.cow

'Hyena had gone to find his food, [but] he found this cow, so he drove it [home]. When he reached the road, he met with Lion; they went together, and when they reached the settlement, Lion said [that] the cow [was] his."'

18 Ta-tac-a   ŋi-tyaŋ   daani,   ta-cal-u-tu
    SEQ-answer-PL   M/PL-animals   all   SEQ-shout-ALL-PL
    they.answered   all.the.animals   they.shouted

    tem-a-si,   "Ko-te   neni,   Munan."
    say-ABL-PL   be-PL   place   kneader
    they.said   it.is.like.this   Kneader

'All the animals answered. They shouted, saying, "It is like this, Munan (=Kneader, i.e., nickname of elephant)."'

Nyepido

19 Ta-tac   nai   Nye-tome   ŋa-kiro,   tem-a,
    SEQ-answer   then   M/SG-elephant   F/PL-matter   say-ABL
    he.answered   then   Elephant   matters   he.said

   "A-bal-a   aaŋ   nya-ate   nya-ka   Na-giri-nyaŋa."
   1SG-say-ABL   I   F/SG-cow   F/SG-of   F/VOC-stripes-yellow
   I.say   the.cow   that.of   Yellow.Stripes

   'Elephant answered the matter. He said, "I say, the cow [is] that of Nagirinyang." '

20 To-nyo-u   Nye-kosowan,   ta-tac   tem-a,
    SEQ-rise-ALL   M/SG-buffalo   SEQ-answer   say-ABL
    he.rose   Buffalo   he.answered   he.said

   "A-bal-a   aaŋ   nya-ate   nya-ka   Na-giri-nyaŋa."
   1SG-say-RFL   I   F/SG-cow   F/SG-of   F/VOC-stripes-yellow
   I.say   cow   that.of   Yellow.Stripes

   'Buffalo rose. He answered, saying, "I say, the cow [is] that of Nagirinyang." '

21 To-nyo-u   Nya-mosiŋ   tem-a,
    SEQ-rise-ALL   M/SG-rhino   say-ABL
    he.rose   Rhino   he.said

   "Nya-ka   Na-giri-nyaŋa   nya-ate."
   F/SG-of   F/VOC-stripes-yellow   F/SG-cow
   that.of   Yellow.Stripes   the.cow

   'Rhino rose. He said, "The cow [is] that of Nagirinyang." '

22 To-nyo-u   Kwee,   ta-tac   tem-a,
    SEQ-rise-ALL   jackal   SEQ-answer   say-ABL
    he.rose   Jackal   he.answered   he.said

   "Nya-ka   Na-giri-nyaŋa.
   F/SG-of   F/VOC-stripes-yellow
   that.of   Yellow.Stripes

   'Jackal rose. He answered, he said, "[It is] that of Nagirinyang." '

23 A-nyo-u   lo   a-nyo-u,
    3SG-rise-ALL   who   3SG-rise-ALL
    he.rose   who   he.rose

    "Nya-ka   Na-giri-nyaṉa   nya-ate."
    F/SG-of   F/VOC-stripes-yellow   F/SG-cow
    that.of   Yellow.Stripes   the.cow

'Rose who rose (= whoever rose) [said], "The cow [is] that of Nagirinyang." '

24 To-nyo-u-tu̱   nai   ŋi-tyaŋ   daani̱   tem-a-si,
    SEQ-rise-ALL-PL   then   M/PL-animals   all   say-ABL-PL
    they.rose   then   all.the.animals   they.said

    "Daani̱   ŋuna,   nya-ka   Na-giri-nyaṉa   nya-ate."
    all   these   F/SG-of F/VOC-stripes-yellow   F/SG-cow
    this.is.all   that.of Yellow.Stripes   the.cow

'All the animals rose. They said, "That [is] all, the cow [is] that of Nagirinyang." '

25 Ani   ku-cut-un-i̱   ŋi-tyaŋ   daani̱   nya-ki-tac
    when   SEQ-end-ALL-RFL   M/PL-animals   all   F/SG-DER-answer
    when   they.ended   all.the.animals   to.answer

    ŋa-kiro,   bu   Nye-kunyuk,   ku-nyum-un-i̱
    F/PL-matter   came   M/SG-squirrel   SEQ-proud-ALL-RFL
    matters   he.came   Squirrel   he.showed.off

    e-nap-iti̱   ŋa-suwa   ka   na-kani̱,   e-nap-iti̱
    3SG-wear-PER   F/PL-iron   at   F/LOC-arm   3SG-wear-PER
    he.wore   iron.coils   around.arms   he.wore

    ŋa-lagam   ka   lo-mosiriŋ,   ta-nap-ite   ŋa-lero,
    F/PL-brass.coil   at   M/LOC-neck   SEQ-wear-SIM   F/PL-beads
    a.brass.coil   around.neck   he.wore   a.necklace

    ŋi-kaboboi   lo-moyo,   ta-nap-ite   nye-gyel-it
    M/PL-ivory.eggs   M/LOC-fingers   SEQ-wear-SIM   M/SG-tusk-SG
    ivory.eggs   on.the.fingers   he.wore   a.tusk

Nyepido

```
ka   lo-keper,            ta-nap-ite      nya-gilae       ka
at   M/LOC-upper.arm      SEQ-wear-SIM    F/SG-lip.ring   at
on   upper.arm            he.wore         a.lip.ring      in

na-kutuku̱,      ŋi-esin         na-ki,          to-ya-i      nya- tome̱
F/LOC-mouth    M/PL-ear.ring   F/LOC-ears      SEQ-be-SG    F/SG-ivory
mouth          ear.rings       in.ears         it.was       ivory.ring

na-kani̱,        ta-nap-ite       nye-kadeŋo   ka    na-abor.
F/LOC-hand      SEQ-wear-SIM     M/SG-belt    at    F/LOC-waist
around.wrist    he.wore          belt              around.waist
```

'When all the animals had finished addressing the matter, Squirrel came with pride/confidence. He had put on irons (= metal coils) around [his] arms, and a brass-coil around [his] neck. At the same time he wore a ceremonial necklace and ivory-eggs on [his] fingers (= thumbs). He wore a tusk [of warthog] on [his] upper arm. He had a lip-ring in [his] mouth, ear-rings in [his] ears, an ivory ring around his hands, and he had put on a ceremonial belt around his waist.'

```
26  Ku-wa-aki̱       ŋi-coroi      lo-kipisi̱,        ku-wal-ite
    SEQ-put-BEN     M/PL-bells    M/LOC-leg         SEQ-wear-SIM
    he.put.on       bells         around.legs       he.wore

    ŋi-konoi        ka na-kou,       ta-nap-ite      ŋa-muk
    M/PL-feathers   on F/LOC-head    SEQ-wear-SIM    F/PL-sandals
    feathers        on.the.head      he.wore         sandals

    ka  na-kejen,      to-lem-a         ŋa-lirwa      ŋa-arei,
    on  F/LOC-feet     SEQ-carry-ABL    F/PL-spears   F/PL-two
    on.feet            he.carried       spears        two

    ta-tap-aki̱        nye-corogat     ka    nya- upwal.
    SEQ-hold-BEN      M/SG-sword      and   F/PL-shield
    he.held           a.sword         and   a.shield
```

'He had put a string of bells around [his] lower legs, had colored feathers on [his] head, and sandals on his feet. He carried two spears, he held a sword and a shield.'

```
27  To-nyo-u,        to-wo,         ta- tac         ŋa-kiro,
    SEQ-rise-ALL     SEQ-stand      SEQ-answer      F/PL-matters
    he.rose          he.stood       he.answered     the.matter
```

```
ki-ne-kin-i,         ku-cum-aki     nye-kumoyin  na-lagam,
SEQ-stretch-BEN-RFL  SEQ-spear-BEN  M/SG-finger  F/LOC-brass.coil
he.stretched         he.speared     finger       into.brass.coil

ki-nene-aki         nya-kani    to-kut-a       ŋa-suwa,
SEQ-stretch-BEN     F/SG-arm    SEQ-blow-ABL   F/PL-irons
he.stretched.out    arm         he.blew.off    irons

tem-a,    "Ko-te   ŋa-kiro           ai?  Tem-a-si     ɲi-tyaŋ,
say-ABL   be-PL    F/PL-matters      how  say-ABL-PL   M/PL-animals
he.said   how.are.these.matters           they.say     the.animals

ba-si      ɲi-tyaŋ           daani  nya-ka    Na-giri-nyaŋa
say-PL     M/PL-animals      all    F/SG-of   F/VOC-stripes-yellow
they.say   all.the.animals          that.of   Yellow.Stripes

nya-ate."
F/SG-cow
the.cow
```
'He rose, he stood [there], answering the matter. He stretched himself, spearing [his] finger into the brass coil, stretching [his] arm. He blew [the dust from his] iron coils, and said, "What are these matters? The animals all say [that] the cow [is] that of Nagirinyang."'

28
```
Tem-a     nai    iŋesi,  "Ee,  a-bal-a       aaŋ
say-ABL   then   he      yes   1SG-say-ABL   I
he.said   then   he      yes   I.say         I

    nya-ate    nya-ka    Na-kitoŋo."
    F/SG-cow   F/SG-of   F/VOC-scavenger
    the.cow    that.of   Scavenger
```
'He said, "Yes, [but] I say the cow [is] that of Nakitongo." (= Scavenger, i.e., nickname of Hyena)'

29
```
To-kulya-u     Nye-ŋatuny,  ta-nap-akin-i
SEQ-boil-ALL   M/SG-lion    SEQ-charge-BEN-RFL
he.boiled      Lion         he.charged.against

    Nye-kunyuk,     ku-wok-or-i         Nye-kunyuk,
    M/SG-squirrel   SEQ-run-ABL-RFL     M/SG-squirrel
    Squirrel        he.ran.away         Squirrel
```

    ku-ruk-okin-i̠   ka   Nye-ŋatuny (wir, wir, wir).
    SEQ-chase-BEN-RFL   with   M/SG-lion   IDEO
    they.chased.each.other with   Lion

'Lion boiled [with anger], he charged at Squirrel, Squirrel ran away, they chased each other *wir, wir, wir.*

30 To-lom-a   Nye-kunyuk   na-dui   (pir).
      SEQ-enter-ABL   M/SG-squirrel F/LOC-hole   IDEO
      he.entered   Squirrel   into.a.hole

'Squirrel entered *pir* into a hole.'

31 To-kur   Nye-ŋatuny   nya-dui.
      SEQ-scratch   M/SG-lion   F/SG-hole
      he.scratched   Lion   the.hole

'Lion scratched the hole (= started to dig).'

32 Ani   e-pap-un-i   nya-ku-rum-un   Nye-kunyuk,
      when   3SG-be.close-ALL-IMP   F/SG-DER-catch-ALL   M/SG-squirrel
      when   he.got.close   to.catch   Squirrel

        ta-naŋ   Nye-kunyuk   nya-dui   ka   na-aye,
        SEQ-reach   M/SG-squirrel   F/SG-hole   at   F/LOC-other.side
        he.reached   Squirrel   a.hole   on.the.other.side

        ku-wok-or-i̠,   tem-a   na-dui   na-ce   (pir).
        SEQ-run-ABL-RFL   say-ABL   F/LOC-hole   F/SG-other   IDEO
        he.ran.away   it.said   into.another.hole

'When he got close to catching Squirrel, Squirrel reached the [exit] hole on the other side, he ran away, he said *pir* [disappearing] into another hole.'

33 To-kur   Nye-ŋatuny   nabo.
      SEQ-scratch   M/SG-lion   again
      he.scratched   lion   again

'Lion scratched again (= started to dig again).'

34 Ani   e-pap-un-i   Nye-kunyuk,   ta-naŋ
      when   3SG-be.close-ALL-IMP   M/SG-squirrel   SEQ-reach
      when   he.got.close   to.Squirrel   he.reached

Nye-kunyuk   nya-dui,   ku-wok-or-i̱,   to-dok-a
M/SG-squirrel F/SG-hole   SEQ-run-ABL-RFL SEQ-climb-ABL
Squirrel   hole   he.ran.away   he.climbed

lo-moru   lo   e-ya-i   nya- guruwoc
M/LOC-mountain   which   3SG-be-SG   F/SG-crevice
onto.a.mountain   which.had   a.very.deep.crevice

na-ti-kooyen,   to-lom-a   na-guruwoc.
F/SG-very-DER/long/SG   SEQ-enter-ABL   F/LOC-crevice
                             he.entered   into.the.crevice

'When he got close to Squirrel, Squirrel reached [another] hole, he ran away, he climbed a mountain in which there was a very long (= deep) crevice, he entered the crevice.'

35 Ani   e-bun-i   Nye-ŋatuny, to-rip-aki̱   Nye-kunyuk
    when   3SG-come-IMP M/SG-lion   SEQ-look.for-BEN M/SG-squirrel
    when   he.came   Lion   he.looked.for   Squirrel

    ka   na-guruwoc,   ki-ŋit   Nye-ŋatuny   Nye-kunyuk
    in   F/LOC-crevice   SEQ-ask   M/SG-lion   M/SG-squirrel
    in.the.crevice   he.asked   Lion   Squirrel

    tem-a̱,   "Lo-cooro,   i-ye-i   iyoŋ   ai?"
    say-ABL   M/VOC-stripes   2SG-be-IMP   you   where
    he.said   Long.Stripes   you.are   you   where

'When Lion came, he looked for Squirrel in the crevice, Lion asked Squirrel, he said, "Locooro (= Long Stripes, i.e., nickname of Squirrel), where are you?" '

36 Ta-tac   Nye-kunyuk,   tem-a̱,   "A-ya-i   aeoŋ ne."
    SEQ-answer   M/SG-squirrel say-ABL   1SG-be-IMP   I   here
    he.answered   Squirrel   he.said   I.am   I   here

'Squirrel answered, he said, "I am here." '

37 Tem-a   Nye-kunyuk   Nye-ŋatuny,   "Ki-piri-un-i
    say-ABL   M/SG-squirrel   M/SG-lion   IV-jump-ALL-RFL
    he.said   Squirrel   to.Lion   jump.here

    ka   ina."
    from   there
    from   there
'Squirrel said to Lion, "Jump from there [and get me if you dare]." '

38 Ki-piri-or-i   nai   Nye-ŋatuny,
    SEQ-jump-ABL-RFL   so   M/SG-lion
    he.jumped   so   Lion

    to-bilibil-ar-i   tooma   na-guruwoc.
    SEQ-break/INT-ABL-RFL   inside   F/LOC-crevice
    he.got.smashed   inside.the.crevice
'So Lion jumped, he was smashed completely [intensive] in the crevice.'

39 To-bil   nye-mosiriŋ,   to-bwaŋ-a   ŋa-moru   nya-kou,
    SEQ-break   M/SG-neck   SEQ-crush-PL   F/PL-rocks   F/SG-head
    it.broke   the.neck   they.crushed   the.rocks   the.head

    to-twan   nai   Nye-ŋatuny.
    SEQ-die   so   M/SG-lion
    he.died   so   Lion
'[His] neck broke (= he broke his neck), the rocks crushed his head (= he smashed his skull on the rocks), so Lion died.'

40 To-dok-u   nai   Nye-kunyuk,   to-boŋ-o,
    SEQ-climb-ALL   then   M/SG-squirrel   SEQ-return-ABL
    he.climbed.back.up   then   Squirrel   he.returned

    ku-nyum-ar-i   lo-pido.
    SEQ-proud-ABL-RFL   M/LOC-assembly
    he.went.proudly   to.the.assembly
'Squirrel climbed back up, he returned, he went proudly back to the assembly.'

41 To-nyo-u-tu̱   nai   ŋi-tyaŋ   daani̱,   ta-cal-u-tu̱
    SEQ-rise-ALL-PL   then   M/PL-animals   all   SEQ-shout-ALL-PL
    they.rose   then   all.the.animals   they.shouted

    tem-a-si,   "A-be-ikin-i̱.   A-be-ik-i
    say-ABL-PL   3SG-hit.target-BEN-RFL   3SG-hit.target-BEN-IMP
    they.said   it.is.right.on   he.hit.the.target

    Lo-cooro   ŋa-kiro   ŋuna,   e-ra-i
    M/VOC-stripes   F/PL-matters   these   3SG-be-SG
    Long.Stripes   in.this.matter   it.is

    nya-ate   nya-ka   Na-kitoŋo."
    F/SG-cow   F/SG-of   F/VOC-scavenger
    cow   that.of   Scavenger

'Then all the animals rose, they shouted, they said, "Right on! Locooro hit the point [in] this matter, the cow is that of Nakitongo." (= Scavenger, i.e., another nickname of Hyena)'

42 Ki-al-ar-i̱   nai   ŋi-tyaŋ   daani̱,   e-baa-si,   "Meere
    SEQ-scatter-ABL-RFL   so   M/SG-animals   all   3PL-say-PL be-not
    they.scattered   so   all.the.animals   they.said   is.not

    mono   ŋu-tuŋa   lu   a-kuryan-it-o   Nye-ŋatuny-a?
    only   M/PL-people   these   3PL-afraid-PER-PL   M/SG-lion-QUE
    only   these.people   they.were.afraid   of.Lion

    K-e-ji-i   karamae   Nye-kunyuk,   a-be-ik-i
    ?-3SG-clever-IMP   really   M/SG-squirrel   3SG-hit.target-BEN-IMP
    he.is.clever   really   Squirrel   he.hit.target

    karamae   ŋa-kiro   ka   nya-ate."
    really   F/PL-matters   of   F/SG-cow
    really   regarding.the.matter.of.the.cow

'So all the animals scattered, they said, "Was it not that these people were only afraid of the Lion? Squirrel is really clever, he really hit the point [in] the matter of (= dispute over) the cow." '

References

Allwood, J., L. G. Andersson, and Ö. Dahl. 1977. *Logic in linguistics.* Cambridge: Cambridge University Press.
Anderson, T. 1988. Ergativity in Pari, a Nilotic language. *Lingua* 75:289–324.
Aoun, J. 1979. *On government, case-marking, and clitic placement.* Mimeographed. MIT.
Aoun, J., E. Benmamoun, and D. Sportiche. 1994. Agreement, word order, and conjunctions in some varieties of Arabic. *Linguistic Inquiry* 25:195–220.
Baker, M. C. 1988. *Incorporation: A theory of grammatical function changing.* Chicago/London: The University of Chicago Press.
Bearth, T. 1995. Wortstellung, Topik und Fokus. In G. Miehe and W. J. G. Möhlig (eds.), *Swahili-Handbuch,* Afrikawissen-schaftliche Lehrbücher, 7:173–206. Cologne: Rüdiger Köppe.
Belletti, A. 1988. The case of unaccusatives. *Linguistic Inquiry* 19:1–34.
Besten, H. den. 1983. On the interaction of root transformations and lexical deletive rules. In W. Abraham (ed.), *On the formal syntax of the Westgermania,* 47–131. Amsterdam: John Benjamins.
Besten, H. den. 1985. The ergative hypothesis and free word order in Dutch and German. In J. Toman (ed.), *Studies in German grammar,* 23–64. Dordrecht: Foris.
Black, C. A. 2000. *Quiegolani Zapotec syntax: A Principles and Parameters account.* SIL International and University of Texas at Arlington Publications in Linguistics 136. Dallas: SIL International.

Blake, B. J. 1994. *Case.* Cambridge Textbooks in Linguistics. Cambridge: Cambridge University Press.

Borer, H., and L. Tuller. 1985. Nominative/agreement complementarity and VSO order in Standard Arabic. *Studies in African Linguistics,* Suppl. 9:27–32.

Bouchard, D. 1984. *On the content of empty categories.* Dordrecht: Foris.

Brody, M. 1990. Some remarks on the focus field in Hungarian. *University College London Working Papers in Linguistics* 2:201–226.

Burton-Roberts, N. 1986. *Analysing sentences: An introduction to English syntax.* London/New York: Longman.

Burzio, L. 1981. *Intransitive verbs and Italian auxiliaries.* Ph.D. dissertation, MIT.

Buth, R. 1981. Ergative word order - Luwo is OVS. *Occasional Papers in the Study of Sudanese Languages* 1:79–90. Juba, Sudan: Summer Institute of Linguistics.

Bybee, J. 1985. *Morphology: A study of the relation between meaning and form.* Typological Studies in Language 9. Amsterdam: John Benjamins.

Carnie, A., and E. Guilfoyle, eds. 2000. *The syntax of verb initial languages.* Oxford Studies in Comparative Syntax. Oxford: Oxford University Press.

Catsimali, G. 1990. Case in Modern Greek: Implications for clause structure. Ph.D. dissertation, University of Reading.

Chafe, W. 1976. Giveness, contrastiveness, definiteness, subjects, topics, and point of view. In N. C. Li (ed.), *Subject and topic,* 25–55 New York, San Francisco, London: Academic Press.

Chomsky, N. 1957. *Syntactic structures.* The Hague: Mouton.

Chomsky, N. 1965. *Aspects of the theory of syntax.* Cambridge, Mass.: MIT Press.

Chomsky, N. 1971. Deep structure, surface structure and semantic interpretation. In D. Steinberg and L. Jakobovita (eds.), *Semantics: An Interdisciplinary reader in Linguistics, Philosophy and Psychology.* Cambridge: Cambridge University Press.

Chomsky, N. 1980. On Binding. *Linguistic Inquiry* 11:1–46.

Chomsky, N. 1981. *Lectures on Government and Binding (The Pisa Lectures).* In J. Koster, and H. van Riemsdijk (eds.), *Studies in Generative Grammar.* New York: Mouton de Gruyter.

Chomsky, N. 1982. *Some concepts and consequences of the theory of Government and Binding.* Linguistic Inquiry Monographs 6. Cambridge, Mass.: MIT Press.

Chomsky, N. 1986a. *Knowledge of language.* New York: Praeger.

Chomsky, N. 1986b. *Barriers.* Linguistic Inquiry Monographs 13. Cambridge, Mass.: MIT Press.

Chomsky, N. 1991. Some notes on economy of derivation and representation. In R. Freidin (ed.), *Principles and Parameters in comparative grammar.* Current Studies in Linguistics 20:417–454. Cambridge, Mass.: MIT Press.

Chomsky, N. 1993. A Minimalist Program for linguistic theory. In K. Hale and S. J. Keyser (eds.), *The view from Building 20: Essays in linguistics in honor of Sylvain Bromberger.* Cambridge, Mass.: MIT Press.

Chomsky, N. 1995. *The Minimalist Program.* Current Studies in Linguistics 28. Cambridge, Mass.: MIT Press.

Chomsky, N. 1998. *Minimalist inquiries: The framework.* Cambridge, Mass.: MIT Press.

Comrie, B. 1989. *Language universals and linguistic typology: Syntax and morphology.* Chicago: The University of Chicago Press.

Cook, V. J., and M. Newson. 1996. *Chomsky's universal grammar: An introduction.* Oxford: Blackwell Publishers. [First edition 1988.]

Cole, P., and J. M. Saddock, eds. 1977. *Grammatical relations.* Syntax and Semantics 8. New York: Academic Press.

Creider, C. A. 1989. *The syntax of the Nilotic languages: Themes and variations.* In B. Heine and W. J. G. Möhlig (eds.), Language and Dialect Studies in East Africa 9. Berlin: Dietrich Reimer.

Crystal, D. 2003. *A dictionary of linguistics and phonetics,* fifth edition. Oxford: Blackwell Publishers.

Derbyshire, D. 1986. Topic continuity and OVS order in Hixkaryana. In J. Sherzer and G. Urban (eds.), *Native South American discourse,* 237–306. Berlin: Mouton de Gruyter.

Dik, S. C. 1978. *Functional Grammar.* Dordrecht: Foris Publications.

Dimmendaal, G. J. 1983a. *The Turkana language.* Publications in African Languages and Linguistics 2, Dordrecht: Foris.

Dimmendaal, G. J. 1983b. Turkana as a verb-initial language. *Journal Of African Languages and Linguistics* 5:17–44.

Dimmendaal, G. J. 1986. Prominence hierarchies and Turkana syntax. In G. J. Dimmendaal (ed.), *Current approaches to African linguistics,* 3:127–148. Publications in African Languages and Linguistics 6. Dordrecht: Foris.

Dimmendaal, G. J. 1995. The emergence of tense marking in the Nilotic-Bantu borderland as an instance of areal adaptation. In *Time in Languages,* 29–42. Center for Theoretical Study – the Institute of Advanced Studies at Charles University and the Academy of Sciences of the Czech Republic.

Dimmendaal, G. J. 1996. Attitude markers and conversational implicatures in Turkana speech acts. *Studies in Language* 20:249–274.

Dixon, R. M. W. 1979. Ergativity. *Language* 55:59–138.

Dixon, R. M. W. 1994. *Ergativity.* Cambridge Studies in Linguistics 69. Cambridge: Cambridge University Press.

Dooley, R. A., and S. H. Levinsohn. 2000. *Analyzing discourse: A manual of basic concepts.* http://www.und.nodak.edu/dept/linguistics/textbooks/DooleyLevinsohn.pdf

DuBois, J. 1985. Competing Motivations. In J. Haiman (ed.), *Iconicity in syntax,* 343–365. Amsterdam: John Benjamins.

DuBois, J. 1987. The discourse basis of ergativity. *Language* 63:805–855.

Emonds, J. 1976. *A Transformational approach to English syntax.* New York: Academic Press.

Emonds, J. 1980. Word order in Generative Grammar. *Journal of Linguistic Research* 1:33–54.

Emonds, J. 1985. *A unified theory of syntactic categories.* Dordrecht: Foris.

Fairclough, N. 1989. *Language and power.* London: Longman.

Fasold, R. 1990. *The sociolinguistics of language.* Oxford: Basil Blackwell.

Firbas, J. 1966. On defining the theme in Functional Sentence Perspective. *Travaux Linguistique de Prague* 1:267–280.

Frajzyngier, Z. 1984. Ergative and nominative-accusative features in Mandara. *Journal of African Languages and Linguistics* 6:35–45.

Givón, T. 1976. On the SOV reconstruction of Southern Nilotic: Internal evidence from Toposa. *Studies in African Linguistics,* Supplement 6:73–91.

Givón, T. 1984. *Syntax: A functional-typological introduction.* Amsterdam: John Benjamins.

Green, G. 1975. How to get people to do things with words. In P. Cole, and J. Morgan (eds.), *Speech acts.* Syntax and Semantics, 3:107–141. New York: Academic Press.

Greenberg, J. 1963. Some universals of grammar with particular reference to the order of meaningful elements. In J. Greenberg (ed.), *Universals of language.* Cambridge, Mass.: MIT Press.

Grimes, J. 1975. *The thread of discourse.* The Hague: Mouton.

Haegeman, L. 1994. *Introduction to Government and Binding Theory,* second ed. Oxford: Blackwell.

Haegeman, L., and H. van Riemsdijk. 1986. Verb projection raising, scope and the typology of rules affecting verbs. *Linguistic Inquiry* 17:417–466.

Hale, K., and S. J. Keyser. 1986. *Some Transitivity Alternations in English.* Lexicon Project MIT Working Paper 7. Center for Cognitive Science.

Hale, K., and S. J. Keyser, eds. 1993. *The view from Building 20. Essays in linguistics in Honor of Sylvain Bromberger.* Cambridge, Mass.: MIT Press.

Halliday, M. A. K. 1967. Notes on transitivity and theme in English. Parts 1 and 2. *Journal of Linguistics* 3:37–81, 199–244.

Harlow, S. 1981. Government and relativisation in Celtic. In F. Heny (ed.), *Binding and Filtering.* Cambridge, Mass.: MIT Press.

Harris, Z. 1988. *Language and information.* New York: Colombia University Press.

Hawkins, J. 1983. *Word order universals: Quantitative analysis of linguistic structure.* New York: Academic Press.

Heine, B. 1981. The non-Bantu languages of Kenya. In H. Heine, and W. J. G. Möhlig (eds.), *Language and Dialect Atlas of Kenya 2.* Berlin: Dietrich Reimer.

Hopper, P. J., and S. Thompson. 1980. Transitivity in grammar and discourse. *Language* 56:251–299.

Hornstein, N., and A. Weinberg. 1981. Case theory and preposition stranding. *Linguistic Inquiry* 12:55–92.

Horvath, J. 1981. Aspects of Hungarian syntax and the theory of grammar. Ph.D. dissertation, UCLA.

Horvath, J. 1995. Structural focus, structural case, and the notion of feature-assignment. In K. É. Kiss, *Discourse configurational languages,* 28–64. Oxford Studies in Comparative Syntax. New York/Oxford: Oxford University Press.

Huang, C.-T. J. 1984. On the distribution and reference of empty pronouns. *Linguistic Inquiry* 15:531–574.

Huang, Y. 1994. *The syntax and pragmatics of anaphora. A study with special reference to Chinese.* Cambridge Studies in Linguistics 70. Cambridge: Cambridge University Press.

Huddleston, R. 1976. *An introduction to English transformational grammar.* London: Longman.

Hymes, D. 1974. Why Linguistics needs the sociologist. In D. Hymes (ed.), *Foundations in sociolinguistics: An ethnographic approach,* 69–82. Philadelphia: University of Pennsylvania Press.

Jackendoff, R. 1972. *Semantic interpretation in Generative Grammar.* Cambridge, Mass.: MIT Press.

Jackendoff, R. 1990. *Semantic structures.* Current Studies in Linguistics 18. Cambridge, Mass.: MIT Press.

Jaeggli, O. 1982. *Topics in Romance syntax.* Dordrecht: Foris.

Jaeggli, O., and K. Safir 1989. *The null subject parameter.* London: Kluwer.

Jones, M., and A. R. Thomas. 1977. *The Welsh language: Studies in its syntax and semantics.* Cardiff: University of Wales Press.

Kayne, R. S. 1983. The antisymmetry of syntax. ms. CUNY.

Keenan, E. 1978. The syntax of subject-final languages. In W. P. Lehmann (ed.), *Syntactic typology: Studies in the phenomenology of language.* Austin: University of Texas Press.

Kiss, K. É. 1995. *Discourse configurational languages.* Oxford Studies in Comparative Syntax. New York/Oxford: Oxford University Press.

Koopman, H. 1984. *The syntax of verbs.* Dordrecht: Foris.

Kuno, S. 1980. The scope of the question and negation in some verb-final languages. *CLS* 16:155–169.

Labov, W. 1972. The transformation of experience in narrative syntax. In W. Labov (ed.), *Language in the inner city,* 297–353. Philadelphia: University of Pennsylvania Press.

Lambrecht, K. 1987. On the status of SVO sentences in French discourse. In R. S. Tomlin, (ed.), *Coherence and grounding in discourse,* 217–261. Amsterdam: John Benjamins.

Larson, R. K. 1988. Subjects and the Theta-Criterion. *Natural Language and Linguistic Theory* 6:1–18.

Lasnik, H., and M. Saito. 1992. *Move α: Condition on its application and output.* Current Studies in Linguistics 22. Cambridge, Mass.: MIT Press.

Li, N. C., and S. A. Thompson. 1976. Subject and topic: A new typology of language. In N. C. Li (ed.), *Subject and topic,* 457–498. New York, San Francisco, London: Academic Press.

Lyons, J. 1968. *Introduction to theoretical linguistics.* Cambridge: Cambridge University Press.

Mallison, G., and B. J. Blake. 1981. *Language typology: Cross-linguistic studies in syntax.* Amsterdam: North Holland.

Marantz, A. P. 1984. *On the nature of grammatical relations.* Linguistic Inquiry Monographs 10. Cambridge, Mass.: MIT Press.

Mathesius, V. 1915. O pasívu v moderní angličtině [On the passive in Modern English.] Sborník Filologický 5:198–220. Prague.

Matthews, P. H. 1991. *Morphology.* Cambridge: Cambridge University Press.

McCawley, J. D. 1970. English as a VSO language. *Language* 46:286–299.

McCloskey, J. 1983. A VP in a VSO language? In G. Gazdar, E. Klein, and G. K. Pullum (eds.), *Order, concord, and constituency,* 9–53. Dordrecht: Foris.

Miller, C. L., and L. Gilley. 2001. Evidence for ergativity in Shilluk. *Journal of African Languages and Linguistics* 22:33–68.
Nichols, J. 1986. Head-marking and dependent-marking grammar. *Language* 62:56–119.
Nyombe, B. G. V. 1987. Argument-bearing affixes in Bari. Ph.D. dissertation, CUNY Graduate School.
Oerhle, R. 1975. The grammatical status of the English dative alternation. Ph.D. dissertation, MIT.
Ouhalla, J. 1991. *Functional categories and parametric variation.* London/New York: Routledge.
Payne, D. 1990. *The pragmatics of word order: Typological dimensions of verb initial languages.* Empirical Approaches to Language Typology 7. Berlin/New York: Mouton de Gruyter.
Payne, T. E. 1982. Role and reference and ergativity in Yup'ik Eskimo and Tagalog. *Studies in Language* 6:75–106.
Payne, T. E. 1997. *Describing morpho-syntax: A guide for field linguists.* Cambridge: Cambridge University Press.
Philippaki-Warburton, I. 1985. Word order in Modern Greek. *Transactions of The Philological Society* 2:113–143.
Pike, K. L. 1975. *Phonemics: A technique for reducing languages to writing.* Ann Arbor: The University of Michigan Press.
Plank, F. 1979. *Ergativity: Towards a theory of grammatical relations.* London: Academic Press.
Plank, F. 1985. *Relational typology.* Berlin: Mouton.
Pollock, J. Y. 1989. Verb movement, UG and the structure of IP. *Linguistic Inquiry* 20:365–424.
Quirk, R., S. Greenbaum, G. Leech, and J. Svartvik. 1985. *A comprehensive grammar of the English language.* London: Longman.
Radford, A. 1992. *Transformational Grammar.* Cambridge: Cambridge University Press.
Randal, S. 2000. Tennet's ergative origins. *Occasional Papers in the Study of Sudanese Languages* 8:67–80. Nairobi: Summer Institute of Linguistics.
Reh, M. 1996. *Anywa language, description and internal reconstructions.* Nilo-Saharan 11. Cologne: Rüdiger Köppe.
Reinhardt, T. 1991. Elliptic conjunctions – Nonquantificational LF. In A. Kasher (ed.), *The Chomskyan turn.* Oxford: Blackwell.
Reinhardt, T. 1982. Pragmatics and linguistics: An analysis of sentence topics. *Philosophica* 27:53–94.
Rizzi, L. 1982. *Issues in Italian syntax.* Dordrecht: Foris.
Rizzi, L. 1990. *Relativised Minimality.* Cambridge, Mass.: MIT Press.

Rothstein, S. 1983. *The syntactic forms of predication.* Bloomington: Indiana University Linguistics Club.
Rude, N. 1983. Ergativity and the Active-stative typology in Loma. *Journal of African Languages and Linguistics* 14:265–283.
Schiffrin, D. 1994. *Approaches to discourse.* Oxford: Blackwell.
Schröder, H. 1988a. *Kisyau nyakimar. [Learn to read].* Toposa Alphabet Book. Trial edition. Juba, Sudan: Summer Institute of Linguistics/Institute of Regional Languages.
Schröder, H. 1988b. *Kimar Ŋatoposa. [Read Toposa.]* Toposa Primer. Trial edition. Juba, Sudan: Summer Institute of Linguistics/Institute of Regional Languages.
Schröder, H. 1988c. *Nyekokor ka nyakoloŋ. [Chicken and Sun.]* Toposa Reader I. Trial edition. Juba, Sudan: Summer Institute of Linguistics/Institute of Regional Languages.
Schröder, H. 1988d. *Teachers' handbook – Toposa literacy. Nyabuk ka ŋiketatamak - Nyakimar ka nyakigir ka Ŋatoposa [Teachers' book - Reading and writing Toposa.]* Juba, Sudan: Summer Institute of Linguistics/Institute of Regional Languages.
Schröder, H. 1994. The Toposa verb phrase: A Government and Binding approach to a verb-initial language. M.A. thesis, University of Reading.
Schröder, M. C. 1988. *Toposa spelling guide.* Nairobi: Summer Institute of Linguistics.
Schröder, M. C. 1989. The Toposa verb in narrative discourse. *Afrikanistische Arbeitspapiere.* Schriftenreihe des Kölner Instituts für Afrikanistik 20:129–142.
Schröder, M. C. 1993a. *Toposa traditional texts: Phonemic version with a free translation.* Nairobi: Summer Institute of Linguistics.
Schröder, M. C. 1993b. *Ŋiemuto lukaalak. [Many stories.]* Toposa Reader II. Trial edition. Nairobi: Summer Institute of Linguistics.
Schröder, M. C. 2000. *Dictionary Toposa–English English–Toposa.* In Bilingual dictionaries of Sudan, No. 2. Nariobi: Summer Institute of Linguistics.
Schröder, H., and M. C. Schröder. 1986. The Toposa verb. *Occasional Papers in Sudanese Languages* 5:1–47.
Schröder, H., and M. C. Schröder. 1987. Vowel harmony in Toposa. *Afrikanistische Arbeitspapiere,* Schriftenreihe des Kölner Instituts für Afrikanistik 12:27–35.
Schröder, M. C., and H. Schröder. 1987. Voiceless vowels in Toposa. *Afrikanistische Arbeitspapiere,* Schriftenreihe des Kölner Instituts für Afrikanistik 12:17–26.

Schwartz, B. D., and S. Vikner. 1989. All verb second clauses are CPs. *Working Papers in Scandinavian Syntax* 43:27–50.
Spencer, A. 1991. *Morphological theory.* Oxford: Blackwell.
Sproat, R. 1983. *VSO languages and Welsh configurationality.* MIT Working Papers 5. Cambridge, Mass.: MIT Press.
Tsimpli, I. M. 1995. Focusing in Modern Greek. In K. É. Kiss (ed.), *Discourse configurational languages.* Oxford Studies in Comparative Syntax, 176–206. New York/Oxford: Oxford University Press.
Tucker, A. N., and M. A. Bryan. 1956. *The non-Bantu languages of North-Eastern African Linguistics.* London: Oxford University Press.
Tucker, A. N., and M. A. Bryan. 1966. *Linguistic analyses: The non-Bantu languages of North-Eastern Africa.* London: Oxford University Press (for the International African Institute).
Vallduví, E. 1992. *The informational component.* New York/London: Garland Publishing.
Vossen, R. 1981. The classification of Eastern Nilotic and its significance for ethnohistory. In T. C. Schadeberg and M. L. Bender (eds.), *Nilo-Saharan. Proceedings of the First Nilo-Saharan Linguistics Colloquium, Leiden, September 8–10, 1980,* 41–57. Dordrecht: Foris Publications.
Vossen, R. 1982. *The Eastern Nilotes: Linguistic and historical reconstructions.* Kölner Beiträge zur Afrikanistik 9. Berlin: Dietrich Reimer.
Vossen, R. 1983. Comparative Eastern Nilotic. In M. L. Bender (ed.), *Nilo-Saharan language studies.* Monograph 13:177–207. Committee on Northeast African Studies, African Studies Center, East Lansing, MI: Michigan State University.
Watters, J. 1976. Focus in Aghem. In L. M. Hyman (ed.), *Aghem grammatical structure.* Southern California Occasional Papers in Linguistics 7:137–186.
Wiesemann, U. 1996. *Discourse analysis.* Holzhausen: Seminar für Sprach-methodik. Prepublication typescript.

SIL International and
The University of Texas at Arlington
Publications in Linguistics
Recent Publications

141. Aspects of morphology and phonology of Kɔnni, by Michael C. Cahill. 2007.
140. The phonology of Mono, by Kenneth S. Olson. 2005.
139. Language and life: Essays in memory of Kenneth L. Pike, ed. by Mary Ruth Wise, Thomas N. Headland, and Ruth M. Brend. 2003.
138. Case and agreement in Abaza, by Brian O'Herin. 2002.
137. Pragmatics of persuasive discourse of Spanish television advertising, by Karol J. Hardin. 2001.
136. Quiegolani Zapotec syntax: A Principles and Parameters account, by Cheryl A. Black. 2000.
135. A grammar of Sochiapan Chinantec: Studies in Chinantec languages 6, by David Paul Foris. 2000.
134. A reference grammar of Northern Embera languages: Studies in the languages of Colombia 7, by Charles Arthur Mortensen. 1999.
133. The geometry and features of tone, by Keith Snider. 1999.
132. Desano grammar: Studies in the languages of Colombia 6, by Marion Miller. 1999.
131. The structure of evidential categories in Wanka Quechua, by Rick Floyd. 1999.
130. Cubeo grammar: Studies in the languages of Colombia 5, by Nancy L. Morse and Michael B. Maxwell. 1999.
129. Aspects of Zaiwa prosody: An autosegmental account, by Mark W. Wannemacher. 1998.
128. Tense and aspect in Obolo grammar and discourse, by Uche Aaron. 1998.
127. Case Grammar applied, by Walter A. Cook, S. J. 1998.
126. The Dong language in Guizhou Province, China, by Long Yaohong and Zheng Guoqiao, translated from Chinese by D. Norman Geary. 1998.
125. Vietnamese classifiers in narrative texts, by Karen Ann Daley. 1998.
124. Comparative Kadai: The Tai branch, ed. by Jerold A. Edmondson and David B. Solnit. 1997.
123. Why there are no clitics: An alternative perspective on pronominal allomorphy, by Daniel L. Everett. 1996.

For further information or a full listing of SIL publications contact:

International Academic Bookstore
SIL International
7500 W. Camp Wisdom Road
Dallas, TX 75236-5629

Voice: 972-708-7404
Fax: 972-708-7363
Email: academic_books@sil.org
Internet: http://www.ethnologue.com

www.ingramcontent.com/pod-product-compliance
Lightning Source LLC
Chambersburg PA
CBHW051523230426
43668CB00012B/1718